ON THE GRID

ON THE GRID

GRID

] *LIFE BEHIND THE SCENES OF FORMULA 1* [

LUKE SMITH

 HARPERVIA

An Imprint of HarperCollinsPublishers

HarperCollins books may be purchased for educational, business, or sales promotional use. For information, please email the Special Markets Department at SPsales@harpercollins.com.

FIRST EDITION

Designed by Janet Evans-Scanlon

Library of Congress Cataloging-in-Publication Data has been applied for.

ISBN 978-0-06-337352-5

25 26 27 28 29 LBC 5 4 3 2 1

For Mum

CONTENTS

The Grid

Move out of the way!"

I have been covering Formula 1 and motorsport for more than ten years all around the world, and I still have moments when I accidentally break the golden rule: When reporting from the starting grid, stay out of the way of the cars and their crews.

The mechanic who just yelled at me is part of a group of eight men helping push through the green Aston Martin of star driver Fernando Alonso, who has just finished his warm-up laps for the Bahrain Grand Prix, the first race of the 2023 season. As each car—ready to be raced hard for the very first time—is wheeled from the rear of the grid, the sea of bodies armed with wheel guns and tire warmers grows, completing their final preparations.

In the forty minutes before lights out, the starting grid is where you'll find anybody who is anybody in F1. Today the air is thick with sweat, engine fumes, and the smell of heated tire rubber as the sky turns orange, the sun over the Bahraini desert beginning to set. Tens of thousands of fans are already watching on, cheering for the drivers as the cars come to their starting positions. Once in place and with their helmets and headrests carefully removed, each driver hoists themselves out of their cars, dodges the throng of camera lenses, and turns their attention to discussing their final race plans, which have been meticulously laid out with their strategists and engineers to account for every eventuality.

I watch as Alonso gets out of the Aston Martin, his new car for this season after switching teams last winter. The two-time world champion, at forty-one, is the oldest driver on the grid, yet he has been one of the quickest drivers all weekend. Aston Martin's team owner, billionaire Lawrence Stroll, an imposing figure with big expectations and an even bigger checkbook, is there to greet his star signee. They embrace and share a few words. They could be in for a great result today: the start of a happy marriage of driver and team.

I continue to walk around the grid, the mass of bodies ebbing and flowing as people go about their business. It's a patch of asphalt fifteen yards wide tucked between the wall that divides the track from the pit lane, where all the teams have their garages, and the catch fencing on the other side next to the grandstand. There's little room to get around. I watch as rival team designers carefully study one another's cars up close, and the power brokers of the sport circulate, posing for pictures with the right people, shaking hands, and making pleasantries. CEOs of billion-dollar sponsors chat with sheikhs, princes, and prime ministers, all closely tailed by security guards. I may not recognize some of these people, but the *snap-snap-snap* of camera flashes tells me they're VIPs.

One by one, I watch as the drivers snake through the crowds and head back to their garages, escaping the noise for a moment of respite. There's Alonso again, the legend in the final chapter of his career. There's Lewis Hamilton, the seven-time champion and superstar whose name has transcended F1. There's Max Verstappen, the young gun who dethroned Hamilton as the current world champion. There's Oscar Piastri, the rookie who wasn't even born when Alonso started his first F1 race, and his teammate, Lando Norris, the British star hoping to take the world by storm.

As I move largely unnoticed through the crowd of bodies, I spot my friend Rupert, the trainer for Carlos Sainz, and wish him good luck with a thumbs-up. He smiles, but I know he can't hear me. His red headphones are tuned in to the team's prerace chatter, ensuring every final detail is addressed: what tires are used, what visor is on Sainz's helmet (it changes depending on weather conditions), even if the driver is wearing the right balaclava or fireproof underwear. Rupert approaches the tool-filled cart next to Sainz's car, picks up a powerful handheld fan, and holds it into the cockpit; keeping it cool will make the seat more comfortable for his driver. No detail is too small.

I weave my way toward the front of the grid, pulling my elbows close as I squeeze past those heading in the opposite direction. It feels like Oxford Street on Black Friday, only instead of rabid shoppers, it's the who's who of the F1 world with whom I'm jostling for space. A row of security guards holds a rope cordoning off the front of the grid, where the drivers are now rushing to line up in time for the national anthem. Lateness results in a fine; even they're not immune to a telling-off.

A booming voice calls on the crowd to stand, and all goes silent. The engines cut out; the chatter stops. Then a marching band springs into life as a woman in a white dress bellows out the national anthem of the Kingdom of Bahrain. When she finishes, to a rousing round of applause, necks and iPhones lurch skyward to capture the flyover: A Boeing 787-9 Dreamliner belonging to Gulf Air, the title sponsor of the race and Bahrain's national airline, is flying over the starting grid, a tradition dating back almost twenty years. As it nears the first corner, the right wing pitches downward, and the plane circles back over the paddock, which, as the base for all the teams' activities over a race weekend, serves as the center of F1's little universe.

And then a siren at the front of the grid blares: It's fifteen minutes until the race starts—time for anyone who doesn't need to be on the grid to get off it. Most definitely me.

I head toward one of the open gates along the pit wall as people stream through, again making sure not to get in the way of the drivers, who will be going for their final bathroom breaks. Most have headphones on, locked in their own little worlds. Hamilton speeds past on a push scooter, while others walk alongside their trainers, who pass final words of advice to their drivers. After crossing the pit lane, I find a small corridor leading back into the paddock, which is now eerily quiet.

Walking toward the media center, I pass Mohammed Ben Sulayem—the president of the FIA, F1's governing body, and one of the most powerful men in the sport—jumping into a golf cart along with the Crown Prince of Bahrain. Both wear pristine white thobes, traditional dress for the region. Ben Sulayem chuckles as the golf cart zooms past me to complete its journey to the other end of the paddock, barely a few hundred yards. "I'm lazy!" he says. No judgment here. I know our difference in standing. While he'll be watching the race from the FIA's hospitality suite overlooking the start line, I'll be in the media center, typing away, noting down every moment of action from the race.

I take my seat back at my desk, the adrenaline still flowing, and watch the TV cameras panning down to the grid, now empty bar twenty drivers and their cars, waiting for the start lights to blink out.

I've always vowed that the instant the grid stops being the best part of my race weekend, it's time to stop working in F1. It's where everything about the sport is distilled in one go: the sounds, the smells, the tension, the glamour, the people, the sacrifices; they all combine for only a moment.

Then out go the lights on the grid. The wheels spin, the engines roar loud, the crowd even louder, and the cars speed away. But what happens on the track is only a tiny part of the story. Whether you're a seasoned fan who hasn't missed a grand prix in decades or a newcomer to F1, I want to show you why this is a sport—a way of life, even—like nothing else on the planet.

1

Smoke and Mirrors

As I climb up the stairs of the Haas Formula 1 team's hospitality unit, its home-away-from-home at race tracks around the world, I'm directed to a door slightly ajar on my right-hand side.

At his desk, Guenther Steiner, the team principal, is peering at some paperwork. It's the start of pre-season testing in 2023, one of the busiest periods of his year. Steiner looks up as the door rattles gently in response to my knocking and invites me to come in.

We shake hands as the team's communications chief, Stuart, follows me into the room. "I've not had time to explain the interview, Guenther, but Luke's writing a book. And it's going to be great," Stuart says, quickly adding: "You were inspired by Guenther, weren't you?"

Steiner raises an eyebrow as I go along with the joke. "Yes, yes. That's exactly it."

On one side of Steiner's desk sits a stack of books along with a capless Sharpie pen that he's using to sign these copies of his best-selling book on a year in the life of an F1 team principal and make them that little bit extra special.

"And you want my help to then beat my book? You bastard," Steiner says. He flicks his hands skyward in disgust. "Why should I help you?! Fucking hell . . ."

He breaks into a grin and laughs, eyes crinkling at the corners as he waits for my reaction.

It's this kind of humor that has made Steiner one of the biggest characters in F1. Haas is among the smallest teams on the grid, lacking the financial might or prowess that the leading outfits like Red Bull, Ferrari, and Mercedes can boast, yet he made a name for himself through his forthright and jovial nature. When F1 opened its doors to Netflix's cameras for the *Formula 1: Drive to Survive* documentary that debuted in 2019, Steiner went from one of the paddock's best-known characters to a cult hero representing the sport.

I hit record on my voice memo app and place my phone on Steiner's desk before taking a seat opposite, then explain that yes, I am writing a book about F1, one that is intended to shine a light on some of the lesser-known stories and aspects of a sport that has given him, me, and so many other people so much in our lives. In recent times, F1 has undergone a dramatic transformation, in no small part thanks to the success of *Drive to Survive* in taking mainstream a sport so often shrouded in secrecy and mystery. The drivers and teams have gained a new level of exposure, many achieving celebrity status they'd previously not thought possible. Interest in F1 has surged, making a ticket for a grand prix one of the hottest in town.

Yet there are so many rich, remarkable stories still to be told that, I tell Steiner, I want to bring to life. F1 has a unique culture, one that has continued to shift and evolve since the first F1 world championship race in 1950, with traditions that make it unlike anything else in global sport. There is so much around F1 that, to those of us on the inside, seems day-to-day or normal when, in reality, they're the aspects that make it so appealing to hundreds of millions of fans around the world. Be it the sacrifices the drivers and teams will go through each year just to keep racing, off the back of a long, arduous journey to get there in the first place; or the brilliant minds that exist within our world, and how they benefit so much far beyond F1 itself; or how the fans and traditions that give color to F1 have changed over the years; or where the sport is going in the future—there is so much depth beyond what we see on the race track, so much more to love and respect beyond the twenty drivers racing wheel-to-wheel in their cars.

Steiner nods and smiles. "It's a sport where you have a mix of everything," he says. "It's a sport first, but you have the politics, you have the technology, you get the glamour. For nearly everyone in the world, F1 has something that they can be interested in. Therefore it attracts so many people. There's a lot of good racing series around, but you don't have the other four or five factors that F1 has got. That's what is special, and people love it. We're a good sport, and good entertainment together. A sport on its own is difficult to sell."

Neither he nor I know it at the time, but Steiner is starting what will be his last F1 season in charge of Haas; at the end of the year, he'll part ways with the team after a disappointing season where it finishes last in the championship. But when we speak at the start of the season, there is still a wealth of opportunities and, above all else, hope for the season to come. This could be the year when things are different, no matter what team you race or work for.

It all starts in testing, which gives the F1 teams the chance to try out their new cars for the first time. Alongside their racing commitments through the previous year, the designers have worked relentlessly to make modifications to the upcoming model, developing new parts and finding ways to try to make the car quicker for the two drivers. If you stand still or don't make enough progress in F1, your rivals are going to easily move ahead; this is a sport where what is best today is often nowhere near good enough tomorrow.

The winter between seasons offers teams a chance to reset and put in hours away from the race track to bridge the gap to their rivals. It can be one of the toughest points of the season, forcing teams to work around the clock in their factories to get the cars ready. They need to comply with the tight regulations that define what is and, more important, is not allowed with the car designs, and pass all the required safety tests. Right until the start of testing, when the cars get their first extensive running, teams will be working to squeeze every last 0.01 percent of performance, shaving off every ounce of weight or making whatever refinement their computer simulations suggest could be a performance benefit.

It's a story that rings true for all ten teams in F1. Months of effort often come down to just a few days of testing that then lay bare the harsh reality of life on the grid. Subtle differences in car shapes, even down to the thickness of a sidepod or the curvature of a front wing, could be worth precious tenths of a second that decide victory or defeat.

The untrained eye will be able to identify obvious differences between cars, but it is not until they actually go on the race track that the time sheets reflect a right and wrong way to design an F1 car. Modern F1 design buzzwords such as *gurney flaps* (a lip on the edge of a rear wing to divert airflow), *monkey seats* (a small wing between the rear wing and the diffuser), and *coke bottle* (where the rear of the car narrows the farther back you go, similar to the neck of a bottle of Coke) point to the linguistic creativity required to describe F1's ever-evolving, innovative design nature.

It didn't used to be so complicated.

■ ■ ■

Compared to the cars that took part in the first F1 world championship race seventy-five years ago, the 1950 British Grand Prix at Silverstone, the modern machines look like spaceships. Back then, no one obsessed over aerodynamics like they do today. A quote regularly attributed to Enzo Ferrari from 1960 is: "Aerodynamics are for people who can't build engines." It perfectly sums up the racing mentality of the era: So long as the car was powerful enough, it would be quick. The driver was still sat high in the cockpit at the rear of the car, exposed to the elements and not required to wear full overalls; a T-shirt, a helmet, and some goggles would do. Seatbelts weren't even mandatory until 1972.

F1's seventy-five-year history is a tale of innovation, adaptation, and competition. Ferrari's quote would be disproven within a decade: As engines grew more powerful through the '60s, designers sought ways to find more grip, leading to the idea of adding wings to a car. Lotus was the first team to successfully mount wings to a car for the 1968 Monaco Grand Prix; driver Graham Hill's victory from pole would ignite a new, important era of F1 car design. The embracing of complex aerodynamics and new car production concepts, such as the carbon fiber monocoque—far lighter, stronger, and safer than the aluminum chassis—changed the game. The wings grew larger, the cars got quicker and safer, the engines got louder and meaner, and F1 leaned on the increasing levels of computerized technology. Nowadays, around 500 GB of data is picked up by the sensors on the cars through a race, tracking everything from g-forces to engine temperature to tire wear. They are supercomputers on wheels.

For manufacturers like Ferrari, Mercedes, and Honda, F1 is a high-speed laboratory—offering great potential for technology transfer to their road cars. It's also a way to prove themselves as the superior carmaker. With the start of a new season comes another chance to stake that claim.

F1 will typically change its car design regulations every four to five years, starting a new technical "era" in a bid to make the sport more competitive on the track and the cars safer for the drivers. Each time this overhaul occurs, the most recent having been in 2022, teams are essentially left with a blank sheet of paper from which to interpret the rules, instead of evolving their old designs year after year. It keeps engineers and designers on their toes as they look for new ways to design their cars and find performance. As exciting as it may be, it does not mean changes to the rules are easy for the teams to handle: The only part of the pre-2022 cars that could be transferred to the new ones was the steering wheel.

The start of a new rule cycle often yields different car design concepts or ideas. In early 2022, the three leading teams—Red Bull, Mercedes, and Ferrari—all debuted cars with noticeable differences, particularly on the sidepods that sit either side of the cockpit. Red Bull had an aggressive cutaway at the bottom of the sidepod, creating a bigger gap to the floor below; Ferrari's design was aptly dubbed the "bathtub"; Mercedes barely had a sidepod at all, going for a radical slimline approach. Each believed theirs to be the right design concept. Ultimately, Red Bull's results were impossible to ignore. Within eighteen months of the new ruleset being in force, most of the teams had adopted a Red Bull–style design. Even Haas, which has a technical partnership with Ferrari and far lowlier aspirations as an independent team—regular top-ten finishes can be deemed a success—eventually shifted its car design to look more akin to Red Bull's.

The technical battle is never-ending, reaching its height at the start of each season. Teams work hard to protect their secrets, often revealing their "new" cars with fake bodywork or even using computer-generated renders to not give away the small differences in their designs that might catch the eyes of their rivals.

It all makes for an intense time of the year. After finalizing the launch specification of the car, teams will put them on-track for the first time in what is called a shakedown. This is a private test limited to 100 km (62 miles), or one-third of a grand prix distance. It's not a lot of track time, but at least it's a first opportunity to ensure that all systems are working properly, to identify any obvious problems, and to give the drivers an initial feel for their new car's characteristics. It is a major landmark in a team's season. More than seventeen thousand components have come together to form the machine; now, it's alive, and the next nine months will be dedicated to making it go as quickly as possible.

"When the car rolls out of the garage for the first time and makes it out of the pit lane, that in itself is a huge hurdle, even before you start looking at stopwatches," said Peter Crolla, the team manager for Haas, where he serves as the team principal's right-hand man. He plays a critical role in every aspect of the team's preparation for a new season and knows how important it is. "It affects not only the two hundred forty people within our own business, but it's also the wider supporting businesses. Everybody's got an interest in it. From a psychological perspective, so many people are putting in so much effort in the run-up to that point. It's absolutely huge."

F1 types are competitive animals. It's their nature. So even through the limited mileage of a shakedown on a cold day in the middle of February at Silverstone, there's an eye on the stopwatch. "As the car starts to circulate and lap times come down, then you start to realize, okay, not only have we done a good job to get it out there, but let's see how good a job we've *actually* done in how the car intrinsically performs," said Crolla.

The first opportunity to run the car for real comes in preseason testing. This typically takes place over three days in a hot country such as Bahrain so the weather won't hinder teams' preparations. (The Circuit de Barcelona-Catalunya in Spain has also been used, but a snowy day in 2018 that halted testing left all of us wondering why we weren't in Bahrain.) Through testing, eight hours of track time are allocated each day for teams to use as they wish, but they will split crews within their team so there is a day shift and a night shift, meaning they can work nonstop to try to make the car quicker and perfect their preparations. It's an exhausting—quite literally testing—time of the year. As the cars are all out there together and the lap times are visible to everyone, it offers the first indication of how the teams are stacking up ahead of a new season: Who has used their winter wisely to leapfrog their rivals, and who has fallen behind?

Yet F1 is never, ever that simple. Testing often descends into a game of smoke and mirrors. Teams may no longer be able to hide the designs that are now in full view of TV cameras and photographers, many of whom are employed by teams to snap shots of their rivals' designs. But there's plenty else they can do to try to mask their true level of performance. As testing is not a competitive session, there isn't the same kind of incentive for teams to get the maximum performance out of their car, nor are there the usual rules and regulations that must be adhered to. Running more fuel in the car makes it heavier and therefore slower, an effective way to hide performance—a practice known as sandbagging. The drivers themselves may also deliberately slow at points on certain laps, meaning quick cars don't always look that way going solely off the timing screens.

"People do for sure play some psychological games through preseason testing," Crolla explained. "There are so many variables that can be implemented through testing in terms of tire wear, fuel choices, the type of running that we're doing. Are we looking for short-run pace? Are we looking for race pace? It's not really until you get to the first race that you truly know where you stand in comparison to other teams."

F1 history has plenty of cautionary tales of preseason prospects looking too good to be true. In the ten preseasons between 2014 and 2023, the fastest team in the final winter test won the opening race of the season five times and would go on to clinch the Constructors' Championship on only four occasions. While the times are a helpful guide, they are rarely the full picture.

■ ■ ■

One of the strongest examples of misleading testing times comes from back in 2001, when Prost Grand Prix—the team owned and run by Alain Prost, a four-time F1 champion who raced in the 1980s and early 1990s—looked like one of the most competitive teams ahead of the new season. This was an era when test running was largely up to the teams to arrange and there were fewer restrictions on how much they could put their cars on-track ahead of a new season. Prost endured a miserable season in 2000, not only finishing last in the championship but also failing to score a single point. After striking a deal with Ferrari to buy their engine in 2001, the team hoped its fortunes would turn around, and when its new car hit the track, it looked fast. Surprisingly fast. The only team that was faster in the main collective test in Barcelona was Ferrari, whose best lap was a mere three-tenths of a second quicker than Prost driver Jean Alesi's. Yet the car was also noticeably bare of the sponsors that ultimately help fund smaller racing operations. Putting two and two together, the theory was Prost had opted to exaggerate its speed—using minimal fuel to make the car lighter, or perhaps even running under the minimum weight limit, given testing is not subject to a grand prix's technical requirements—in order to get headline lap times that might attract fresh sponsorship ahead of the new season. When it came to the opening race of the season in Australia, the team's lack of speed was revealed: Alesi qualified three seconds off Michael Schumacher's pole position time. Prost would score just four points all season and, still lacking the sponsorship and financial backing it needed, fold at the end of the year.

But sometimes the testing picture that seems too good to be true is, in fact, real. Miracles do happen.

Since taking complete ownership of its British American Racing (BAR) customer team in 2006, Honda had been set on conquering F1. Hundreds of millions of dollars were poured into the team and the design of its cars, only for it to score a single victory up to the end of 2008. The team finished that year ninth out of eleven teams, scoring a paltry fourteen points and just a single podium finish to its name. With an overhaul of the technical regulations due for 2009, the team bosses decided to switch focus as soon as possible to the next year, sacrificing development through the second half of the 2008 season. Short-term pain for long-term gain.

The Honda bigwigs back in Tokyo had other ideas. At the end of the year, and with the Great Recession impacting the car industry hard, Honda's board pulled the plug on its F1 team with immediate effect. The entire workforce was laid off, and the F1 facility in

Brackley, England, was put up for sale for a grand total of one pound. Honda didn't care about getting its money back. It simply didn't want to keep funding the team.

But the development of the car for 2009 had been extensive, using three different wind tunnels and coming up with some innovative design concepts, such as a double diffuser at the rear of the car used to generate greater levels of downforce, which increases the level of grip. The team members knew it was going to be a good car—too much hard work and money had gone into it for the story to turn out otherwise—and were adamant all their hard work would not go to waste. "It was an interesting emotional journey," said James Vowles, who worked for Honda as a chief strategist at the time and is now the team principal of Williams. "We all lost our jobs in December 2008. But everyone stayed in the factory, every single person, to basically go on to build the car." Ross Brawn, the team principal of Honda, stepped in to save the day. He purchased the team and secured enough investment to just about keep it going, rebranding it as Brawn GP. The car would not go to waste.

The bare-bones operation that remained went to Silverstone in early March to give the car a first outing, working out of a single articulated truck. Mercedes provided a last-minute engine supply deal for Brawn. When their engineers turned up for the first Silverstone test and asked where to set up their laptops, Vowles told them: "Anywhere you like particularly—we have nothing!" The team did not have a single sponsor when it started, running its car in an all-white design with some fluorescent yellow trim. Such humble beginnings hardly had the makings of a quick car, yet the fifty-lap test completed by Jenson Button was still a major landmark for the Brawn team. Three months after the team looked dead and buried, it was literally back on-track.

A greater breakthrough came three days later when Brawn joined the other teams in Barcelona for a collective test session. "As cars got released, we started looking at them, going: 'That's odd, that's what our car looked like a year ago or six months ago. . . .'" said Vowles. Button was sent out on the same set of tires he'd used at Silverstone, and soon came back into the pits, reporting the balance of the car felt terrible through the corners, making it hard to fully trust his steering inputs. "We made some adjustments, sent him back out, he came back in again and said: 'No, sorry, the car balance still isn't there,'" recalled Vowles. "We walked over to the timing screen, and he was three and a half seconds a lap faster than anyone. Oddly enough, the car balance was fine after that!"

That was the moment Brawn knew it was onto something. In true F1 spirit, it didn't want to totally give the game away. It ran higher fuel than normal for the rest of testing in a bid to hide its true pace, downplaying expectations ahead of the opening race of the F1 season in Australia. Its car—now carrying a couple of sponsors, giving merit to the bandwagoning effect the likes of Prost tried yet failed to capture—was utterly dominant, qualifying and finishing the race first and second, led by Button. He would win six of the opening seven races and go on to become world champion, while Brawn won the Constructors' Championship. At the end of the year, the operation was bought by Mercedes, becoming the team that would go on to dominate F1 under current team principal Toto Wolff. "It was a fairy tale really," said Vowles, who stayed on and became Mercedes's strategy director. Greater things followed for the team, yet those early testing days in 2009 will always be where the fairy tale started.

A Brawn doesn't happen every year. More often than not, preseason testing is an incredibly stressful time for the teams. There's always the constant doubt and uncertainty about how a car is really performing given the enormous amount of effort teams put into getting their cars ready for the new season. The hundreds of people involved in a car project will get an idea of where things stand but cannot know for sure until that first race. No matter how committed or united people may be, the on-track fortunes do impact morale and motivation. "People thrive on good results," said Crolla. "Equally, bad results have a complete opposite effect. And that's where you've got to work harder, when things are going badly and you're up against it."

Crolla laughed when I asked if working out the picture of where everyone stacks up is part of the fun of the buildup to the opening race. "I don't think 'preseason' and 'fun' are two terms that I'd really put together!" he said. "They're long, hard days, and it's not got the buzz and excitement of a race weekend. It's a big, long hurdle that you've got to get over."

As a journalist roaming the paddock, it can be an exciting time trying to piece together a competitive picture and get a read for what the season to come may look like. It gives you the chance to earn bragging rights at the end of the year for correctly predicting a team's success—or, as I found out a few years ago, to look very silly. After a poor initial test in Bahrain, I said in a video that Alpine would be the biggest disappointment of the season after I'd heard one of its drivers was pretty downbeat about his feeling behind the wheel, albeit based off a single day of testing. In the end, the team far outstripped my low expectations and enjoyed a decent year, scoring podium finishes and regular points. About an hour after the checkered flag in Abu Dhabi, when it had secured fourth in the championship at the season finale, I ran into Alpine's CEO and sporting director in the team motor home. "We've just been watching your video!" they said gleefully. "Such an expert, aren't you!" I shook their hands and said well done, feeling humbled.

So how can you tell which teams are actually good or not in testing? One of the best rules of thumb is the number of laps completed. If a car is racking up good mileage and running without any problems, then it's a sign of a solid, reliable base. Teams can complete upward of two grand prix distances in a single day of testing, providing an enormous amount of data. They will also be keeping an eye on the opposition to try and understand who is looking competitive and if their pace is genuine.

If the data can therefore be misleading, watching the cars with your own eyes is often the best way to do it. It's rare to get a lot of time to actually see the cars on-track when covering a grand prix, given the wealth of TV footage and data available in the media center, where I'll be stationed for much of a weekend. It means the long testing days are a great chance to get trackside and see the cars pushing hard. You can pick out which drivers are able to brake later into a corner than others; the difference in the pitch and yaw of cars going through the corner, some looking far more balanced and smooth; which car gives drivers the confidence to really get their foot down and push at the exit of the corner.

It was what made Aston Martin's progress heading into the

2023 season so obvious. Bankrolled by billionaire owner Lawrence Stroll, the team secured a marquee signing in two-time world champion Fernando Alonso to race alongside Lance Stroll—Lawrence's son—and help achieve its goal of becoming an F1 front-runner by 2026. In 2022, the team had finished seventh in the championship, fighting for points but rarely bothering the leading teams. Yet as more whispers emerged about the performance gains the team was making in the wind tunnel used to design its car, and with the computer simulations suggesting the car would be quick, the excitement around its prospects grew. Testing did little to change that. Alonso's laps were not only competitive, but the car looked fast on-track. As I chatted to team members, the positivity was hard to ignore, even if it was always tempered with the caveat of "but it's only testing."

Come the opening race in Bahrain, when the teams hide no more and unleash the full performance of their cars, Aston Martin's incredible step forward was confirmed. Alonso finished the race in third place, trailing only the dominant Red Bull cars. He even overtook the Ferrari and Mercedes cars, in a different league a few months earlier, en route to the podium. For a team that hadn't even been in the picture for points at the same race the previous year, it was a total turnaround in its potential, one the team itself scarcely dared to believe until the cards were laid down at the opening race.

"You never know where you are compared to the others," said Mike Krack, Aston Martin's team principal. "We knew when we had the first laps with this car that it was a step forward. You have your data, you have the drivers that give you this feedback. But then obviously you have no competition. So you are always a little bit in doubt: Where are you? It is only in race one where we realized that the car was competitive."

For the drivers in the cockpit, they'll typically have an idea from the early stages of their test running. Since their earliest days racing at the age of four or five in go-karts, they've built an innate understanding of how a car should feel underneath them. They know what characteristics they like: Is the rear end of the car stable enough? Is there enough confidence under braking to go for a daring overtake? Is it balanced enough to take this corner flat out?

Sometimes, as Button's initial complaints about the handling of the Brawn prove, even if a car doesn't *feel* quick, it can be considerably better than the opposition—or vice versa. In the days after my chat with Steiner, the picture of the pecking order starts to become clearer. Red Bull, the reigning champion team, is a step ahead of the opposition again, and will go on to enjoy the most dominant season in F1 history by winning twenty-one out of twenty-two races. Mercedes, just two years removed from winning an eighth championship in a row, the kind of run that marks an F1 dynasty, is lagging far behind. George Russell, one of Mercedes's drivers, wasn't even sure where the pace was lacking at first. Behind the wheel, it felt pretty good. "The car can sometimes feel great, but the lap times aren't representing the feeling and vice versa," he later reflected. "Even championship-winning cars, they may not also feel perfect. We're just driving around at a slightly higher pace. It was when we saw that the lap times weren't translating into what we expected."

Ferrari's Charles Leclerc felt the same way. After finishing as runner-up to Verstappen in the championship the previous year, he was seen as the most likely candidate to have a car capable of mounting a serious, sustained challenge—only for the car to not give him what he needed. It was more inconsistent to drive than the previous year's model despite Ferrari's tireless efforts to make it quicker. The car also chewed through its tires at a rate that made it difficult for Leclerc to push hard throughout a race and keep up with the Red Bull car; drivers will lose time by having to come into the pits and change tires more than others. The areas that needed fixing were obvious, but doing so was another matter. Leclerc later admitted that Ferrari already knew in testing, despite all the intrigue and guessing games, that it was far behind Red Bull and instead in a similar ballpark to Mercedes. "But then in testing, you're always cautious because you're always like, What if they do something different this year, and they just want to scare us?" he said. "You always try to focus on yourself."

That focus on the self can seem like an easy deflection through the gamesmanship of preseason testing. But there is a large degree of truth to it, especially for the ones actually driving the cars. While the mechanics and engineers back at the factory burn the candle at both ends to get ready for a new season, the drivers will be doing the same, training hard to get themselves into peak physical and mental condition for the long year of racing to come.

Except things don't always go as planned.

■ ■ ■

The F1 paddock loves to gossip, particularly during testing, when speculation and educated guesses become the currency everyone deals in.

As I do the rounds at the end of the final day of testing in 2023, not long after my chat with Guenther Steiner and with darkness long descended and the lights of the Bahrain International Circuit illuminating the last chats before the opening weekend of the season, the one driver everybody is talking about hasn't driven a car. He hasn't been at the track, and he isn't even in Bahrain. He's more than three thousand miles away in Spain with one wrist broken and the other fractured, a broken big toe, and serious doubts over his participation in the opening race. While Aston Martin's optimism was building for the new season thanks to Alonso's performance through testing, his teammate and the son of the team owner, Lance Stroll, was in a race against time to make it to Bahrain at all following a cycling accident.

All F1 drivers will use the winter break to switch off from the high-pressure demands of a full season. After a run of twenty-two races, the three-month gap between the final race—typically in late November or early December—and the start of the new season in early March offers some brief respite. While the intensity of their training can afford to ease a little bit in the first few weeks of the winter break, as the new year begins, a stricter regime comes into force to get ready for the new season.

Stroll will typically spend the early part of his winter doing a mixture of physical activities, his favorites being mountain biking and, being Canadian, some snowboarding. It is the job of his performance coach, Henry Howe, to oversee the training program, which needs to be stricter than for most drivers. At six feet, Stroll is one of the tallest on the grid, making him naturally heavier—not a good thing when every ounce counts in an F1 car. To show how great the swing can be, Yuki Tsunoda, the shortest driver at five feet three inches, is over fifty pounds lighter than Stroll. F1's regulations do add ballast to avoid penalizing the heavier drivers, but even so, the lighter you are, the better.

It means Howe has to ensure Stroll gets the right mix of training to prepare for the demands placed on the body by an F1 car, without putting on too much muscle mass. "Lance looks at a dumbbell, and he puts on muscle," said Howe. "It's a good problem to have if you're not a racing driver!" In the weeks leading up to a new season, they'll focus on building his strength—particularly in the neck, which bears the brunt of the high g-forces keeping the head steady through high-speed corners—before embarking on a final training camp. This will be around a week of intense workouts and physical activity, the final push of total commitment from the driver to be in the best possible condition for the new year of racing. Ahead of the 2023 season, Stroll, Howe, and the rest of their support team went to Málaga in Spain for the final training camp. "We were having a successful trip," said Howe. "Day one, he did four hours on the bike. Day two, he did three hours on the bike and an hour in the gym. And then it was day three he had the accident."

Upper-body strength is the priority for F1 drivers, and this extends to their hands and wrists. A deft, dexterous touch is required to maintain close car control. So once Stroll's injuries became clear after coming off his bike, the early part of his season was thrown into doubt. "Lance's initial thing was just asking me: 'How many races [will I miss]? How long does this take?'" recalled Howe. "It's not fair to start putting stuff like that in anybody's head. You can have an idea, but you don't want to hang your hat on it until you see what the first week of recovery looks like really." A trip to the local hospital in Málaga made it clear Stroll had sustained fractures to his wrists. Howe quickly got in touch with Rob Madden, Stroll's physiotherapist back in London, who had worked with high-profile boxers such as British world champion Anthony Joshua and seen his fair share of wrist injuries. It isn't a common F1 injury. Stroll remembered a friend from his junior career, Dani Juncadella, once told him about breaking his collarbone and then managing to get back in the car five days later thanks to the help of a sports-injury specialist. His name was Dr. Xavier Mir, one of the best in his field, who had dealt with motorcycle riders, golfers, and tennis players, all disciplines prone to wrist and hand injuries. And he was based in Spain. As Howe put it: "We fucked up, but we fucked up in the right country."

By the time Stroll and Howe met with Mir, they were already expecting to miss the opening three races of the season. The one-month gap that followed in the calendar would give a greater window for recovery. Bone injuries typically take fifty days to heal. Stroll had fifteen before the start of the race in Bahrain. It seemed out of reach. Yet when he awoke from surgery on his right wrist two days after the accident, Mir told him: "Maybe Bahrain." There was a chance.

From there, "Project Bahrain," as it became known between Stroll, Howe, and the supporting medical team, kicked into full effect. Aston Martin had confirmed publicly that Stroll had been injured in a cycling accident and would not be taking part in preseason testing but remained tight-lipped on any further information, citing his privacy. Rumors had gotten out that his right hand was in a cast, but little more was known, only adding to the speculation doing the rounds in the paddock. The theories abounded over how the injuries were sustained and whether Stroll would make it for the opening race. The team's performance through testing increased the spotlight, as did considerations over who might step in if he could not race.

"We were camped out in a hotel, trying to avoid the media," said Howe. "It was a bit of a secret operation. The reason it was like that was because, fundamentally, drivers give—not to be rude—people such as yourself, they give them a lot. It's very different to any other sport. But your health is private."

For fourteen hours per day, Stroll and his team worked on rehabilitation to get him in a position to return to the cockpit the following week. Any exercise that might give even the smallest percentage of improved healing or movement in his wrists was explored, chasing marginal gains. Performance coaches from British boxing, Ian Gatt and Mike Loosemore, helped Howe and Madden guide the recovery program, calling on their expertise in dealing with similar injuries. A private chef ensured Stroll was getting the right nutrition to aid recovery, including plenty of calcium and vitamin D. Howe was there all the while not only helping with the training but doing simple things Stroll could not do because of his injuries, such as untucking his bed after housekeeping made up his room and, he said deliberately without going into detail, "helping him with everything else you can possibly think of." Although the focus was on his wrists, Stroll also had to maintain his general fitness, meaning he was still doing hours each day on the exercise bike with a broken big toe. Howe smirked retelling the story, calling Stroll a "lunatic."

Once the cast came off Stroll's right hand and the scans showed the recovery was going well, Bahrain became a real possibility. He returned to the team's factory in the UK and completed a session in the simulator, which showed he'd be able to navigate the tight confines of the cockpit and—more importantly for not only his own safety but for that of the other nineteen drivers sharing the same piece of race track—control the car as normal. With the doctors also satisfied, Aston Martin put an end to speculation by confirming Stroll would be entered to the race weekend as normal.

His arrival in Bahrain was the big story ahead of the opening race. Cameras followed him as he walked gingerly down the paddock, still nursing his broken toe, which, after a week of wearing slides and flip-flops, now had to be crammed into his race boots. There was still one major hurdle for Stroll to overcome: the FIA's jump-out test. For a driver to be cleared to race, they must prove they can get themselves out of the cockpit of their car unaided within seven seconds. The test is designed to ensure the drivers can quickly get out of the car in the event of a fire or a bad accident. To get out of the cockpit, the driver must remove their steering wheel, lift their hands toward the Halo structure above the cockpit, then pull themselves upward until standing upright, before putting their weight on the Halo and vaulting over the side of the cockpit.

Stroll passed, but the strain it put on his wrists meant he was in more pain than he'd been in since coming off the bike. "It wasn't a nice moment," said Howe. Nevertheless, "Project Bahrain" could be deemed a success. They'd passed all of the required tests. Howe and company could take heart in the fact they'd made the impossible possible.

It's a very F1 way of thinking. The sport has a can-do attitude and approach to problem-solving that makes it unique. Howe had had a long career in sports science and worked with a number of elite athletes prior to entering the F1 world a few years ago. Had this environment changed his way of thinking about medicine?

"Probably, yeah," he said, "in so much of being limitless. There is a way. And just being a bit more open-minded, I guess. The sport I worked in before was track-and-field sprinting. It's very low budget, and that's guiding everything. You come into F1, and the budget far exceeds the budget of sports medicine."

■ ■ ■

When Stroll comes to the media pen after the race in Bahrain, his face and hair glistening with perspiration, the only outward sign of his injuries are the small white plasters on both his wrists. He's spent the weekend battling through the pain, helped by medication, and put in a gallant drive to sixth place. Eight precious points. All without any testing.

"Aside from the pain, it was fun," he tells us. He spent part of the race battling George Russell, a driver he'd been far, far behind the previous year, and eventually overtook the Mercedes to finish a second clear at the finish line. They're the kind of close fights F1 drivers thrive off. But it's not enough of a buzz to stop the pain being Stroll's overriding feeling. "Even with adrenaline," he says, "broken bones still hurt."

After giving his final answers, he returns to his garage to celebrate with his team. With Alonso on the podium and Stroll sixth, the team is second in the championship. Even without the remarkable backstory to Stroll's recovery, it has been a good day for the team. A few days later, Stroll would share images and videos of his recovery on Instagram. Shots show him laid on his back in a hospital bed, stood wearing a patient's gown, X-rays with pins in his wrist. It's a rare show of vulnerability for an F1 driver whose commitment has often been questioned. After all, he's the son of a billionaire who owns the Aston Martin team. Does he really need to fight as hard as the other drivers?

"I know how tenacious he is," said Howe. "You only have to work with him for one weekend to know that. Everybody's got their ideas about Lance, and hopefully those ideas have been satisfied by this point. There was no need for him to try and get back, but he wanted to. That's why he shared that fairly candid post on Instagram. I was proud, for sure. I've not seen anything like it. I don't think Formula 1 has seen anything like it."

Walking through the paddock at the end of the opening race feels like the calm after the storm. As the team members put all of the garage equipment into boxes, ready to transport to the next race, some have more to celebrate than others. Music blares from the back of the garages of the teams who enjoyed good days. Red Bull celebrates a race win with a team photo, Max Verstappen front and center of the crowd alongside his winner's trophy. Aston Martin toasts Fernando Alonso's podium and, with careful embraces, Stroll's comeback performance that *feels* like a victory. Down at Haas, it's been a more difficult day: thirteenth and fifteenth place for drivers Kevin Magnussen and Nico Hülkenberg means zero points to start the season.

Following a hard winter of work, sacrifice, and second-guessing their rivals, at long last everyone knows where they stand. The chips are down. You can tell from the body language of the drivers which ones know they're in for a long, arduous season, struggling to get the kind of results they want. The same goes for the team members, who will do all they can to help turn things around. It's only round one of a twenty-two-race season. There's a long way to go, for better or for worse.

Even getting to that first race can be a monumental achievement for the drivers, often decades in the making. The hard training over the winter or the competitive frustrations over a lack of performance are nothing to what they've known on their way up the ladder, giving up everything for a shot at making it to F1.

No story is the same. And some have it far harder than others to simply get to the start line.

2

The Billionaire Boys' Club

A s the sun began to set over the track, the incoming darkness bringing a natural end to the test day, French driver Esteban Ocon and his father, Laurent, would watch as the other drivers and their parents packed up their equipment, including their go-karts and the canopy tents that served as garages, into their vans before setting off on the drive back home.

Before Esteban and Laurent would do the same, they'd have a look around to see what the others had left behind. Tires, an expensive, precious commodity in go-kart racing, were something many of the wealthier kids would go through at an astonishing rate. After a single test session, a look at the tread would be enough to say they were past their best, and therefore not worth keeping. They'd get thrown into the large dumpsters at the track and forgotten about. A fresh set would be fitted the next time the go-karts went on the track, offering maximum grip and, as a result, quicker lap times.

To the Ocons, the discarded tires looked just fine. Sure, they'd done a decent number of laps and wouldn't offer the kind of grip that you'd get from a fresh set of rubber. But they would still be perfectly usable for testing, meaning the Ocons' brand-new tires could be saved for races. Laurent would fit the tires to Esteban's go-kart—which was also secondhand—for the tests, and he would set lap times comparable with the kids using the fresh tires that would inevitably be thrown away once again. Come the competitive events, with the fresh tires he'd saved, Ocon would win. The other kids might have had better equipment and deeper pockets, but Esteban had the talent. And nothing was going to trump that.

"Even if we had the smallest tent and we were doing it all by ourselves, we were the enemies of everyone," recalled Ocon. "And that was good because we were beating everyone."

To discuss going to such lengths just to save a few hundred euros on a set of tires with someone who is now an F1 driver may seem strange, given the sport's big-spending, extravagant nature, and the lifestyles that come with it. On an average F1 weekend, each driver will go through thirteen sets of tires, so fifty-two in total, costing around thirty-five thousand dollars, a small outlay compared to a car worth millions.

But Ocon's story is one that makes him something of an outlier on the F1 grid. He didn't enjoy the endless means many of his peers and rivals did growing up and through their junior careers. His family sacrificed a great amount for him to keep racing when he was young, giving up everything—including the family home—in aid of his dream of one day making it as an F1 driver.

I'm sat with Ocon in the Alpine hospitality unit, his team at the time. It's a long way from his basic karting setup, serving as the home at the track to the sixty operational staff on his F1 car, including engineers, mechanics, strategists, and the pit crew, plus all the additional team members ranging from communications to catering on a race weekend. Ocon begins to open up about the hard years and the journey he's been on with his family, and when he speaks about it, there is no sense of frustration or heartache about the tough times, simply a frankness and acceptance. "There's nothing we can regret now," Ocon tells me. "It's all good. I'm living my dream, day in, day out. It's been a crazy ride if you think about it, how many sacrifices that we had to make." Yes, the story gets a happy ending. It doesn't mean the hard times weren't hard.

From a young age, Ocon was surrounded by cars. His father owned a garage, and to enter the family home, you had to walk through Laurent's workshop. Ocon would leave for school in the morning with his father toiling over an engine that would not start and come home to find it had kicked into life. They were the sounds and smells of his childhood. He became "addicted" to racing, as he puts it, when he first tried out a go-kart at the age of four. Ocon was too young to drive the go-kart, but he jumped in anyway and zoomed away from the track staff trying to get him out. "The people couldn't stop me for fifteen minutes!" he says. "I was going around them as if they were cones! From then on, I couldn't wait to get back in a go-kart."

Ocon received a go-kart for Christmas and entered some exhibition events, where he showed enough talent to convince his father it was worth looking at some competitive races. Aged seven, he dominated the regional series on the outskirts of Paris, putting him on the path to compete on a national level. Winning became the only thing that mattered. With a tinge of embarrassment, Ocon remembers deliberately crashing into the back of another driver after being defeated in one out of twenty-five races in a season, leading to what Ocon describes as a "bad telling off" from his father. "But that's how much anger I had in me when I was losing," Ocon says. "I think if I was not born competitive like that, we would probably not have had the motivation to get to where we are here."

At this time, money wasn't such a make-or-break issue for the Ocons, who could operate on a par with the kids and families they were racing. "My parents could keep up in a way because my dad was doing all the mechanic work, building the tent, he was doing the truckie work," Ocon says. "He was doing the jobs of four different people. My mom was doing all the catering, the physio stuff, she was doing all of that. So we could keep up at a very low cost until the national championship. We won that with a used go-kart that we bought from another driver from the year before."

The national karting championship victory attracted the attention of Gravity Sports Management, a talent agency led by future Lotus and McLaren F1 team principal Éric Boullier and Gwen Lagrue, a prolific scout who now oversees Mercedes's young-driver academy. Although Gravity could supply some of the budget to fund Ocon's racing efforts, the family was forced into a tough decision around this time: selling their house to release funds to keep him on the track. They moved into a caravan that they would take around Europe, going from race to race, committing everything to realizing Esteban's dream.

"That's where we really decided *Okay, there is an opportunity here,*" says Ocon. "I'm saying that as if I was twenty at the time . . . but that's the discussion we really had. I knew that to get to my dream, there was going to be a lot of weight on my shoulders from a very young age." There was a time when Ocon had a bed set up in the medical center of a go-kart track in France. He would wake up each morning, shower in the caravan, and then get on-track, practicing the craft he and his parents hoped would make such sacrifices worthwhile. There was no safety net or plan B, no great wealth in which to retreat if things went wrong. "We couldn't fail," Ocon says. "It would have had big consequences."

Even as Ocon moved up from go-karts to open-wheel race cars, there was always a need to prove himself, a need to fight. He won the European Formula 3 title in 2014, beating Max Verstappen, but the collapse of Gravity meant he faced an uncertain future. Mercedes came to the rescue, saying it would fund him for a year in GP3—a series equivalent to F3—with the remit he had to win the championship to continue with its academy. He did exactly that, and would debut in F1 the following year for the back-of-the-pack Manor team, which then closed its doors at the end of the season. Ocon had impressed enough to land a seat at Force India, only for that team to also eventually face financial tumult until it was purchased by Lawrence Stroll, whose son, Lance, then replaced Ocon for the 2019 season and left the Frenchman on the sidelines. The kid looking for tires in a dumpster with his dad was always scrambling for security.

"Every year I had to perform, I had to prove to people that I deserved to be on the grid and deserved to have a seat," Ocon says. "When you get to Formula 1, you have to redo that all over again. It's always stressful. But it's nothing that I haven't faced before. I've faced such difficult times that now, I know how to get through them."

It would not be until 2020, when Ocon signed a multiyear contract with Renault (now Alpine), that he would get true career security for the first time. And the 2021 Hungarian Grand Prix, a chaotic race featuring crashes and heavy rain at the start, ended with Ocon on the top step of the podium: He was a grand prix winner. Besides winning a world championship, victory in a grand prix is the greatest joy a driver can experience. Ocon is an established part of the F1 grid, now racing for Haas. And, significantly, he's been able to give back to his parents after all the sacrifices they made. He even received the car he won the race in Hungary with in 2024, causing his father to shed a tear when it was delivered.

"My parents have a secure future," he says. "They have a new house, they work for me and with me, which is just awesome. For sure, it was tough to get here, but the highs are just mega. We're just obviously blessed and happy to be where we are now."

And some things remain the same. Even with their financial security, Ocon's father continues to work on cars. To enter the family home, you still have to pass through Laurent's workshop.

■ ■ ■

For all of us, our parents or parental figures play a significant role in shaping our personalities and our characteristics, for better or for worse. F1 drivers up and down the grid recognize the financial lengths that their families went to when they were younger to help them realize their dreams. But they also cite the core values and commitment to winning that were instilled in them at a young age as being key factors in making them who they are today and helping them succeed.

In the case of Verstappen, becoming a racing driver always seemed to be his destiny. His mother and father both raced competitively, with dad Jos driving in F1 between 1994 and 2003. Although that meant there was a degree of wealth supporting Max when he started out, there was no bottomless pit for the family to delve into, nor did Jos ever let him rest on his laurels. Together they would tour around Europe as Max raced in the top go-karting categories. They were the years that would lay the foundations for him to become a multiple F1 champion and be on course to keep breaking records.

"It's hard to explain how much he has dedicated to me," said Verstappen. "I probably still don't even understand how much he did. He was preparing everything—go-karts, engines—and then driving all the way to Italy with me, in between school, then back. I probably only will fully realize how much he has done for me when I have kids. Then you start to understand this kind of relationship."

Jos was not easy on Max. Not easy at all. Stories of Jos not talking to Max for a week because of a crash in a go-kart race, or leaving him behind at a gas station when he tried to defend a mistake that cost him a win, are common knowledge. Verstappen saw it as proof of the seriousness with which his father took his career, all important formative moments that made him the man and driver he is now.

"Without him, I would not be sitting here today," Verstappen said. "He has taught me so much and prepared me so much from a very young age, where sometimes I thought, *Why does it need to be so serious straightaway?* Maybe you want to play around a bit more and have fun. But he was working towards this goal. He had this goal set for me to be first of all better than him [as a driver], and then to get to Formula 1."

One of the key figures involved in junior motorsport and the progression of future F1 talents is Trevor Carlin, who ran his eponymous Carlin racing team in junior series for over twenty-five years until the end of 2023. Carlin hailed Verstappen as "the ultimate example" of a driver working incredibly hard from a young age to forge their talent. "His dad worked hard and gave him the equipment for go-karting, and then he had enough money to do karting well," Carlin said. "But Jos was super hard on Max. Max had a really tough upbringing, and he had to work his ass off. He built his own kart, his own engines, and that's why Max is now the driver that he is, because he's worked so hard. He was never given anything. He had to earn it.

"Now he's had the best car, the best training, the most pressure, and he's going to become possibly one of the greatest drivers of all time. It's that adversity that's helped him become that."

It was a similar kind of will to win that Ocon's father bred in him, knowing the importance of giving everything to make it in a hypercompetitive world when the odds were already stacked against them. "My dad was good in sports but never really had the opportunity to get the right people around him," said Ocon. "He thought, *One day, if I have a kid and he's good at doing what he does, I'm going to do everything I can to get him where he wants to go.* And together with my mum, he's done that, and even beyond."

Ocon's gratitude when talking about his parents was clear. He always knew the sacrifices they had made meant he could do something extraordinary, even at a young age. "I was *racing a go-kart* at the age of six or seven, so I'm already a superlucky person," Ocon said. "Not many people have the chance to drive a go-kart in the real world.

"That's the value that my parents have instilled in me: Always feel lucky for what you have. The competitive spirit is probably the biggest thing that differed our family to all the other kids on the grid at that time."

All twenty F1 drivers may now live vastly different lives to what they knew growing up, staying in the best hotels and flying first class—if not private jets—around the world. In the case of Lewis Hamilton, F1's biggest star with a celebrity status unmatched by any other in the sport's history, his contracts have been mooted to be somewhere around the $50 million per year mark for some time. It's an impossible amount of money to imagine, and a very different life to what he knew growing up, when he'd be sleeping on the couch in his father's one-bedroom apartment, and a day would start with a bacon sandwich or instant noodles while watching highlights of the sport that Anthony hoped his sacrifices would one day make Lewis a part of. Make no mistake: That past is never lost on Hamilton.

"He sacrificed everything for me to be here today, so I continue to try and make him proud," Hamilton said. "I know how hard it was for him with everything that he faced because I was right there with him.

"The ultimate dream is always to be like your father. I want to be like my father."

■ ■ ■

The lengths that Ocon's family went to just to keep Esteban racing are rare in F1, a sport that has fostered its glamorous reputation for big personalities and bigger wallets. Ultimately, this is a sport that has incredibly high barriers to entry, perhaps more so than any other. If a kid wants to throw a football or kick a soccer ball around, so long as they have the one required piece of equipment—the ball—and enough space, then they can do exactly that. But to be a racing driver? Even at the base level, you need a go-kart, a race suit, a helmet, gloves, and the track itself to drive on. It automatically prices out a very large percentage of the population.

As the drivers get older, the go-karts get more powerful and the competition increases, so does the spending and budgets involved. At the top levels of go-karting in Europe, a budget could be around $300,000 for a season. Once a driver has proven themselves in go-karting, they'd look to move up to car racing in the lowest category, Formula 4, where budgets for the national categories start nudging toward $400,000. Working up the racing ladder, they would move into Formula 3 ($1 to $1.5 million) then Formula 2 (as much as $3 million) before even having a chance to make a case for one of the twenty seats in Formula 1. And remember, each of those figures is *per season*. It is a long, expensive—and therefore sacrifice-laden—road.

It is for that reason all young drivers will look to raise funding to help them go racing, either by attracting sponsors or, for the most talented drivers, getting picked up by one of the F1 teams that has an academy for its juniors. All ten F1 teams have some kind of young-driver program, and a few look as far down as go-karting in their efforts to try to secure the next great talent. The support offered by a program can extend to funding to help them progress up the racing ladder. Lewis Hamilton was supported by McLaren and Mercedes in the early part of his single-seater career, and he went on to win championships for both teams. Max Verstappen was briefly a member of the Red Bull Junior Team at the age of sixteen, only for his talent to convince the team's management that he needed to be in F1 the following year, debuting at seventeen. It's a record that will likely never be beaten, given F1 reacted by introducing a rule insisting drivers had to be eighteen and hold a valid road driver's license—Max was too young to get one in his home country—but Verstappen's subsequent success has more than rewarded Red Bull's confidence in him.

But even drivers who are members of an academy will look for sponsorship to help meet the considerable costs involved. Just as F1 teams have cars and race suits covered in sponsors who help bolster their budgets, the same goes for young drivers. Financial backers will sometimes look for a percentage of future earnings or a continued promotion of their company should the driver they work with make it to the top level.

"A majority of the drivers here [in F1] make it with money," said Guenther Steiner, the former team principal of Haas. "They can show their talent to somebody who then invests money. As with everything else that you do, if you invest something, you don't want to lose your money. You take a risk, and if it pays off, you get some benefit."

The fact that motorsport is a rich man's game is nothing new. In the early days of automobile racing, long before the rise of professional competition, it was a pursuit reserved for those who could afford to purchase a car and compete. Upon the launch of the F1 world championship, manufacturers would work with elite drivers known for being among the best in the world, as is the case today. But there was also room on the grid for one-off entries from wealthy drivers, even extending to royalty. Prince Bira of Siam (now Thailand) was a regular competitor on the European racing scene before and after World War II, and made nineteen F1 world championship appearances, the last handful of which came in a Maserati 250F car that he owned. Bernie Ecclestone, who would go on to become F1's commercial chief in the late 1970s and mold the sport into the globe-trotting, financial behemoth it would become, used his personal wealth from investment and selling secondhand cars to twice attempt to qualify for grands prix in 1958, only to find out his talents in motorsport were better applied off the track.

Even world champions had to lean on financial support to make the initial step up to F1. Niki Lauda won three titles (1975, 1977, and 1984) en route to establishing himself as one of the all-time greats, enjoying close rivalries with James Hunt and Alain Prost. Yet without a bank loan he took out while racing in F2, secured against his life insurance, he would not have been able to keep racing. Lauda used the loan to secure a race seat in F1 that helped kickstart his career before he caught the attention of Ferrari, who signed him in 1974. It was a short-term bet on himself that he made work, leading to a remarkably successful career on and off the track in F1 that lasted until his death in 2019 at age seventy, having spent his final years in a senior management role at Mercedes amid its F1 domination.

In the past, some have enjoyed the benefits of government support or of large national corporations, who see success on a global scale in motorsport as a way to raise the profile of their country. Pastor Maldonado raced in F1 between 2011 and 2015 with backing from Venezuela's state oil company, PDVSA, and dropped off the grid when the funding dried up as global oil prices tanked and the country faced economic issues. Sergio Pérez, a grand prix winner with Red Bull and Racing Point, has received backing from Mexican telecommunications magnate Carlos Slim throughout his career. Slim helped fund Pérez's racing dream through to F1, with Slim's company, Telmex, becoming a long-serving partner through Pérez's career, its logos featuring on all his cars. Even when racing for the best and richest teams, drivers who can bring either financial backing or are commercially lucrative may have an edge over those rivaling them for a seat.

Those who perform well at junior levels will often attract top sponsors who want to be associated with the next great talent, but in order to race at junior levels in the first place, they have to find money of their own. Teams in F2 and F3 will sell each of their seats to drivers who cover the cost of racing. Although all drivers get the same cars in these championships, meaning there's no disparity in the performance of their machinery as there is between F1 teams, some junior teams have better operations than others and are therefore the most attractive to youngsters, meaning those teams can also command a higher fee. Drivers with more backing will also be able to complete more private testing than their rivals, giving them an advantage.

Alex Albon, an F1 podium finisher who has raced for Toro Rosso, Red Bull, and Williams, was picked up by Red Bull's junior team when he was in karting. He emerged as part of a group of incredibly talented drivers that now reads as a who's who of the F1 grid, including the likes of Ocon, Verstappen, George Russell, and Charles Leclerc. "In those years, it was usual that maybe one driver per age group made it to F1, if that," Albon said. "So then to have four or five of us make it, even more, it was a golden generation." Today the drivers enjoy a friendship and camaraderie rarely seen before in F1, something Albon attributed to their time together in go-karting. "Outside of the circuit, not only were we close, but we also ended up being teammates a lot of the time," he said. "That's why we're particularly close with each other. A lot of days were spent in hotel rooms, you can imagine, just like kids, mucking around, running down the hallways, that kind of thing."

But racing kids have to grow up quickly. It was something Albon found out when he was dropped from Red Bull's program after a tricky first year in single-seaters in 2012, leaving him with a deep hole in his funding to keep racing. "I was kind of in the weeds," he recalled. "I didn't have the money to keep going. In one year, my life turned around so quickly. I wasn't prepared going into single-seaters. I wasn't prepared for what was going to happen after, once I got dropped, and had to really scramble around." In the same year, Albon's mother went to prison for luxury car fraud, a deep personal challenge for a young man of sixteen to deal with while trying to piece his career back together.

Albon met with Lagrue, the Mercedes talent scout, whom he knew from his time racing up against Ocon. "I told him my issue," Albon said. "He believed in me, saw my results in karting. He said, 'Okay, first we've got to get you on the grid, find some money, and get you back in.' He put his own money in as well, he really committed on that. I'm always very thankful for that." British-born but racing under the Thai flag through his mother, Albon even spent time in Thailand trying to raise local sponsorship, successfully getting the money together to continue racing.

It wasn't until Albon's third year in single-seaters that he felt back to his old self. He puts part of the tricky adjustment down to not being able to afford a dual program in his final year in go-karting, which would have allowed him to do half a year in Formula 4 cars and do some testing to help bridge the gap to his first full season in car racing and reduce the learning curve. "If I had a kid, I know exactly what I would do differently," said Albon. "Unfortunately, it's come to a point now in motorsport where the more money you can spend, and the more testing you can do, the better you're going to be."

In 2016, Albon finished second to Ferrari junior hotshot Leclerc in GP3, allowing him to step up to F2 the following year. But as the budgets took another step up, the pinch to find money became increasingly hard. By the start of the 2018 F2 campaign, his team, DAMS, would only sign him to a race-by-race deal. If a driver swooped in with more cash, then he would be replaced.

Albon's impressive on-track performances convinced the team to keep him in the seat. He not only completed the full season, but he also became a surprise contender for the championship, eventually finishing third behind Russell and Lando Norris. Crucially, he also did enough to land an F1 seat, joining Red Bull's junior team, Toro Rosso, for the 2019 season. To make things even better, twelve races into his F1 career, he was handed a shock promotion to the senior Red Bull team. In the space of eighteen months, Albon had gone from not knowing if he would even be at the next F2 race to driving for one of F1's leading teams. Albon would only last one-and-a-half seasons with Red Bull before being replaced as he struggled to match Verstappen's results across the garage, the speed of his rise arguably being too fast. He still can't comprehend how his fortunes changed so quickly.

"It almost feels surreal," Albon said, looking back. "I'm someone who believes in karma, and I feel like almost no one would be lucky enough to be given these opportunities if it was down to the natural world."

But for those born into wealth, those opportunities are more likely to come and make the route up the ladder a little bit easier.

■ ■ ■

"This sport has become a billionaire boys' club."

Lewis Hamilton's comment to a Spanish newspaper, *AS*, in the spring of 2021 painted a stark and rather sorry picture of the state of F1. But there was a heavy dollop of truth in it.

Family backing is nothing new in motorsport. It's something a large percentage of the grid had while transitioning into their single-seater careers, to wildly varying degrees. One example is Lando Norris. He was a member of McLaren's junior program starting in 2017, but prior to that, much of the financial support that kept him racing was his father's wealth.

At the time Hamilton made his "billionaire boys" comment, three F1 drivers—so 15 percent of the grid—were sons of billionaires: Lance Stroll, Nicholas Latifi, and Nikita Mazepin. Each had got their F1 seat on merit, to a degree, due to an important rule governing who can become an F1 driver. Since 2016, the FIA has operated a points system that requires a certain level of success in junior categories in order to qualify for the Super Licence—think of it as an elite driver's license—that is required to race in F1. It means not just *anybody* can buy their way to a seat, and, as Stroll's remarkable efforts to be ready to race for the 2023 season showed, there is no guarantee of an easy life upon getting there.

Stroll's father, Lawrence, made his money investing in fashion brands like Tommy Hilfiger and Michael Kors in the 1990s, taking them international. His penchant for motor racing filtered through to Lance, whose racing career in go-karting he supported and funded before then investing in Prema Powerteam, the F3 team with which Lance won the European championship in 2016. When Lance moved up to F1 with Williams the following year,

Lawrence again brought financial backing to help Williams move forward, only for the team to struggle to compete with the leading teams and slump to last in the championship in 2018. By the middle of that year, Lawrence had acquired his own F1 team. After Force India went into administration, he formed a consortium that bought the struggling outfit for just $117 million—the team is now worth beyond the billion-dollar mark, making it a very savvy investment—and saved the jobs of everyone working at the team, which became known as Racing Point until its Aston Martin rebrand for 2021. Lance was signed as a Racing Point driver in 2019, displacing Ocon.

Latifi's case is a more curious one. He did not start go-karting until the age of thirteen, late compared to many of his peers. His father, Michael Latifi, is the CEO of Sofina Foods, a Canadian food manufacturer, and runs an investment company on the British Virgin Islands that has shares in McLaren. After rising up the junior motorsport ranks, Latifi spent four years in Formula 2 (including one year when the series was known as GP2) and was runner-up in the championship in his final year, scoring four victories, before graduating to F1 with Williams. Unlike Stroll, he did not win a championship at any level en route to F1.

The same was true of Mazepin, whose father, Dmitry, regularly featured on the list of Russia's wealthiest businessman as the owner of chemicals company Uralchem and Uralkali, the world's largest potash producer. Mazepin progressed through the European karting championships before moving through single-seaters, finishing as runner-up in GP3 (which would later become F3) and then fifth in Formula 2 ahead of graduating to F1 with Haas the following year. A sign of the financial considerations involved came with the rebranding of Haas as "Uralkali Haas F1 Team" as Mazepin's father's company took over the title sponsorship of the American outfit in a deal worth more than $20 million per season—money that Haas badly needed at that time.

We've already established that just because a driver has money, or has unconventional means with which to raise it, it does not mean they aren't qualified to race in F1. But how did the "billionaire boys" stack up in F1, given none of them displayed the red-hot, impossible-to-ignore form that made the likes of Leclerc and Russell such hot property through their junior careers? And would they have even made it to F1 without such deep pockets?

Stroll has cemented himself as a mainstay on the F1 grid. He is the second-youngest driver in F1 history to score a podium (after only Verstappen), the second-youngest points scorer (behind Verstappen, again), and the sixth-youngest driver in F1 history to score a pole position, a memorable result coming in wet conditions at the 2020 Turkish Grand Prix. Yet he has struggled to outperform his experienced teammates through his career, most notably when alongside Pérez and Fernando Alonso. Alonso, who was forty-one upon becoming teammates with Stroll, always stated it was his ambition to help form the succession plan at Aston Martin by building the team into a position where, once he retired, Stroll could take over as the de facto team leader on the race track and become a championship contender. Question marks linger over the likelihood of that happening and whether Stroll has the natural ability that makes the best drivers stand out, but there isn't the same kind of doubt over his place on the grid that there always was with Latifi and Mazepin. Of the three, he is the only one to have extended his F1 career beyond three seasons.

Latifi debuted in 2020 for Williams, a team that found itself lagging far behind the rest of the grid as years of underinvestment took its toll, leading to a car design that was significantly slower than everyone else's. In Latifi's three seasons, Williams finished last in the championship twice, and failed to score any points at all in 2020, meaning he never got the kind of car that might have allowed him to show more potential. But the biggest question mark about his form came in his comparison to his teammates, Russell (2020–2021) and Albon (2022). In sixty-one races for Williams, Latifi outqualified his teammate—who had the exact same car, remember—on only six occasions. While Russell and Albon stood out for doing the best they could with a substandard car, clawing points where possible, Latifi's F1 career ended up being mainly remembered for his late crash in the 2021 Abu Dhabi Grand Prix. The subsequent safety car would spark a rule fumble by then-race director Michael Masi, whose erroneous restart with one lap to go allowed Verstappen to pass Lewis Hamilton and win the world championship. Latifi would face unwarranted abuse and death threats for an innocent mistake, and after losing his Williams seat at the end of 2022, he stepped away from motorsport altogether, eventually pursuing a master's degree in business management at university in London.

Mazepin's F1 career was even more fleeting and was embroiled in controversy before it started. In December 2020, just eight days after Haas announced Mazepin would be part of its lineup for the 2021 season, a video was posted on Mazepin's Instagram Stories in which he reached from the passenger seat of a car and groped a woman's chest. The woman raised a middle finger at the camera in reaction. The video was quickly deleted from Mazepin's account, and the woman would later claim she posted it herself on Mazepin's Stories as a joke. His actions were condemned by Haas as "abhorrent," and Mazepin issued an apology, saying he had to "hold myself to a higher standard as a Formula 1 driver." Haas conducted an investigation and said the matter was "dealt with internally" and kept him as part of its lineup for 2021, later unveiling a new car livery that was in the colors of the Russian flag linked to the sponsor, Uralkali. It was an extremely visible sign of the importance of the money Mazepin brought to the team.

On-track, Mazepin would do little to properly justify his place on the grid. Preferring to divert resources to the 2022 car, Haas opted against any car development through 2021, accepting it would be in for a difficult year and finish last in the championship. Neither Mazepin nor his teammate, fellow rookie Mick Schumacher, scored any points, but Schumacher outqualified Mazepin twenty times in twenty-two races. As debut seasons go, Mazepin's had few redeeming features. Even the *Drive to Survive* episode about him attempted to play up his performance at his home grand prix in Russia by portraying him judging the clouds to know when to change to rain tires ahead of an incoming downpour—he still finished last. The episode also included a point where his father, Dmitry, threatened to pull his company's funding over concerns Nikita wasn't getting the same machinery as Schumacher. The influence of the pay driver's backers in F1 can be considerable.

The reality of F1 means teams sometimes have faced no choice but to take the money and hire a driver who, were financial considerations not such a factor, would not typically be a serious contender. It is something that Steiner, the former Haas team principal, acknowledged when I brought up the 2021 driver lineup decision with him. At that point, the team was in serious need of financial backing after seeing its revenues impacted by the Covid-19 pandemic, prompting the top management to question whether it would even be possible to continue racing. To help remedy the situation, the team parted company with Kevin Magnussen and Romain Grosjean, two experienced racers who knew how to get on the F1 podium, at the end of 2020 in order to bring in Mazepin and Schumacher, both of whom brought sponsorship.

When I asked Steiner if the team's position meant the commercial factors swung a bit further than they normally would, he raised his eyebrows at me and laughed: "'A bit' is quite a light way to put it, leave 'a bit' out!" he replied, honest as ever. "It swung in a commercial direction, seeing what [sponsorship] they could bring with them." On Mazepin, Steiner admitted: "He would have struggled to get the seat without the commercial considerations, or the title sponsor he brought with him."

Come 2022, Haas would have to survive without the Mazepin money. Following Russia's invasion of Ukraine in the February of that year, both the Uralkali sponsorship agreement and Mazepin's contract were terminated due to Dmitry's ties to Vladimir Putin, and both Mazepins would be placed on the UK sanctions list. Haas wasted little time removing the Russian colors from its car, literally scraping off the stickers midway through preseason testing, as it swooped to re-sign Magnussen, who had raced for the team between 2017 and 2020. It was an extremely popular decision and one that immediately paid off: After a year out of F1 altogether, Magnussen finished his first race back in fifth place. Peter Crolla, the Haas team manager, coyly noted that "the level of enthusiasm changed massively" among the Haas workforce when the switch was made: "The driver lineup has a massive impact on people's kind of emotional output."

It can sometimes be a difficult pill for drivers to swallow, seeing their F1 dream end because a driver with more money has come along and displaced them. At the end of the 2021 season, Alfa Romeo dropped Italian driver Antonio Giovinazzi in favor of Zhou Guanyu, who graduated from F2. Zhou became China's first F1 driver and had some backing from China, prompting Giovinazzi to react to the decision by posting on Instagram: "F1 is emotion, talent, cars, risk, speed. But when money rules, it can be ruthless." His team looked askance on the comments, pointing out he'd had three seasons on the grid and plenty of opportunities to make a case for being retained, while Zhou would quickly justify the decision by scoring a point in his first race in 2022 and getting a contract for the following year.

But even at the lower levels of junior motorsport, it can be a challenge for young drivers to stand out and display their true talent when they're racing against wealthier drivers. It was something Albon found upon his move from go-karting to single-seaters. Drivers who had deeper pockets and could spend more money on private testing were at an immediate advantage. "People I was comfortably beating in karting were suddenly beating me in single-seaters," he recalled. "I was a bit like . . . 'I'm doing something wrong here.' I guess in some ways, you had an expectation of your talent, and even though if I wasn't the most arrogant guy, I thought to myself, *I'm losing out to people who wouldn't even be in the top fifteen in karting, never mind beating me in single-seaters.*" Albon made clear that it was "never jealousy" he felt toward the wealthier drivers, instead using it as a "little bit of a reality check" of what he needed to do to raise his performance and rise to the top. "I put it very much on myself," he said. "I wasn't blaming or looking at other people, it was, I've got to get my act together here, and figure out what's going on."

On the discussion of talent versus money being the biggest influence on performance among youngsters, Trevor Carlin thought wealthy drivers "can get to the doors of Formula 1 by always having the best stuff" at their disposal. "But when they get into Formula 1, all of a sudden, it really is a meritocracy," he said. "Some of them just can't cope."

Around a quarter of the current F1 grid once raced for Carlin in their junior careers, the likes of Lando Norris and Daniel Ricciardo being the standout stars from the hundreds who have passed through his teams. But when discussing those who bring a lot of money to the table, Carlin acknowledged there is "a whole lot of entitlement with some drivers" he has encountered, albeit without wishing to name names.

"If they're not fast, then the first thing they do is come to me and blame my team, my engineers, or the engines, things like that," he said. "If it is a problem with us, the team or the car or the engine, then we're the first ones to want to fix it. But now as I've become a little bit older and wiser, I tell the drivers, 'No, it's you.' It is a sport at the end of the day, and they are the athlete, they're the skilled person, they have to be the best they can. And some of them just aren't good enough. It's as simple as that.

"But their dads believe they are, so they keep throwing money at it. It's not always the right thing to do. Some of them are a bit spoiled, I have to say."

When I reminded Hamilton of his billionaire boys' club comment two years later, and asked if he thought anything was changing, he was fairly blunt. "No, it's getting more and more expensive," he said. "Do you see any other working class youngsters here? That's probably not going to be the case, unfortunately."

■ ■ ■

If the picture surrounding the talent of young drivers is often clouded by the amount of money they have behind them on the road to F1, how do the best still rise to the top regardless of their circumstances? And what can be done to try and fix the system to make it cheaper and more transparent?

It is something James Vowles, the team principal of Williams, "kept hypothesizing" during his time at Mercedes, when he was heavily involved in young driver development as Toto Wolff's right-hand man. Although his focus was on F1, Vowles took an interest in young drivers going right the way down to go-karting, where he was and remains staggered by the costs involved. "It is ludicrous in many regards that we're spending a quarter of a million for a sensible karting team," he said. According to Vowles, the Italian national go-karting championship is the series where drivers know they will be racing up against the best, making it the only one F1 teams pay close attention to with their scouting. "You can win the British championship, and it doesn't mean anything," he said, claiming that even though it's half the price of racing in Italy, it is impossible to truly judge how good a driver could become. The same goes with the move up to single-seaters: In F4, drivers need to be racing in the Italian championship, then graduate to Formula Regional before moving up to F3. As this is the only path drivers can realistically take to make it up to F1 nowadays, the budgets involved are understandably higher.

One thing Vowles believed can bring costs down is a reduction in testing, but he acknowledged there isn't an easy or practical way to do it. "There are people whose livelihood it is to run a kart team, and they can't run a kart team for half of the year," he said. Even with cuts to testing in F2 and F3, Vowles said drivers are "talking about two million" for a season and that "clearly, no normal human being would be able to afford that."

It means to go racing at the highest levels, Vowles thought drivers need to be "at the mercy of being involved with an F1 team, or being so wealthy that it doesn't make a difference to you. Or you've sold your soul to the devil! All three exist, and you've seen drivers recently do all three. All of this is a roundabout way to say . . . that I'm afraid I don't have a solution at the moment. I don't think we're working towards a solution either, as teams and organizations. We're just accepting that it is the way it is. I hope in time that we can think of a better way of doing this."

Steiner agreed that it is "very difficult" to bring the costs of racing down. But he believed the most talented and capable drivers will always make it to the top. "Yes, it's a rich man's game, but it's not only a rich man's game," he said. "Look at all the teams. There are very few people who come from very rich families." The definition of "very rich" is a loose one here; to Hamilton's original point, there are few (if any) other drivers who could really be called "working class" even if they're not coming from billionaire families, which has skewed the concept of what wealth looks like in our sport. "Obviously if you do a good job, you have the talent and market yourself well, you can still find the support you need from an individual, a wealthy one, or from a junior program from one of the manufacturers," Steiner added.

That could be the solution to racing's financial problem: the money at the top trickling down to support young drivers with the talent to really shine. Because there is no escaping that, to make a young driver's racing career happen, with all the travel and associated costs involved, there's always going to be a need for deep pockets.

"You need to have backing of some sort," said Ocon. "There's no secret that this has to be the case. There are still great people around that are helping the young drivers, there are a lot of academies that are helping, a lot of big sponsors that are still involved. But in a way, it's still too expensive. It would be nice if it's more affordable for everyone, and there would be many more surprises, I'm sure, if that was the case.

"But it's motorsport. Anything that goes fast with wheels, from radio control cars to motorbikes to go-karts to cars, it's going to be expensive."

Something money cannot buy young drivers is the characteristics that set them apart to succeed. Trying to analyze and evaluate kids in go-karting can be a challenge, given how quickly young people develop through that time in their lives, even without the pressures of being involved in competitive motorsport. Their results will speak for themselves, but a young racer's attitude and demeanor are things that Vowles believed can offer good insight into whether a young driver has what it takes to one day make it to F1. Every team is searching for the next Verstappen or Hamilton, meaning they need to identify what separates the great from the good at a very early stage.

"Do they have the capability to go all the way?" Vowles pondered. "Do they have the determination to make it? Do they have the behavioral patterns you're looking for, so performance under pressure? And of course, do they have the performance in a kart? Already by age eleven, you'll have normally three years of racing in a kart, so you can start to see probably where they are.

"You clearly look for performance, but even if they're not winning but they have performed under pressure, you want to see the right culture. When there's a problem and a failure, they haven't won a race or they've been knocked off or something's happened, they internalize what they could have done better, here's how I could have improved, these are the steps I'm going to be taking. How do they behave with the team afterwards? For me, it's 50 percent cultural, and 50 percent performance."

One of the shifts that may make it possible for there to be more money trickling down from teams toward supporting young drivers, and an emphasis in going for talent over all commercial considerations when selecting their lineup, is F1's recent boom in popularity and, as a result, its income. From the tricky days of the

Covid-19 pandemic when multiple teams were unsure if they would even be racing the following season, revenues are now at a level where every team on the grid is stable. Now that sponsors are flocking to the grid and paying sizable sums to get their logos put across the car, there is less of a need for teams to rely on funding associated with a driver. Some drivers may still bring sponsorship or backing, but a team like Haas would now never need to consider going solely down the route of hiring drivers based chiefly on the money they bring in order for the team to survive.

Performance can also go a long way to make up for any financial shortfall in the form of prize money. Each position in F1's Constructors' Championship is worth somewhere in the region of $15 million, meaning a stronger driver is more likely to help a team up the table. "If you had the choice between a driver who you know can score you points, and a driver who is okay and he *could* score you points but he brings ten or fifteen million, you still take the other one," Steiner said. "Because the ten to fifteen million, with one position in the championship, you make it up. And by doing that, having better results, your partners are happier, and you enjoy going racing.

"In the end, every race team is not run because of the commercial benefits. They are run to go racing. And if you do racing well, you will make money. You will be successful."

Vowles was hopeful the investment from teams at the lowest junior levels will help to form more of a "meritocracy" through junior championships. "I think this concept of taking a few million to put someone in the car is not the way that we can perform these days," he said. "Otherwise, you'll fall back."

It is an approach that Carlin believed is already shaping the current F1 grid, helping raise its quality. "The money shot is when you get a driver that's really, really good, and has money as well," Carlin said. "That's a Norris-type scenario where he is just supremely talented and kept his independence so he could pick and choose which Formula 1 team he went to. That's the magic sauce, when they've got the money and the talent. I think we've seen the level of Formula 1 drivers get higher and higher now, I really do."

It is a correct assessment due to all three factors: the Super Licence system requiring a certain level of success and, therefore, performance; the increased investment from F1 teams in young talent at an early age; and the reduced need for them to take a pay driver because of their uplifts in income. Should that stay in place over time, there is hope that junior motorsport can become more of a meritocracy—even if it will always remain an expensive meritocracy.

3

Off the Grid

Melbourne, Australia's second-largest city, is one of my favorite places in the world.

We're fortunate in this job to travel to some of the most spectacular places and countries on the planet, experiencing different cultures, cuisines, and climates, even if only on fleeting visits for a few days at a time over a grand prix weekend. But if you had to ask me to pack my bags and move anywhere at the drop of a hat, it would have to be Melbourne. In a heartbeat.

I love Melbourne for its charm and culture; its vast-ranging food; its European-style architecture; the friendliness of the locals; the blend of a buzzing, metropolitan city within easy reach of beaches and countryside. And there's no better place in the world to get a good brunch. As much as the rivalry may roll on between

Melbourne and Sydney for the accolade of Australia's best city, I'm firmly on the Melbourne side.

When the Covid-19 pandemic really set in through the March of 2020, hitting F1 when we were all down under and causing the Australian Grand Prix to be canceled just hours before practice was due to begin, there was uncertainty over when we might return. The severity of Australia's restrictions through its pursuit of a Covid-zero policy meant the 2021 race didn't stand a chance of happening. Melbourne endured one of the toughest Covid-19 lockdowns and spent more days in lockdown—262—than any other city in the world. There was a strict 9 p.m. curfew, and people were only allowed to leave home for essential work, to go shopping, or to briefly exercise.

So to be back as soon as the spring of 2022, roaming the streets I'd been longing to see again during the darkest depths of lockdown in my tiny London apartment, felt as invigorating as it did strange—especially as Melbourne's restrictions had been lifted only four months earlier. With the grand prix weekend now complete and a couple of vacation days booked, I'm taking in all the sights and sounds I've missed for the past two years. I've checked out the graffiti on Hosier Lane. I've run down to St Kilda beach. I've gone for brunch at St. Ali, a favorite locale of Finnish F1 driver Valtteri Bottas, who through his Australian partner has become an adoptive son of the locals in Melbourne. The following year, he'll even launch his own coffee beans with St. Ali and adopt a mullet hairdo to really lean into the stereotype. Even little things like the sound of the kookaburra bird used for the road crossings, the confusing different sizes of beers—from small to big, it goes pot, schooner, then pint—or the free trams in the middle of the city stir a feeling of belonging that has been absent for over two years. At last, in my unconventional life on the road with F1, normality has resumed.

But there's one thing at the top of my list today: I want to eat the best croissant in the world.

I know what you're thinking: in Australia? Surely France is the place you'd want to go for the greatest pastries? Well, if the line outside Lune on Collins Street in Melbourne's Central Business District is anything to go by, stretching up the block and around the corner, then this could well deliver on that promise.

As I join the rear of the line, I'm braced for a long wait. We edge forward slowly, the anticipation of the groups in front of me growing with each step. A passerby on the phone tells the person on the other end: "I reckon it's about an hour. . . . Not bad, you want me to wait?"

After forty-five minutes, I am at the threshold and see the different croissants on display behind the counter. A group of eight or nine workers dart around, pulling fresh pastries out of massive batch ovens, ensuring each one is ready to serve at the optimum temperature. Upon reaching the counter, I ask for an almond croissant, which is handed back to me in a brown paper bag warmed by its contents. The line is now even longer than when I joined it. How did I know this would be worth the wait? I was going off the *New York Times*, which in 2016 wrote a feature about Lune entitled "Is the World's Best Croissant Made in Australia?"

I find a sunny spot in Fed Square around the corner, opposite the beautiful Flinders Street station. Obligatory "before" pictures for Instagram taken, I take my first bite into the croissant—and it's everything I wanted it to be. The almond filling is still warm, and the layers of pastry are more tightly packed than any croissant I've eaten before. It's light and buttery, yet perfectly chewy and a little bit crunchy on the outer layer, the almond flakes arranged so perfectly it reminds me of a porcupine. You'd regret eating such a beautiful creation if it didn't taste so good. Every second in that line had been worth it. I can't vouch for it being the best croissant in the world, but I can certainly vouch for it being the best croissant I have ever eaten. Lune is now my first port of call upon returning to Melbourne.

And without Formula 1, Lune's world-famous croissants would never have come into existence.

As with so many who end up working in the sport, Kate Reid was exposed to racing incredibly young—in fact, before she was even born. Her father raced in Formula Vee (an amateur, low-level single-seater series), and while pregnant, her mom would go and watch. "I think she blames the fact that I probably got the smell of petrol and the sound of cars from a very early age," Reid said.

It would be the start of a shared passion between Reid and her father. Since they lived in Melbourne, the F1 races would be on late at night, making it a novelty to be allowed to stay up and watch. "It was this incredibly exciting carnival that represented the height of technology in the automotive world, traveling around the most glamorous cities and countries," Reid said. "I was going from my lounge to Montreal and Monaco and Spa. It was a special way to virtually travel around the world with my dad." When the Australian Grand Prix moved to Melbourne in 1996, Reid's dad got her the day off school so they could go and watch practice. It was the first time she'd seen an F1 car in the flesh and heard the sound of the piercing V10 engine sweeping by. It would be all the confirmation she needed: "I still remember that moment of 'oh my God, this has to be my life!'"

Reid embarked on a career to become an aerospace engineer with a view to working in the aerodynamics department of an F1 team. It is one of the most crucial departments to help make a car go faster. Intricate changes to the design of a front or rear wing—adjusting the slope of a winglet to manipulate the airflow as it takes corners at full throttle, the downforce being generated sucking the car to the ground—can make all the difference. Upon completing her degree and working for Ford Australia, as well as volunteering for a Formula 3 team in Melbourne to gain some motorsport experience, Reid sent off her resume to all the F1 teams and inquired about volunteering ahead of doing a specialist master's in the UK, and waited to hear back. When she did, there were a lot of nos. "I realize now that it's impossible—no F1 teams have space for someone with no experience to come and volunteer!" she said. "Everyone in the team is too important to the progression of the performance of the car." But Williams replied to say it was looking for entry-level aerodynamicists, and that it wanted to talk to Reid. One successful phone interview later, she packed up her life to follow her dream in the UK.

The reality of F1 would be far different to what Reid had pictured as an eager-eyed kid watching races late at night with her dad. Based entirely at the factory and spending three out of four weeks per month in the office, the fourth being in the wind tunnel,

Reid struggled to fit in with the engineers around her who were happy to spend all their time knuckling down with work at their computers. "It was probably very evident from early on that engineering in general wasn't a great fit for my personality," she said. "The general type that suits engineering is relatively introverted and doesn't mind long periods of time by themselves working on a computer. Engineers are engineers for a reason, and there are some outliers like me. The office was very high pressure and a negative environment to work in, I guess because we weren't winning." A move to Force India, a team that was even less competitive in the championship, only made things worse. It ended up having a big mental and physical toll.

"Subconsciously I was starting to realize the picture that I painted of F1 was different to the reality," Reid said. "I'd put ten years of my life into it. I'd left behind my family. I'd left behind Australia. And it wasn't diagnosed, but I definitely developed depression at that stage, and it ended up manifesting into an eating disorder." Reid became so sick that her partner at the time called her parents in Australia, and her dad flew to the UK to bring her home.

"When you have an eating disorder, all you can do is think about food, because it's essentially your starving body sending signals to your brain all day to eat, and it's torture," Reid said. "All you can think about is food but it's the thing you don't want to do, you don't want to eat. But also, you don't really think about health food. You don't dream about lettuce or salad, you dream about the thing that you really want to be eating, and I really wanted to be eating baked goods. In particular, pastries."

Reid would get home from work and put her ideas for pastries into motion, all with an engineering mindset. Like the aerodynamic evaluations she would do in the office for the parts of a front wing, changing one variable at a time, she'd do the same with her pastries. The ingredients would be weighed out perfectly, the eggs, the sugar, the flour, and it would all come together into something far greater and far more delicious than the sum of its parts. She also took fulfillment from the joy it would bring her colleagues when she took the pastries into the office the next morning, all while applying her engineering mindset to baking. "I guess I was living vicariously through the process of even just working with the ingredients," she said. "I was marveling at the things I was creating."

When Reid returned to Melbourne, penniless but determined to pursue her passion, baking was what she turned to. She took a cash-in-hand job for fifteen dollars an hour at a bakery and asked if she could bake simple goods like cakes and cookies, to which the owner said yes. It would be her first foray into baking professionally, providing a sense of happiness and belonging that had been missing toward the end of her time in F1. But she still wanted more of a challenge. She took out a book called *Paris Patisseries: History, Shops, Recipes* from the library to learn more about French pastry. Sitting on her living room floor, she flicked through the pages and landed on a zoomed-in photo of a stack of *pains au chocolat*. "I was so moved by the photo that I shut the book, walked to the nearest travel agent, and booked a ticket to Paris."

In Paris, Reid would further her technical skills as an apprentice at the same boulangerie where that photo had been taken and, more importantly, try her hand at making croissants for the first time. "From day one, it was totally clear to me I had found my perfect crossover of baking and engineering," she said. "Croissants are the hardest pastry to make. If you do it properly it's a three-day process, and there are dozens and dozens of processes within those three days that are technical and scientific and precise." When she returned to Melbourne three months later, she was disheartened by the lack of good croissants in a city renowned for its world-class coffee. "I got thinking: *Maybe I learned enough in Paris to do this myself?* And Lune was born!"

Reid signed a lease for her first Lune shop in the bayside suburb of Elwood and began recipe testing, but there was an issue: She didn't know the full process of how to make a croissant. The head pastry chef at the boulangerie had never let her go beyond making the dough. "I tipped it out on the bench, and I remember staring at it and going: 'Oh my God, I don't know what to do next!'" she said, recalling the horror of that realization. "There were massive parts of the process that I had no idea how to do. I'd spent my meager life savings setting up the bakery, and I was like, well I can't really just leave all of this and go and do an apprenticeship, and I can't go back to school because I can't afford it. So at this point in time, I'm probably going to have to put my engineering hat on, and figure out how to reverse engineer this process."

In the next three-and-a-half months, Reid adjusted every variable possible with her recipe, tweaking the temperature by half a degree per day before finally getting a product she wanted to take to market. The results were spectacular: Within six weeks, people were already lining up when the shop opened at 8 a.m. As word got around Melbourne, the lines and waits got longer, prompting Reid and her brother, who had joined her to make the bakery customer-facing, to place caps on how many pastries people could buy—and they'd still wait from as early as 2 a.m. to get their hands on a Lune croissant. When a barista Reid knew asked if he could bring a friend to come and try a pastry, she sternly told him: "Yes, you can have one, so make sure you pick carefully!" Said friend turned out to be a *New York Times* journalist, who wrote the article that put Lune on the map worldwide.

Lune has grown rapidly from those humble beginnings. The business employs over two hundred staff and produces around thirty-eight thousand pastries per week across its Melbourne stores, and has expanded to other Australian cities with plans to go international. Each morning, Reid walks her black Labrador, Lily, to one of the Melbourne stores to go and see the staff, and marvels at the long lines. "Sometimes I have mornings where I walk past, and I just get really emotional," she said. "I think, wow, they are all here for a pastry I created. I feel so humbled and lucky."

Reid remains grateful for her time in F1, and her passion for the sport is still strong. She watches as many races as she can, and takes heart in seeing the Williams team she once worked for racing out on-track, as well as giving thought to the hundreds of people working behind the scenes back at the factory, once like her. The Australian Grand Prix is a permanent fixture in her calendar as "the happiest four days of the year." The organizers of the race even invited her to become an ambassador for the race, representing the combination of Melbourne's food culture and F1's cutting-edge approach to engineering. "It was really magical, both my worlds colliding in such a special way," she said. "Being able to represent

Melbourne, and the food and hospitality community, and to celebrate my technical background in F1, it was really a celebration I never imagined: that the two careers came together." At the 2024 race, Lune had its own stall in the fan zone for the first time, selling freshly baked pastries throughout the race weekend. The lines were longer than anywhere else around the circuit.

To this day, Lune operates like an F1 team. The pastries are its cars; the chefs are the engineers. And the mentality is the same as it was for Reid and the other aerodynamicists she once worked with: design is ever-evolving, and if you make a change to your baseline design that makes it better, that becomes the new baseline.

"I don't think Lune would exist in the format that it is now without my F1 background," Reid said. "I am going to be as bold as to say the existence of Lune has changed the way the entire world approaches croissants and production. People didn't care about croissants before Lune, maybe except in France. They were just a token menu item on most people's counters. But now people have realized that you don't have to settle for the centuries-old techniques. Everything is open to critical analysis and improvement."

It is precisely that kind of thinking that enables F1 to give so much to the world, even when it comes to reinventing and refining the humble croissant. Yes, it is a sport, yet the brilliance of the minds involved means it can make a far greater contribution to the world. As Reid put it: "Precision and process-driven thinking and problem-solving can be applied to absolutely anything. Lune is a good example of that."

It makes the F1 way of thinking valuable when it comes to far greater challenges facing the world, something acutely felt in those dark days of March 2020 when it was literally a matter of life and death.

■ ■ ■

As the spread of Covid-19 continued apace and the number of people being hospitalized started shooting up, the UK government quickly realized a pandemic was unavoidable. It had to start preparing for the worst and make up for shortages in an underfunded and, as a result, underprepared National Health Service (NHS). If the UK followed a similar trend to China and Italy, two of the first countries to be hit badly by Covid-19, then the eight thousand ventilators available across the country would be nowhere near enough. Technical industries began to shift their expertise and resources to help the nationwide response and produce a high volume of ventilators, known as the "Ventilator Challenge," with a wartime arms race spirit. F1 had its own role to play.

The government turned to the country's leading universities to evaluate potential ways to help. Tim Baker, a mechanical engineer at University College London (UCL), received a call from a fellow professor, Rebecca Shipley, who was involved in the ventilator response and wanted someone to assist on the mechanical side. Both met with one of the university hospital's main intensivists, Professor Mervyn Singer, who had been in touch with peers in China and Italy about what the next few weeks would look like. "It was a pretty scary conversation," Baker recalled. "The government was doing this ventilator challenge, but the reality was we needed something that bridged the gap between nothing and full-on ventilation." One method being used in other countries to keep people off invasive ventilation was CPAP (continuous positive airway pressure). Unlike ventilators, which require sedation and the insertion of a tube into the lungs to pump oxygen directly in while drawing carbon dioxide out, CPAP machines were noninvasive, using a mask that provided a constant flow of oxygen, preventing respiratory failure and getting more oxygen into the bloodstream. By using CPAP, patients were being kept off ventilators, making it an important form of care—but there weren't enough machines. More had to be produced en masse. Baker said they needed "something old school" that would do the job without lots of screens or clever tricks. But the engineering response had to be of a high quality and turn things around in a short timeframe—making F1 an obvious industry to approach.

The next day, Baker put in a call to his former protégé Ben Hodgkinson, who was now the head of mechanical engineering for Mercedes's F1 engine division, known as AMG High Performance Powertrains (HPP). His job was to work with the team designing the power units that helped Lewis Hamilton win races and championships. But with the F1 season on hold and all the engines sealed in Australia, it was unclear what Hodgkinson's next project would be. "I figured with the race being called off, they were going to be twiddling their thumbs, and I started thinking, it's kind of like getting the Blues Brothers back together," Baker said. He'd previously worked with Hodgkinson in F1 and stayed in close contact ever since.

Baker explained the situation to Hodgkinson, who got the blessing of his boss at Mercedes AMG HPP, Andy Cowell, to head down to UCL and learn more about what was needed, as well as pledging engineering support if needed from the Mercedes factory. Hodgkinson packed an overnight bag with three changes of underwear—"I thought it was a three-pant problem," he jokes—and drove down to London imagining the kind of complex contraption Baker might want him to design. His imposter syndrome had him asking whether he'd be capable of designing state-of-the-art medical equipment.

Hodgkinson met Baker in a cafe near UCL, where Baker pulled a CPAP machine that he'd taken from the UCL Hospital museum out of a plastic bag and laid it on the table. "I was like, 'Is that it!?'" recalled Hodgkinson. "It transpired he really just wanted me to reverse engineer and re-create that." He quickly realized it was possible, understanding that it was all about controlling the airflow, and he had experience with manipulating airflow in F1 at Mercedes. "We used it to entrain more gas into the exhaust flow where we were using blowing to energize the rear wing," said Hodgkinson. Knowing he could help, Hodgkinson went back with Baker to the "MechSpace" on UCL's campus, where they started to set about taking the CPAP machine apart so they could better understand how it worked and how it was made, and if they might be able to reverse engineer something better. The model they were looking at, known as the WhisperFlow, had been designed in 1992. The F1 mentality is always "this is good, but how do we make it better?"

Speed was everything at this point. Baker and Hodgkinson would not leave until they had reverse engineered the device and had something capable of going into mass production. They used a band saw at UCL to cut through the machine—Baker recalled "the look of horror" on the face of one of the intensivists as they "calmly sliced through one of his prized possessions"—and another CPAP machine was found on eBay by Cowell. A CT scanner was used to get a detailed look inside, allowing them to work on re-creating 3D models and draw every part that would need to be produced. By now, Hodgkinson had called on some extra Mercedes engineers to join him down in London. The group worked until 4 a.m. before going and getting an hour or two of sleep (or, at least trying) in a nearby empty hotel—London was by then a ghost town, absent of its regular tourists and visitors. Everyone reconvened at 7 a.m. to push on with the design. "None of us slept, our heads were spinning," said Baker. "We just cracked our heads together and kept going."

The collaborative engineering effort was similar to that of an F1 team. Everyone had their own jobs to do toward one end goal, but there was a trust and knowledge of the significance of the work they were doing. "I don't think there was ever an argument about anything, even though it was that pressured," said Baker. "Everyone had this incredible level of trust. Everyone knew what their part was." Some worked on CAD (computer-aided design) drawings of the parts for the machine, like they normally would for wings or aerodynamic F1 bodywork, while others focused on getting parts into production for the first prototypes. Mercedes was fully supportive of the entire project besides lending its engineers. Baker recalled the message he got from Cowell: "'Do not hesitate to call upon the might of what we can do.' That's when it really took off."

Hodgkinson had first met Baker in the cafe near UCL on Wednesday. By Sunday, less than one hundred hours later, they had successfully reverse engineered a CPAP machine, called the UCL-Ventura, and were able to conduct the first tests to ensure it was working. It was designed to be simple enough that hospital staff could learn how to use it during their tea breaks despite being tired from exhaustive shifts, yet an effective way to treat patients.

But the government still needed convincing. Up to this point, all the official guidance had been to focus on using ventilators to treat the worst-hit Covid-19 patients, making them the priority for both funding and resources. CPAP was not even on the health service's pathway as a form of treatment due to concerns over hospital oxygen supplies and the possibility of the virus being transmitted through aerosolization. It meant all the initial research, development, and manufacturing costs of the UCL-Ventura had to be covered by Mercedes AMG HPP and UCL. While Baker and Hodgkinson worked on refining the device further and set about working with Mercedes to put them into mass production, Shipley and her team worked with the public bodies to change the country's political direction toward Covid-19 treatment and ensure CPAP was included. Two days after the first UCL-Ventura prototype was delivered, the NHS issued new guidance approving the use of CPAP. Final regulatory approval for the UCL-Ventura arrived after thirty-six hours instead of the usual eighteen- to twenty-four-month process, and the government placed an order of ten thousand units. To meet such a high number in a short amount of time, Mercedes entirely repurposed its F1 engine facility for the production of the UCL-Ventura at a rate of one thousand devices per week. Within two weeks, the first hospitals were receiving the devices and using them to treat patients.

Mercedes's contribution to UCL-Ventura is something its F1 boss, Toto Wolff, looks back on with pride. "It saved lives," he said. "We got all the people back into the factory that were able to help production. You can see how Formula 1 can contribute, if we are putting all of our efforts into something. In that case, it was a very urgent health issue. That was something to be proud of."

By the time the device was on rapid rollout to hospitals, Baker and Hodgkinson's team had worked on a Mark II device that reduced oxygen consumption by 70 percent, allaying fears about possible shortages in hospitals, and they set about making the designs available online for free. For engineers with F1 backgrounds, where all designs are close-guarded secrets and IP is king, to give it away so freely was an alien experience—yet it spoke to something far, far greater. According to UCL, the design files were downloaded in 105 countries.

"Mercedes were fantastic and released all of the designs open-source so that we had countries all around the world that could access the designs," said Baker. "We had countries that had never made a medical device in their history that used those designs to make Venturas and treat patients."

As I chat to Baker and Hodgkinson three years later, the world is a very different place. Lockdowns are a thing of the past, and mass vaccination has helped the world return largely to normal. F1 is back to its globe-trotting best, going to more countries than ever. Somewhat fittingly, I'm talking to them over Zoom, very much an advent and lasting symbol of the lockdown experience for many, from a hotel room in Singapore, the same country I'd narrowly gotten out of before returning to lockdown in the UK on my way home from Australia. Both Baker and Hodgkinson are also now in different jobs. Hodgkinson left Mercedes to become the technical director of Red Bull Powertrains, tasked with designing the company's first F1 engine, which its team will use from 2026. One of the first people he called up to join his team was Baker. The Blues Brothers were reunited once again.

The UCL-Ventura project was a way for them to implement the best practices of an F1 team to something far more powerful. In an article for *The Lancet* that listed Baker, Shipley, Cowell, and Singer among its authors, they wrote: "The health-care industry can learn some valuable lessons from the motorsports industry in terms of their ability to adapt to ever-evolving situations, their design and manufacturing processes, and their nimble logistic capabilities. Efficient, streamlined, and synergistic partnerships between industry, academia, and health care are needed to break down barriers to innovation and adoption of novel, effective technologies."

As Baker reflects on the UCL-Ventura project, he shows disappointment that the healthcare system "went back to previous behavior" in the years that followed, lacking the collaborative nature and urgency that made the response to Covid-19 so powerful and effective. "You realize that for the big manufacturers, obviously it's all about profit," says Baker. "I think that's why they weren't able to respond quick enough when we got hit by the pandemic, because they're not set up to solve a problem. They're there to make a return for shareholders. We certainly had that different perspective on it, and really focused on the end user, what do they actually need, and being able to respond to that."

Both Baker and Hodgkinson admit they faced a tricky adjustment back to their regular jobs and duties afterward, and that it had a big impact on their perspective on the sport. "In many ways, it was life-changing," says Baker. "We lived on adrenaline for so long. To then just try to go back to normality was really, really hard. I've definitely got a completely different outlook, and I'm still doing things to try and help. Once you see that childhood pneumonia is a bigger killer than Covid was ever going to be in low- and middle-income countries with low resource settings, you realize that there's still a lot that you can do."

Hodgkinson explains that to sustain a long career in F1 such as his, dating back to the early 2000s, he's been able to reframe things by literally saying: "It's not saving lives." It's only racing. But now he was involved in a project that *was* saving lives.

"It's part of the reason why working so hard happened during this event," he says. "When I left at 4 a.m., I felt disappointed in myself, and that's why I got up early again. I thought, *I need to throw absolutely everything into it*. It was highly emotional. My niece is a doctor, and she was telling stories of how she was triaging and not treating the elderly, because it's that serious in hospitals—as if I needed any more motivation.

"I even feel quite emotional just talking about it, actually." He takes a pause to gather himself. "Those three days, there were no arguments. We just knew what we had to do. We knew what we were doing was right, and it was going to help, and we just had to throw everything we could at it. Subsequently, reflecting back on it, it's quite hard to justify spending a career in motorsport, actually."

It's something many within motorsport question: What is my purpose? F1 is glamorous and exciting, but does it actually give anything back to the world? UCL-Ventura proves that yes, it absolutely does. The world needs innovators. It needs inspired people. And F1 is an industry filled with people who are exactly that.

"The reality is that making cars go around a track really quick just inspires me," says Hodgkinson. "To be part of that, it's almost as if I'm addicted to it. It's a bit of a drug really. So being able to point that at something else, to show that we can develop anything fast, just give us the circumstances to make it possible and we'll do it, it was great to be able to demonstrate that to the world."

It's a demonstration that is a vital part of what makes F1 so relevant not only within its own "bubble," where everything comes down to tenths of a second in the heat of competition, but also to so many aspects of life far away from the sport. Being part of something that spends a lot of time, manpower, and money all to be lazily labeled from the outside as just "cars going around in circles" misses the wider contribution that F1 has made. Obviously the manufacturers that involve themselves in F1 do so in part to develop new technologies, with the height of competition allowing for concepts like sustainable fuels or hybrid engines to be pushed to their limits and eventually trickle down to the cars people drive day-to-day. Yet F1 is not only about doing good for the automotive industry. It genuinely can make the world a better place, be it through Kate Reid's delicious croissants, which have Melburnians queuing around the block, or, more seriously, by saving lives thanks to its quick-thinking engineers and the might of the sport coming together in response to Covid-19. F1's mentality has literally saved lives.

"The industry is exciting," says Hodgkinson. "I think it proves again and again that if you make something a competition, your innovation rate can far outstrip any other industry. The creativity and the pace of innovation, you just don't get it anywhere else."

F1 truly is a sport like no other in that regard. Nothing else combines the same degree of engineering and athletic spectacle, pushing both to the very limit. It's a characteristic that has become not only part of its appeal to fans across the world but also ingrained within its history.

But there's also the side of F1 you are more likely to see splashed across the newspapers and social media: the glitz and glamour.

4]

Champagne Problems

t's Saturday night in Monaco. Formula 1 is in town, turning the
tiny principality, once described by the writer William Somerset
Maugham as being "a sunny place for shady people," into one of
the most coveted locations for A-listers, B-listers, Z-listers, and
everyone in between for a few days.

Standing on the top of the Red Bull motor home overlooking
the harbor, I look at the horizon. The high-rise apartment blocks
bunch tightly together in the distance, stretching up the hill and
across the border into France. At their feet lies the port, around
which the F1 track that pulls tens of thousands of people into Monaco for the weekend is strewn like a ribbon, up the hill past the

casino and back down again along the waterfront. The circuit is opened to pedestrians each night, meaning the patches of tarmac in the final sector, where Max Verstappen and Lewis Hamilton were darting their cars between the walls at over 100 mph just hours earlier, are now filled with people drinking and dancing outside the bars. The nearby yachts are blaring music and flashing lights, their owners having paid anything up to $100,000 just for the right to park their boat in prime position in the harbor for the weekend. Considering some of the mega yachts are worth $50 million, the mooring fee is pocket money; it'd be like you or I putting a few dollars in the parking meter.

Being on the inside of the F1 world over the Monaco weekend is one of the strangest experiences of the season, one that is alien to the vast majority of those in the paddock, who would otherwise have zero reason to come to such a place. I spent Friday night dashing between two yachts for media events—companies and oil-rich nations keen to make an impression and lay on the schmooze. I learned the hard way a couple of years earlier that wearing an appropriate pair of socks when in Monaco is important if you are planning to venture onto any of the yachts, as most require you to take off your shoes. The look on the face of the man taking my bags as I stepped aboard one year when I took off my shoes to reveal a pair of Kermit the Frog socks, an old Christmas gift from my mom, stays with me. . . .

It's not real life. That's the thing to remember in all of this. It's the one race of the season where F1 truly leans into its reputation for big parties and putting on a show.

Right now, I'm holding a gin and tonic, pondering the best way to get back to my three-star, $150-a-night hotel in Nice, given it's past midnight and the trains have all stopped. Downstairs there is a DJ playing a set and long lines at the 360-degree bars, service staff in crisp white shirts diving to the guests' every need. The Brazilian soccer star Neymar is playing poker as part of a sponsor appearance at the party.

And I'm starting to sway. No, it's not because I've had too much to drink. Red Bull's motor home in Monaco is in fact a *floater home*, moored in the harbor next to the F1 paddock. In the early days of the team's existence, prior to becoming the serial race- and championship-winning operation it is today, Red Bull wanted to be known as the team that did things differently by bringing a bit of fun and out-of-the-box thinking to F1. The party team, if you will. One of the biggest statements it made to live up to this reputation was to place its motor home, known as the Energy Station, on top of a barge that would then be moored in the Monaco harbor next to the F1 paddock. It's a process that takes more than three weeks to complete: The hospitality unit on the barge is built over forty miles away in Italy before it is transported six hours and squeezed into its spot for the weekend. Not only does it mean the team has all of its regular working space on a race weekend, instead of cramming its usual unit into the limited confines of the Monaco paddock, but the novelty also proved to be a hit. It's become one of the most vibrant, buzzing places across the whole Monaco weekend. There's even a swimming pool on the top that has been the site of many a postrace celebration for Red Bull over the years.

Only in F1 would a floating motor home exist. Throughout its history, the sport has forged a reputation for its outrageous excess, its parties, and, more importantly, its exclusivity. The Monaco grid is no different.

At the start of this book, I wrote about the prerace buildup for the opening race of the season in Bahrain: how the tension and pressure ramp up the closer we get to lights out; how everyone has a job to do—the drivers, the mechanics, all the team members. Well, picture that with about half as much space, and throw in a dose of celebrity pizzazz that has everyone rushing for selfies and brief TV interviews. Then you have Monaco.

It makes the next day one of the highlights of the season. On my way down to the grid, I see Neymar again, walking gingerly. I can't work out if it's due to the injury that prevented him from playing in Paris Saint-Germain's championship-winning fixture the previous night, or the diamond-encrusted trainers on his feet. NFL star Odell Beckham Jr., rapper Bad Bunny, comedian Chris Rock, and even Spider-Man himself, Tom Holland, are all in attendance, seeing the cars and drivers up close in the minutes leading up to lights out. Their pictures will be plastered across the newspapers' showbiz sections the next morning. For those chasing and covering celebrity culture, F1 in Monaco is a gold mine.

It's always interesting to see which celebrities are big on the F1 spectacle and which are there largely because of some sponsorship or commercial requirement. You do get some superfans. Gordon Ramsay is one who comes to mind, his attendance on the grid now feeling like a regular part of a race weekend, even at some of the more rural or obscure events like the Austrian Grand Prix, which takes place in Spielberg, a town in the middle of the Styrian mountains about two hours out from Vienna, a long way from any kitchen nightmares. You do also hear stories about Grammy Award–winning popstars refusing to come out of their VIP suites for even a second, showing zero interest in the racing ahead of their performance later in the day, or the influencers working hard to maximize their time in front of the cameras.

Still, you can bet on Monaco to bring out a regular stream of the same big names year after year, including *Game of Thrones* stars Liam Cunningham—a huge F1 fan who spends most of his time on the grid snapping photos with his professional camera—and Kit Harington, the latter being the only celebrity I've ever had the courage to ask for a selfie back at the height of the show's popularity. He didn't smile or say a word, silently nodding when I asked if I could get a picture, but he was at least kind enough to offer a second of his time.

"The show" is something F1 has to weigh up far more than other sports. The grand prix is not simply what happens on the track but also everything that goes on around it.

■ ■ ■

Monaco is where the roots of F1's glamorous reputation were formed. The grand prix was first held in its streets in 1929, prior to the formation of the F1 world championship, around the time when increasing numbers of European countries and automobile clubs were beginning to take an interest in competitive racing. With the support of the royal family, the inaugural Monaco Grand Prix was held in April and won by William Grover-Williams, a British driver who would go on to be a spy supporting the Allied resistance in World War II. While the course was rudimentary, using hay bales along the side of the harbor to outline the course as recently as 1967—the two-time world champion, Alberto Ascari, famously launched his car into the water after going off the track in the 1955 race; he survived—it proved a hit among the drivers and the locals, quickly becoming a highlight of Monaco's social calendar.

It led to the race gaining a special place not only within F1 folklore but global motorsport. Alongside the Indianapolis 500 and the 24 Hours of Le Mans, Monaco formed the "Triple Crown of Motorsport," a prestigious trio of races that drivers, back when many would take part in more disciplines than just F1, sought to complete. Just one driver, Graham Hill, has ever managed the feat. He gained the nickname "Mr. Monaco" for his five victories around the street circuit, a tally later surpassed only by Ayrton Senna, who won six times in seven years from 1987 to 1993. All the greats have won in Monaco, its tight confines and beckoning walls that punish even the slightest of errors making it one of the hardest circuits on the calendar.

As F1 began to grow into the commercial giant we know today, Monaco quickly became the most significant race on the calendar off-track. It would be where all the team owners would sweet-talk and impress blue-chip sponsors, champagne overflowing on oversize yachts and parties going long into the night. Excess was the name of the game. In 2004, the Jaguar team leaned into the image of the race by putting a diamond worth $300,000 into each of the nose cones of its cars, one of which then crashed on the opening lap of the race. The diamond was never found.

Yet times are changing. Monaco may be considered F1's "jewel in the crown," but from a purely sporting point of view, it is simply one race of twenty-four taking place each year. As F1 starts to explore newer destinations such as Singapore, Miami, and Las Vegas, all of which have their own sparkle that appeals to new fans and draws in big names, there's no longer the same kind of onus on Monaco to be the it-race for F1.

There's even the debate around whether it is really an appropriate place for F1 to still be racing, considering the track hardly lends itself to the most exciting on-track spectacle. As the cars grew wider and heavier, making them less nimble, the drivers found it hard to maneuver around the street circuit with the same kind of agility they once did. Overtaking became nearly impossible, leading to a dip in the on-track action and making Sundays a procession, the order largely set by Saturday's qualifying result. In short, races in Monaco became a bit boring.

Christian Horner, Red Bull's team principal, admitted that "if anybody came up with this track now and presented it, there's no way we'd race here," so unsuitable is it to the modern requirements of F1 cars, now more than six feet wide and weighing close to eighteen hundred pounds. The added trouble with Monaco is that unlike other circuits, which can be widened or adjusted to fit shifting needs, city streets can't be moved and the massive apartment blocks are fixed where they are. The layout is pretty much as good as it can be. F1 has evaluated options to improve it, but it's not been possible to find a better course around the principality.

So if it doesn't have the same kind of unique pull it once had, and the races become sheer formalities once the order is set in qualifying, has F1 outgrown its crown jewel?

"We race here because it's Monaco," said Horner, who once dove into the Red Bull swimming pool in Monaco wearing only a Superman cape after losing a bet. "It's because of the history, the legacy, the backdrop, the glamour, everything. Monaco is a crucially important part of the grand prix calendar and a hugely valuable one. And it's always exciting to come to this venue. The same points apply to all races, but some just have that extra value attached to them. Certainly, Monaco has that."

Not all F1 tracks have a place on the calendar on their racing merits alone. The sport has grown into something far bigger than a pure racing series, even if that occasionally comes to its detriment. It is a business. It's the show. And Monaco embodies so much of that with a history that none of the "new money" events, no matter how grandiose they may be, can boast in the same way.

"It's just a spectacle in itself," Toto Wolff, the Mercedes team principal, said of Monaco. "Even if you were to see no overtakes, it's still the most prestigious, glamorous, and exciting track in the world. Every year we come back, it continues to amaze me."

■ ■ ■

The grid at Monaco is where the two sides of F1 meet: It's the sport getting ready for one of the most intense and challenging races of the season, one steeped in history; yet it's also the show, the star names there to be seen, posing for pictures and giving sound bites to TV crews. No moment of the season better signifies where F1 is right now.

Organizing the grid to make it a memorable moment not only

at Monaco, but the other twenty-three races of the season, is no small feat. Jonathan Nicholas, an executive producer for F1, is the man tasked with overseeing the grid proceedings and helping to build the tension toward lights out, as well as putting the spotlight on the names who have graced F1 with its presence.

"The sport is oozing in big names and VIPs," said Nicholas. "It's always been on my remit or radar about how we televise it and capture it. More recently, it's been looking at how do we enhance the spectacle itself and make it as good as it is for those on-site and in the grandstands for those at home? How do we take the fan energy and transmit that to the world, and get people to actually follow it?"

It is an enormous challenge. The tension that builds in the countdown to lights out is a lot, even without the spotlight and show that buzzes around the drivers and mechanics who are just trying to get ready for a race. As this is the point where the majority of fans will be tuning in ahead of the start, the challenge is to translate everything that is being felt on that strip of asphalt right across the world.

"What we've done is apply this energy to get ourselves in the engines a bit more, and create an atmosphere, whether it's music coming from DJs or orchestras coming from the grid, to bring the energy and amplify it," Nicholas said. "If you're on the grid, you'll feel the heartbeat. When you hear these national anthems, wherever you are on that grid, you hear it, you feel it, it goes through you. You want air displays going over the top. We want all the broadcasters on the grid to say 'I wish you were here.' You essentially take the culture from that venue and bake that into the race."

It is something that has increasingly become a calling card of F1 under Liberty Media, the company that has owned the series since 2017 and under whom there has been more of an entertainment push to make each race something far greater than the sporting spectacle alone. Ranging from DJ sets by Martin Garrix and Tiësto to full orchestras being led by the legendary Dutch violinist and conductor André Rieu, the grid is no longer about simply going through the formalities in the lead-up to the start. Nicholas felt things have changed "hugely" under Liberty. "They are leaders in entertainment, and there was always this vision that we had to embrace that change, and they've unlocked those gates for us," he said. Now, the show before the main event matters.

There can sometimes be a challenge to get the drivers fully on board. The thirty-minute window before the start of the race is arguably the most important of the weekend. All their preparations are laid out to the second, ranging from final exercises with their trainers to when they go to the toilet. While they'll give a few seconds of their time for a quick TV interview, it can be tricky for them to turn on the charm for the prerace show. For the Miami Grand Prix in 2023, F1 tried American-style driver introductions using an orchestra led by will.i.am (he'd written an F1-themed song called "The Formula"), with LL Cool J serving as the hype man for each driver. It drew mixed reviews, and many of the drivers weren't happy about having their focus pulled away at such a critical point, walking out through dry ice while flanked by cheerleaders. George Russell said he was "here to race" and "not here for the show." Lewis Hamilton, on the other hand, said he was in full support of F1 trying new things. "They're not just doing the same thing they've done in the past," he said.

"Drivers need to be part of that journey," said Nicholas. "We've got people like Lewis, who knows how to be the showman. You've got other drivers where it's just not in their interest. They're here to race. There's an element of the sport where we've got to educate the drivers a bit more with their managers and various other stakeholders, that there's a point where a driver needs to feel that moment."

And that show isn't for the drivers. It's an important part of getting F1 outside of its usual lane and reaching wider audiences. One of the few times F1 made it to the pages of TMZ was in 2021, when Megan Thee Stallion's entourage refused to let Sky Sports pundit Martin Brundle, a former racing driver, interview her on the grid. It sparked a strange outcry in the sport that thought anyone on the grid had no right to dismiss a TV interview. Many deep within the F1 bubble spouted it was the best thing that could have happened to her career as they'd never heard of her before. Those who don't live under a rock knew her star appeal reached a very different audience to the sport's typical follower. For context, at the time it happened, Megan Thee Stallion's combined social media following was thirty-three million—eleven million greater than F1's own channels.

Nicholas and F1's other leaders know the importance of F1's celebrity power, and they say it is something the sport wants to double down on in the future. "We've got to do better, we have to showcase those people," Nicholas said. "I think if you have a big name that comes to an event, it's how do we take those people and elevate them in our world?" One example he cited was when Will Smith attended a race as a guest of Lewis Hamilton at the season finale in Abu Dhabi in 2018. Smith not only waved the checkered flag at the end of the race—it's standard now for a celebrity to do that job—but he also went trackside and was even given a chance to use one of the TV cameras for the broadcast. It created content gold for F1 and was a rush for Smith, who has since been a regular visitor to races and is friends with Hamilton.

"We don't want people to come to our sport just to sit in the background and be in a TV shot, we want them to actually experience it," said Nicholas. "You hear them on the grid saying it's the best sport in the world, those to us are gold. I think it's a trend, and we're trending in the right way. We are an appealing sport."

■ ■ ■

As significant as Nicholas's work is in the buildup to lights out and the start of a grand prix, there is arguably no greater symbol of F1 than what happens right after the checkered flag when the race finishes: the podium ceremony and celebrations, especially the champagne.

The drivers have just given their all for close to two hours, dealing with the physical exhaustion and incredible g-forces generated by their cars as they fight for glory. And for the top three finishers, there'll be a refreshing reward at the end of it. Standing on the podium, they not only pick up the trophies for their efforts, but they also get the chance to spray—and, more importantly, taste—the champagne, the most exclusive and well-earned drink of all. Once the formalities of the podium are through, including the playing of the national anthem of the winning driver and team, and then the presentation of the trophies, the drivers grab the oversize bottles that stand waiting for them and start to celebrate, shaking them vigorously to the jaunty music of "Les Toréadors" from Georges Bizet's opera *Carmen.*

Nicholas plays a key role in orchestrating the F1 podium ceremony and how it looks on TV. His goal is for the podiums to be "over the top" and help connect the drivers with the fans. "We want people at home and people on-site to experience this incredible moment," he said. He wants F1 to have more podiums like the one used for the Italian Grand Prix at Monza, which sits above the pit wall and allows thousands of fans to spill onto the main straight after the race in order to be directly under the top three drivers as they celebrate—and in the line of fire for when they shake the bottles of fizz.

Once the dignitaries have quickly made their way off the podium and the call has been given for the celebrations to begin, the drivers can get the chance to let their emotions go and focus on spraying the bottles. It is an opportunity for the drivers to not only enjoy the moment but also pay tribute to their team members, who will assemble underneath the podium to celebrate the result. While watching an F1 podium may look like a haphazard, unchoreographed dance as the drivers try to get one another with the spray and celebrate their achievements together, there is actually some thought that goes into their actions. It lacks any kind of precision comparable to what they've just done behind the wheel, but even when spraying champagne, they have certain tactics or ways to go about things.

So what do you do when you have a three-liter jeroboam—a double magnum equivalent to four standard bottles—in your hands amid the postrace high of a win?

"The first thing is to have a sip," said Valtteri Bottas, who scored over sixty F1 podiums in his time with Williams and Mercedes, helping the latter win five Constructors' Championships. "It would be rude to waste such a fine drink, so you need to try it first. And then . . . you go for it! Give a bit to the team, a bit to the guys on the podium." Bottas said he likes the taste of champagne—but only when chilled. "I've had both on the podium," said Bottas. "I've had cold champagne, like properly like it should be. But then I've had warm. And after a race when it's warm, it's not that nice."

Not all of the drivers are so enamored with the taste of the fizz on the podium. Esteban Ocon doesn't drink alcohol, but when he scored his first F1 podium in Bahrain in 2020, he was able to take a drink from the bottle because it wasn't champagne, but instead rose water, something that is used at all of F1's races in the Middle East. "That was the only time that I did drink out of the bottle," said Ocon. "I fake it otherwise! I have to cheers, and I just put my thumb over the top [of the bottle] and pretend to drink!" It's not only the taste he dislikes; the mixture of postrace sweaty overalls doused in champagne is a pungent one that is hard to get rid of. "It's stuck to you for two hours after because you can't take a shower," Ocon said.

Ocon's advice to would-be podium finishers on what to do with the bottle was "start spraying but keep some for the mechanics." Another F1 tradition is that once the podium festivities are complete, the driver will bring the bottle back to the team so that everyone who has contributed to their success can take a sip of the drink and share in the celebration.

"And don't slip on the podium, which I nearly did in Monaco,"

Ocon added, referring to his third F1 podium at the 2023 Monaco race, where he was greeted by Prince Albert II and his wife, Princess Charlene, who are regular fixtures in the ceremony. (After the 2018 race, Princess Charlene herself was presented the race winner's bottle by Daniel Ricciardo and took a swig.) The amount of liquid on the rostrum can make it hard for drivers to keep their balance. "It was like ice skating, I nearly crashed," Ocon admitted. "It's not the right moment to do some stuff like that, with everyone watching! But when you are there, it's pure joy."

It can also be a sticky situation if you end up getting some of the spray into your eyes. "I can't describe how much it hurts your eyes . . . holy crap!" said Lando Norris, now a podium regular with McLaren. "When this stuff goes in your eyes, you can't see anything. And the more you try and open it, the more it hurts! That's not the nicest thing. Maybe I'll wear goggles next time." It's not as silly as it sounds: In 2012, Red Bull's then technical director, Adrian Newey, was on the podium as the team representative and comically took a pair of ski goggles with him to protect from the spray of the victorious Sebastian Vettel.

F1 podiums have always been about tradition. From the early days of grand prix racing until the mid-1980s, the drivers would also be presented with laurel wreaths to wear in recognition of their achievement, with the tradition continuing to this day in races such as the Indianapolis 500. The practice died out in F1 when it emerged to the power brokers and, more significantly, the team owners that the oversize wreaths were blocking the branding of their major sponsors on the driver race suits at one of the most-photographed moments of the weekend. Although there would be a brief revival of the wreaths for F1's sprint races in 2021, it has sadly become a tradition long consigned to F1 history.

While the podiums have gone from cramped celebrations on an elevated platform on the main straight to one of the most vibrant, carefully planned moments of a race weekend, the tradition of spraying the champagne is something that has endured—even if it was not part of F1's origins. The first time champagne appeared on the podium was at the 1950 French Grand Prix, when the race winner, Juan Manuel Fangio, was presented with a bottle of bubbly to mark his success. Yet at no point was there ever the intention to spray the bottle; it was far too precious a liquor to waste. Some races would present alcohol for the winners to drink. Heineken, which sponsored the Dutch Grand Prix in 1968, gave Jackie Stewart a giant stein of beer to drink on the podium, and the champagne would sometimes be poured into the trophies and sipped from as a way to cool off following the exertions of a race.

The tradition of spraying the champagne did not actually start in F1. Bottles were supplied to the drivers on the podium in all the top racing categories by the 1960s, including the 24 Hours of Le Mans in France. At the end of the 1966 race during the national anthems, the bottle placed next to Jo Siffert, a Swiss driver who had won the two-liter prototype class for Porsche, popped its cork spontaneously after being left out in the sun for too long, causing the pressure inside to build up. Unsure what to do, Siffert grabbed the bottle and started to spray it over the watching crowd, snatching another bottle in his free hand, which he also shook. It was an accidental start to a tradition that would escalate at Le Mans the following year, when American racer Dan Gurney, who had won the race for Ford alongside A. J. Foyt, deliberately took his bottle and shook it up before spraying it over the rest of the podium finishers and dignitaries—including the wife of Henry Ford II. Ford was said to be unimpressed that his immaculately dressed wife had been covered in champagne.

Stewart, a three-time world champion in the 1960s and '70s, was the first driver to bring the practice to F1 in 1969. After winning the French Grand Prix, he was handed a bottle of Moët right after getting out of his car. As with Siffert, the bottle had been left in the sun, so when he popped the cork to have a drink, it started fizzing everywhere. In a bid to try and *save* the drink, he claimed, Stewart placed his thumb over the top of the bottle, only for that to cause it to spray in all directions. Knowing the champagne was lost anyway, the Scot shook the bottle and directed it toward the assembled crowd, thus marking the start of an iconic, symbolic action in the F1 world.

The podium moment is something all drivers aspire to be part of. While some make it a weekly occurrence, enjoying periods of F1 domination where anything but a top-three finish is a surprise, for others, it's an experience they'll get only on a handful of occasions, if ever, through their F1 careers. Alex Albon scored two F1 podiums through 2020 when he was racing for Red Bull. When he rejoined the F1 grid in 2022 with Williams, a team for whom even scoring points was a major achievement, podiums were a far-flung, precious memory.

"You have to enjoy the moment, purely that," Albon said. "It's a rarity, more and more in Formula 1 now, especially being at a team like Williams. So, just savor it. I think sport is a cruel thing—95 percent of doing your sport is negative, 5 percent is positive, and you do it for the 5 percent. So when you can have those moments, you've really got to embrace them and enjoy them. Because they may never come again, or they may take a lot longer to come again. You have to appreciate the good times."

His profound thoughts aside, Albon went on to agree with Ocon that he doesn't like the taste of alcohol. "I like getting other people wet," he said. "I enjoy getting other people intoxicated!"

■ ■ ■

But what if I told you that the champagne on the F1 podium isn't actually champagne at all, but in fact, sparkling wine?

A bottle of fizz can only truly be champagne if it comes from the Champagne wine region in northeast France. From 1966 up to 2000, the French champagne brand Moët & Chandon served as the supplier to F1, its role predating Stewart's first champagne spray in 1969. G. H. Mumm took over from 2000 to 2016 before F1's first sparkling wine provider, Chandon—an Argentine brand—had a brief spell in the role. F1 returned to champagne in 2017, getting bottles from Carbon and then Moët again until the existing supplier, Ferrari Trento, linked up as F1's "official toast" in 2021 and brought sparkling wine back to the podium.

The first thing you may think of with the name "Ferrari" is the car brand—yet it is actually one of the most common names in Italy. Its etymology is linked to blacksmiths, meaning it translates to "Smith" in English. (Had I been born an Italian, I would've been called "Luca Ferrari," which, let's face it, is an infinitely cooler name!) But there is no direct link between Ferrari Trento and Ferrari the F1 team.

Yet there is a history between the two. Founded in 1902, Ferrari Trento was sold to the Lunelli family in the mid-1950s. The company's president, Gino Lunelli, was friends with Enzo Ferrari, the founder of the great car brand, and worked to ensure Ferrari Trento was the go-to drink among the great and the good of Italian society. Lunelli's successor was his nephew, Matteo, who first experienced F1 going to Monza for the Italian Grand Prix as a child. "I have a lot of memories. . . . The opportunity to live in the world of Formula 1, to hear the sound of Formula 1," he said, recalling the reverberation of the engines while walking through the tunnel under the circuit. "Being the toast of Formula 1 had always been a dream."

It was a dream that was realized in 2021. Midway through the Covid-19 pandemic, Ferrari Trento entered a new partnership with F1 to become its official celebratory toast, becoming the first Italian brand and only the second sparkling wine to hold that important role. Ferrari Trento is an Italian mountain wine, its grapes growing at an altitude of up to nearly three thousand feet. During the summer months, warmer temperatures allow for a greater aromatic maturation, and at night and through the winter, the drop to a cooler temperature helps balance out the acidity before the grapes are picked by hand, resulting in a 100 percent chardonnay that has been aged for four years in darkness. Between three thousand and four thousand bottles of Ferrari Trento are served over a grand prix weekend, ranging from the VIP Paddock Club suites to the bottles upon the podium.

According to Lunelli, having sparkling wine on the podium instead of champagne is "a consequence of the fact that more and more opinion leaders and wine lovers recognize that excellence in the sparkling world is not a monopoly of champagne. I think this is also what drove F1 to change from the tradition and innovate, bringing in a brand that is demonstrating excellence and also something new."

Even if some of the drivers may not like the taste of alcohol, all are enthusiastic in their celebrations when they get their hands on a bottle of bubbly. As Albon said, you never know how often it's going to happen, making it important to properly enjoy the moment.

One driver who has fully embraced that is Norris. From very early in his junior career, he adopted a podium celebration that he calls "the smash." Instead of popping the cork out of the top of the bottle and then shaking it, he causes a buildup in pressure by grabbing the bottle by its neck and slamming its base into the ground. The result is a long stream of liquid shooting directly upward into the air, making for dramatic photos.

"I started doing it in F4," Norris explained. "I think one of my friends did it. But then I tried to make it my thing. Pretty much every single podium I've been on, I've done it." He added that he then likes to wait before spraying the other podium finishes. "People spray me, and then I'm like . . . now whatcha gonna do? Boom!" he said with a laugh, gesturing the shaking of a bottle toward me. "Then I can get them."

One question that Lunelli is often asked is whether it's a shame to see the sparkling wine his family has poured over half a century of work into refining get "wasted" and sprayed away. But he loves to see the enjoyment of the drivers on the podium. "Lando wins the award for the most aggressive celebration," Lunelli said. "Sometimes I tell him, pay attention, because the bottle is not made to be thrown on the floor! With our bottle, it's very strong, but still. . . . It's a great celebration."

Sometimes "the smash" can go wrong, even if Norris is yet to injure himself. "I've not smashed these bottles, because they're so thick," he said. "I've not found the true limitation of these. In MotoGP [F1's equivalent for motorcycle racing], I think they have Prosecco. A MotoGP guy saw me do it, so he tried to do it, but the bottles are so thin, he did the smash and lacerated his whole hand . . . ten stitches or something. So I've not done that!" He did, however, accidentally knock Max Verstappen's porcelain winner's trophy off the top step in Hungary a few years ago, caus-ing it to break. A replacement trophy, costing $45,000, was made for Verstappen, who joked that Norris was not allowed to touch it. In a fun nod to what happened, Norris used the same beautiful painted look of the trophies for his helmet design at the next year's race in collaboration with the trophy manufacturers.

F1's glitzy culture was always part of the appeal for Ferrari Trento but especially the opportunity to be at the forefront of that through the podium ceremony. In all the pictures and all the TV coverage, it is its bottle of sparkling wine that is being sprayed by the most famous drivers in the world. "It's the glamorous reputa-tion," said Lunelli. "There are the guests, there is a huge attention on them. And in Formula 1, the podium is really the iconic part. If you think about it, in some sports, when the race ends, they don't even show the celebrations. In Formula 1, the moment of the celebration is really something that everybody watches. Everybody is part of the tradition.

"The F1 podium is the most iconic celebration in the world of sports. It's part of the show."

■ ■ ■

There's that word again, *show*. The showers of fizz that take place after the race provide such strong imagery of what F1 is known for—regardless of where in the world it is racing. Being part of the spectacle is what makes F1 so appealing to the biggest names in music, films, fashion, or any other industry known for its star power and celebrity pull. With the exception of the Super Bowl, no other sporting event goes to the same lengths as F1 to emphasize the entertainment around the action, playing up its exclusivity and the breathtaking action that makes it such a desirable place to be. Bear in mind there is only one Super Bowl per year; F1 goes racing twenty-four times in the space of nine months.

Not every race can be its own Super Bowl. When Liberty Media took over, the new F1 CEO, Chase Carey, said: "We have twenty-one races. We should have twenty-one Super Bowls." It was a statement of the direction he wanted to take the sport in, rather than a firm prediction. Races such as Monaco and Las Vegas are always going to have more star power and appeal on a broader scale than rural events in Austria or Japan, no matter how historic the tracks may be or how high the quality of the racing is.

It is that kind of mix that F1 needs to retain moving forward. The city-based races that automatically draw in celebrities and that extra dose of sparkle must be balanced out by more traditional events. Going to one extreme or the other would saturate the calendar and make those events less special. Like the sparkling wine on the podium, it's all about moderation.

"The glamour is good for Formula 1," said Guenther Steiner, the former Haas F1 team principal. "I think the best thing in Formula 1 is, in having twenty-four races, that they're all different. Because if you had twenty-four Las Vegases, or twenty-four Singapores, people would just get used to it and it wouldn't be glamorous anymore. We've got historic race courses; we've got night races. I think the change in it attracts people to watch because every race has got its particularity. The mix of the races is good."

"The diversity of all these races is great," added McLaren CEO Zak Brown. "You've got all these different countries and the culture of these countries comes out. All the races on the calendar are great and unique in their own way."

Every F1 event has its own pull, and the sport is always going to be more complex than simply appealing to one type of fan or taste. Yet it is never going to solely be about the "purity" of racing, where the only thing people follow are the sporting matters, especially at a time when F1 is pushing to bring in new fans and truly be a great entertainment product, not merely a motorsport.

In truth, that's been the case for seventy-five years. F1 has always been about the big stars on the grid, the champagne showers, the yachts in Monaco. All are powerful images that have only enhanced its identity, taking it into the mainstream and fostering a reputation unlike anything else.

■ ■ ■

And yet for all the money those with the yachts may have, for all the champagne that may be flowing, I bet you I've still got a better view when the cars finally get on-track.

One of the perks of being in the media is that you can get a tabard that allows you to go trackside, standing next to the barriers with the photographers. It's a great way to see the cars up close and tell by watching which drivers are especially quick or committed through particular corners. It's effective at all circuits, yet at Monaco, when it feels like you could reach out and touch the cars because you're so close to the barriers, it takes it to another level. It is why this race remains one of my highlights of the season, especially for qualifying, when the cars compete on a single lap to set the fastest time. It is where you see their skills pushed to the extreme, kissing the barriers with the outside of their wheels as they find the limit in the knowledge a millimeter more would result in a crash.

Each year in Monaco, I make a point to spend one of the practice sessions by the side of the circuit. A race is typically spent in the media center, watching from the TV screens hanging from the ceilings and with just one window at the rear of the building that overlooks the circuit. The opportunity to get trackside is a rare but welcome one. For all the flaws, facades, and fakery of the place itself, this is a circuit unmatched in global motorsport.

As practice begins under the Mediterranean sun, I'll wave my media pass to the security guards and move into the narrow pathway that runs right along the side of the circuit. Starting at the penultimate corner, La Rascasse, the same place filled with partygoers each evening as the bars spill onto the circuit, I work my way backward around the lap. The entry to La Piscine chicane—named after the

large swimming pool on the inside of the track, complete with a diving board—has the drivers flicking left then right at speeds of around
150 mph, making it a thrill to stand on the exit of the corner behind
the barrier and catch fencing, seeing how close each car dares to get
to the exit as they thread the eye of the needle through the walls.
From there, I keep walking along the side of the track, the pathway
tightening to no more than six feet. To my right is the drop into the
water of the harbor, the yachts now filled with guests enjoying their
vantage points. One even has a small barbecue on the go, the smell
of hot dogs filling the air as a man in sunglasses, shorts, and flip-
flops hands them to his guests. To my left, the track, cars zooming
past. It's like walking a tightrope, senses heightened.

After squeezing past the left-hand Tabac corner, the path opens
up and leads toward the Nouvelle Chicane. This is a prime spot for
the photographers, who stand behind the direction of the cars
without a barrier in front of them, giving them wonderful shots of
the cars against the backdrop of the Monaco skyline. I walk past the
small tents filled with security staff on their lunch break, serving a
typical French spread of cheese, bread, tomatoes, and a plate of an-
chovies, before making it to the tunnel. It's the only tunnel on the
F1 calendar, and produces a deafening sound when the cars pass
through. Given F1 used to have ear-piercing V12 engines and these
are "only" V6 hybrids, I cannot imagine what it must have been like
for those making this exact journey forty years ago.

A pedestrian elevator then takes me up to the highest point of the
circuit, Casino Square, before I walk down to the hairpin. In front of
the Fairmont Hotel, the cars reduce to speeds as low as 30 mph for
the tight left-hand corner. I watch as the drivers slowly thread their

cars through the right-hand corner before hitting the brakes, down-shifting, and getting the car stopped in perfect time to sweep to the left, then hitting the gas on exit and shooting away, the rear of the car stepping out as the wheels spin. It is masterful. I look up behind me at the hotel balconies and see the people who have, presumably, paid extortionate amounts of money for such an incredible vantage point, flags out in support of their favorite drivers. There's no way to get closer to the action at any other F1 track.

That is what makes Monaco so special.

No, the circuit is not fit for purpose as it once was. But it is unique within global motorsport. Nowhere else encapsulates everything that makes F1 so evocative in quite the same way as this silly little track that, as Horner said, would get knocked back in an instant were it proposed today. In years to come, there are likely to be regular debates over its suitability, and whether we should go elsewhere, accepting the glamour events are now in new locations. But it would take something quite spectacular to match the pull of Monaco.

It is still the place people want to be seen.

Our Deadly Passion, Our Terrible Joy

n 2019, the F1 community experienced one of its darkest days in recent memory when Anthoine Hubert—a promising French driver who was racing in Formula 2, the category below F1 and racing on the same weekend as the grand prix—was killed in an accident at Spa in Belgium.

My first interaction with Anthoine had come the previous year, when he was racing in GP3, the series below F2 that is now known as Formula 3. I'd been commissioned to do an introductory profile on him for the F1 race program at his home race in France. I fired off an email to the media contact on his website, anticipating, as tends to often be the case, a reply from a manager or publicist, if I were to get one at all. Instead, Anthoine himself replied from his personal email, passing along his phone number to arrange a time to chat on the phone. It was a small thing, but immediately I could see he was doing things differently to so many other racing drivers, even at the lower levels.

The nature of the profile meant the chat was a mix of "light" topics, such as talking through his favorite books and films, and discussing his career progression to date and hopes for the future. He wasn't born into great wealth but climbed up the racing ladder through sheer hard work and impressive results. The French racing federation helped support his early days karting with funding and training, leading him to cross paths with talents including Pierre Gasly and Charles Leclerc, striking up close friendships with both drivers, who were a couple of years ahead of him on the path toward F1.

As I spoke to Anthoine, I was impressed by his determination and commitment to making it to the highest levels, even without the pathways or support enjoyed by some of his peers. But the greatest takeaway was his good nature and character. He lacked the bravado of so many racing at the same level. He was shy and deeply self-aware, even opening up about his frustration over his superstitious nature. If he did well in a session or felt he was driving strongly, he'd try and repeat the exact same routine to the letter before getting back into the car. "I'm not even doing it on purpose!" Hubert told me. "It's a waste of energy." He was, put simply, a good kid.

And he was also quick. Hubert won the GP3 championship a few months after we spoke, securing a graduation to F2. He was a member of Renault's young driver program, the French manufacturer spotting his talent during his title-winning season. Although Hubert lacked the budget to land a seat with one of the best F2 teams for his rookie season, he wasted little time, impressing by scoring victories at home in France, crossing the line to a crowd of fans waving small *tricolores* from the grandstand, and in Monaco, one of the toughest street tracks in the world. His stock was firmly on the rise.

But then came Spa.

■ ■ ■

The Circuit de Spa-Francorchamps, the site of the Belgian Grand Prix, is the longest and one of the most challenging circuits in F1. A 4.3-mile ribbon of asphalt strewn through the Ardennes forest, the track started its life over twice as long, running on the roads connecting various small towns in the area, including Spa and Francorchamps. Over time it evolved into a permanent race track boasting some of the greatest elevation changes and corner speeds in racing, making it a firm favorite for drivers and fans alike. A true season highlight. Yet Spa has regularly faced questions over its safety standards and suitability for F1, and its accompanying series, due to the design of the corners that date back to its origins and the extraordinarily high speeds and g-forces involved, even by F1's usual standards, at the track.

On the second lap of the F2 race on Saturday afternoon in 2019, taking place after F1's qualifying session, Hubert's car was involved in a multicar accident at Raidillon, a blind crest that is one of the fastest points of the circuit. While trying to avoid a driver slowing in the pack due to a puncture, Hubert touched the rear of another car, causing him to spin into the barrier. His car bounced back into the middle of the race track and almost came to a complete halt— into the path of driver Juan Manuel Correa, who crashed into the side of Hubert's car at 135 mph. The crash investigation by the FIA would later report a force of 81.1g on Hubert's car. To put that into context, an astronaut in a rocket launch will experience around 3g. F1 drivers can pull upward of 5g on some of the fastest corners on tracks around the world.

It quickly became apparent the accident was a serious one. The remainder of the F2 race was canceled while medical crews tended to the crash site, reaching Hubert for an initial assessment just fifty-four seconds after the accident. Correa was also found to have sustained life-threatening injuries, such was the severity of the impact.

At 6:35 p.m., eighty-eight minutes after the accident occurred, Hubert was declared dead. He was twenty-two years old.

When the news came through, it hit the F1 community hard. The team buildings at Spa, often abuzz with music and chatter long into the evening, champagne popping and glasses clinking to toast the next day's race, were rendered silent. It was like the air had been sucked out of the paddock as everyone came to terms with such a devastating reminder of the risks that remained in our sport.

It cast a pall over the following day's races. Ahead of the resumption of on-track activity, starting with the F3 race on Sunday morning, the paddock came together on the grid to pay their respects and hold a minute's silence. The usual hubbub of the prerace festivities, soundtracked by music and cheering from the grandstands as engineers complete their final preparations and drivers focus on getting ready for lights out, was totally muted. Hubert was the only person on anybody's mind. At the front of the crowd stood Anthoine's mother, her eyes hidden behind dark sunglasses as she clutched her son's racing helmet, coming to terms with an unfathomable, unimaginable pain.

■ ■ ■

I wrote a few chapters ago about the significance of families in the stories of F1 drivers, their sacrifices and support that make their careers possible. The same goes for everybody throughout the paddock. Time and time again, we talk about the importance of our parents or parent-figures in inspiring our love for the sport, for encouraging us to make it a passion so serious we turn it into a career.

The same was true for me with my mum. When I was ten years old, I stumbled across an F1 race on TV, the 2005 Brazilian Grand Prix. There was a big crash at the start, and it ended with Fernando Alonso becoming F1's youngest-ever world champion. As a sports-mad kid, I was hooked immediately.

It turned out Mum had been a massive F1 fan when she was younger. She attended the British Grand Prix each year through her late teens, becoming a supporter of Ferrari and Gilles Villeneuve, the legendary Canadian driver known for his spectacular driving style and raw, natural speed. In her senior yearbook, which she got her classmates to sign, one even drew a small portrait of Villeneuve, and predicted he would win every world title from

1978 to 2000. Villeneuve was tragically killed in an accident at the Belgian Grand Prix in 1982, leaving a legacy of being widely regarded as one of the greatest F1 drivers never to win a championship. Being an unaware ten-year-old mistaking his name for the female "Jill," my reply to her story was: "But Mum, girls don't race cars!" Such ignorance was quickly drummed out of me. . . .

My rainy Sunday TV find not only sparked a fresh interest for me, but it rekindled Mum's love for F1, something that had waned as she started a career and focused on having a family. We'd watch every F1 race together and go to our local race tracks to see everything from Minis to truck racing, where her boss worked as the circuit doctor. Weekends became dedicated to motorsport.

And there was one thing Mum, who devoted her life to nursing, was always quick to point out to me: the danger of racing. On the back of every single ticket you purchase to attend a racing event, there is a message, usually in red capital letters, that will be some version of: "Motorsport is extremely dangerous." It's a reminder that what you are watching is not a "normal" sport. Nothing else is this high speed, this exhilarating, which is why you love it. And nothing else carries the same degree of risk. It is undoubtedly part of the appeal of motorsport, both for those watching and those competing.

Danger is part of F1's DNA. Enzo Ferrari, the founder of the great Italian manufacturer, famously called racing "our deadly passion" and "our terrible joy." Everyone involved in the early days of grand prix racing knew the risks they were taking, particularly in an era when safety standards were nowhere near as strict and regulated as they are today. Helmets covered only the top of the head, and most raced in a T-shirt in the eras before overalls. Hay bales were used to line the side of a track. Death was common. Yet they raced on.

Between F1's first year as an international championship in 1950 and 1990, twenty-nine F1 drivers were killed at world championship races, even as safety standards evolved through changes to the cars and the circuits. In the past thirty-five years, a further three have died: Roland Ratzenberger and Ayrton Senna, both of whom were killed on the same weekend at Imola in 1994 on consecutive days; and Jules Bianchi, who died nine months after sustaining severe head injuries in an accident at the 2014 Japanese Grand Prix.

If you were to plot the number of deaths at F1 grands prix on a chart, there is a sharp drop as time goes on, becoming a total flatline in the twenty-one years between the deaths of Senna and Bianchi. As the sport evolved and technology improved, so did the safety standards. Cars became far safer, protecting the drivers when they got into accidents. New devices that would seem ancillary to protecting the body of the driver were introduced, such as a support device attached to the helmet designed to prevent neck injuries, or biometric technology woven into the lining of the gloves the drivers wear that can keep a track of their vitals and help doctors at the race track in their assessment of accidents.

Circuits were also modified to become safer, reducing speeds and installing barriers that could absorb the energy of an impact instead of sending it through the car or the driver's body. Each time there was a notable accident, steps were taken. In the wake of Bianchi's accident, F1 introduced the "Halo," a wishbone-shaped structure placed over the cockpit, designed to protect the drivers' exposed heads. It has unquestionably saved numerous lives since its first usage in 2018.

One of the most dramatic accidents in recent F1 history was French driver Romain Grosjean's at the 2020 Bahrain Grand Prix. Grosjean's car spun off the track on the first lap and into a barrier before splitting in half, lodging the cockpit in the middle of the barrier. Grosjean was trapped inside the car for twenty-seven seconds as flames started to engulf the chassis, but astonishingly he pulled himself out of the wreckage using the Halo that had already saved his life in the initial impact. For such a ferocious accident to end with Grosjean only sustaining severe burns to his hands from his emergence from the fire shows just how far safety standards have come.

A number of drivers were initially uneasy about the Halo's introduction, proof of how integral some believe risk to be to the nature of F1. They felt the structure on top of the car went against the spirit of open-cockpit racing. Some even suggested it should be optional, leaving it up to the drivers to decide whether or not they were comfortable with the risks of their helmets remaining exposed. In an era when serious driver injuries were so rare, the debate often surrounded F1 becoming *too safe*, not increasing safety standards. F1's regulator, the FIA, has always maintained a fierce commitment to making racing safer because, tragically, we are served occasional reminders of why it remains such a deadly passion and a terrible joy.

■ ■ ■

The dangers of motorsport mean that loss never feels that far away in F1. For Charles Leclerc, the Ferrari driver rightly regarded as one of the best among the younger generation on the grid, it has been something he has sadly been reminded of through his racing career.

Growing up in Monaco, F1 was always part of Leclerc's world. His bus route to school wound through many of the same roads that made up the grand prix track, and some of his earliest memories of the race in Monaco include the red cars—the Ferrari cars—catching his eye while he was looking down from the balcony of an apartment.

There was also a deep familial connection for Leclerc and racing. His father, Herve, was close friends with Philippe Bianchi, the father of Jules Bianchi. It was Jules, who was Charles's godfather, who would help further Leclerc's love of motorsport and get him racing competitively in go-karts. Leclerc would spend as much time as he could at the Bianchi family's go-kart track to learn everything there was to learn from Jules.

"He was extremely important," Leclerc told me in a 2018 interview, back when he was an F1 rookie racing for Sauber. "I drove for the first time karting on his track, and he was there. Then I think we were meeting up every Wednesday"—French schools have Wednesday afternoons off for extracurricular activities—"and on weekends just to drive rental karting. These are probably the best memories I have in racing. It was so much fun, and I learned a lot." Even with an eight-year age gap, Leclerc wanted to soak up all the knowledge he could, even to try and beat Bianchi, himself a rising star in junior motorsport. "He was older than me, so I always pushed myself to beat him," Leclerc said. "They are very good memories. But he was more than a mentor. He was also an extremely close friend. A bit like family."

Bianchi seemed destined to one day race in red for Ferrari, having become a member of its young driver academy. He graduated to F1 in 2013 with Manor, one of the smallest teams that stood no real chance of success, making his ninth place finish at the 2014 Monaco Grand Prix a landmark result, taken as proof of his star status.

Tragedy cruelly struck a few months later at the Japanese Grand Prix. In heavy rain, Bianchi's car slid off the Suzuka track and into the path of a recovery tractor that was pulling another car out of the gravel. The Frenchman sustained severe head injuries in the accident to which he would succumb nine months later in July 2015 at the age of twenty-five.

Leclerc was starting to make a name for himself in junior racing around this time. He was managed by Nicolas Todt, who was also Bianchi's manager, and signed in 2016 to Ferrari's young driver academy, the same one that had set Bianchi on the path toward F1. That in itself was a special moment for Leclerc, a fine tribute to his godfather. But as he kept racing and kept winning, securing a move to F1 with Sauber for 2018 after back-to-back titles in GP3 and Formula 2, it became clear he'd be Ferrari's next young star.

The significance of his path toward Ferrari was never lost on Leclerc, even in 2018, when it was merely talk linking him to one day racing in those famous red overalls. He never tired of the speculation or questions about Ferrari but always noted it was the opportunity he felt rightfully belonged to Bianchi. "He probably deserved this place more than I do," Leclerc said in the same 2018 interview. "If one day I have the chance to be there, I will try to do everything I possibly can to win the titles that he deserved to win." A few months after that interview, Leclerc received his chance: Ferrari announced he would join its team from the 2019 season, only his second in the sport, making him the youngest driver since 1961 to race in F1 for Ferrari.

It's an opportunity that Leclerc quickly seized. Without an engine issue, he'd have won his second race for Ferrari in 2019. That maiden victory eventually arrived at Spa—the day after Hubert's death. Leclerc had been friends with Hubert since they were racing in the same junior circles, calling him "Tonio," a nickname he carried on the rear of his steering wheel for the race. "We grew up together," Leclerc said moments after getting out of his car. "My first ever race, I did it with Anthoine when we were younger. So I can't enjoy fully my first victory. But it will definitely be a memory I will keep forever."

More and more success has followed. While Ferrari hasn't been in a position to fight for championships, Leclerc has led its efforts season after season, quickly establishing himself as a driver enshrined within its rich F1 history. Even with the arrival of Lewis Hamilton as his teammate for 2025, Leclerc is very much the man who will mold Ferrari's long-term future. None of that would've been possible without Bianchi's support and influence.

Nor would it have been doable without the other figure Leclerc regards as having the greatest impact on his career and life: his father, Herve.

The friendship of Herve Leclerc and Philippe Bianchi brought their sons together, but Jules was not the only racing driver that young Charles looked to for advice. Herve had raced in Formula 3 himself during the 1980s, giving him a decent understanding of how to race. He was there beside Leclerc right through his success in go-karting and his early junior days. But when he grew ill in 2017, the year Leclerc, at the age of nineteen, was racing in F2, it was apparent he may not get the chance to see his son realize his F1 dream.

So Charles decided to tell a white lie. Soon before his father passed away, Charles told Herve that he'd done it: He'd be racing in F1 the following season, as he'd signed a contract with a team—except he hadn't.

A few days after Herve died in June of 2017, Leclerc was scheduled to take part in the next round of the F2 season in Baku, Azerbaijan. It was never even a question whether he'd race: Leclerc knew what his father would have wanted. Running with a tribute message on the side of his helmet, "*je t'aime papa*," Leclerc put in an emotionally charged and utterly dominant display on the track. He was on pole position by over half a second—a lifetime in racing terms, but even more so when you consider all drivers in F2 have the same car—and then scored victory in the main race. He revealed his dad, unsurprisingly, had been on his mind constantly as he dedicated the win to him on the podium after the race. "It's a good way to thank him," Leclerc said. "It won't bring him back. But it's a satisfying thing for me this weekend."

A few months later, by signing for Sauber, Leclerc achieved what he'd prematurely told his father: He would be racing in F1. And through all the success that has since followed, from his standout rookie season that prompted Ferrari to promote him so quickly, the victories and spectacular performances that have come since then, Leclerc gladly attributes so much of that to his father's influence. Upon scoring an emotional home victory around the streets of Monaco in 2024, Leclerc admitted he was struggling to see at points in the final laps of the race due to his eyes welling up as he thought about his father.

When I brought it up with Leclerc a couple of years ago, how pivotal a role his dad had played in his career, he was more than happy to talk about it. While he noted the on-track technical skills he'd learned in order to be a good racing driver, the greater take-away was how Herve helped nurture such an organic, healthy love for racing in his son.

"He would teach me the basics of the sport, which obviously helped, especially at such a young age," Leclerc said. "But what I am the most grateful for is he never really pushed me or never forced me to keep going. It's always been a real pleasure for me to drive. This I think has helped me massively for the future. He made me the person I am."

It is also testament to Leclerc's character that he has carried such an enormous amount on his young shoulders throughout his racing career. Drivers are attuned to the risks they are running and the consequences of being part of such a dangerous sport. Yet it can never truly brace anyone to deal with loss when it does happen, especially handling it at such a young age like Leclerc has.

■ ■ ■

March 2021. As is standard at the start of a new F1 season, I'm spending my days chatting to the F1 drivers and team principals about their hopes and expectations for the coming campaign, which was about to start that weekend in Bahrain.

Except I'm not in Bahrain. I'm in my bedroom in West London, still wearing pajama bottoms.

We're in the depths of the Covid-19 pandemic, meaning all of our media duties are taking place via Zoom, even if you're at the track—making attendance of the grand prix itself of limited worth at the time. We're midway through a press conference with the then Haas F1 team boss, Guenther Steiner, whose face fills my computer screen as he talks. He's only interrupted when the camera switches to each journalist asking a question. Steiner is his usual, chatty self, even as he admits his team is in for a tricky season.

Halfway through the call, my phone rings. It's the doctor from the hospital in my hometown.

"You need to come now."

A few days prior, my mum had been rushed in after experiencing a sharp downturn in her health. Due to the severity of the Covid-19 lockdown enforced by the government at the time, the same one that had kept us apart at Christmas, I wasn't allowed to go and see her in the hospital until they knew for certain what was going on—or until the situation was dire enough. The breast and skin cancer she'd been fighting for the past five years, and that she thought she had beaten, had come back and spread rapidly. Now, there was nothing they could do, besides manage her pain and, at last, make an exception for me to finally go and visit.

I hurriedly log off the call with Steiner, change into some jeans, grab the prepacked bag of clothes I'd been dreading the need for, and run to the tube. I can't make the Underground journey, nor the two-hour train ride back home, go any quicker, so I'm left to sit and ponder what is about to happen. I know by now how all of this ends. But do we have weeks? Days? Hours?

My dad picks me up from the train station. Just when I think all the tears had flooded out of me on the train, my eyes stinging and puffy, his reassuring hug starts a fresh wave. I have no idea what to think, what to hope, what to pray for. A kind doctor meets me at the ward entrance, sits me down, and talks me through the situation. The underlying message is to make the most of every moment I have left with my mum.

I put on a mask, an apron, and a plastic visor, all pandemic-forced requirements of visiting in the hospital. The visor steams up quickly as I sniff to hold back tears, trying to compose myself while entering the ward.

Mum looks up from her bed, small and weak. The corners of her mouth curve into a resigned smile.

"Oh, Luke. What have we done?"

As I sit with Mum by her hospital bed, so much rushes through my head. It's the first time in my young life that I'm truly contemplating what loss this close looks like; what to do or to think when you know you're about to lose the person at the center of your universe. And what to say? How do you comprehend any of it?

So we sit and we talk, just as we'd done all those years ago when we were at the race track, those lazy Sunday afternoons soundtracked by engines, the smell of petrol and burnt rubber in the air. And now, just as then, between the various rounds of doctors and nurses coming to check on her, run tests, and care for her, so many of our conversations come back to racing. It doesn't take long after showing up that Mum says: "But it's a race weekend. . . . Aren't you working?"

As though it matters. F1 often exists in a bubble that feels so far detached from real life. It's what we dedicate so much of our time and our lives toward following, going from race track to race track, country to country. It's far from an ordinary sport, nor an ordinary way of life. Yet there is no escaping the life events that impact all of us at one time or another.

But it's being in that bubble that gives us such strong bonds to the people with whom we share that passion, be it for the drivers going wheel-to-wheel against one another, the teammates devoted to success on the track, or even the friends and family with whom we spend our time watching F1. The creation of a community that reaches far beyond those within the F1 paddock.

For me, Mum is the person who helped ignite and further that love for F1, setting me on the path for this career, this life. And in this hospital room, sat coming to terms with the loss to come and all the accompanying emotions, I feel a tiny glimmer of joy.

Among the items in my "go" bag prepared for when I could finally see Mum, I'd put a gift for her intended for Christmas. A few months earlier, a friend working at Mercedes had found out she was a big F1 fan and suggested organizing a special present: a cap signed by Lewis Hamilton, one of her favorite drivers (the others being Fernando Alonso, whom she always called "my Spaniard," and Leclerc, given that he raced for Ferrari and she thought he was "really up and coming").

Under the circumstances, it seemed silly to include it with the other, more practical items I needed upon getting the call to go and see her, like clothes and toiletries to tide me over for an indefinite, uncertain amount of time. But after a few hours and once my spinning head had started to slow down ever so slightly, I remember: The cap is in my bag.

So in the ward of the hospital, on this painful, heartbreaking day, I pull out a white cap with the Mercedes star on the front, signed by Hamilton and addressed to my mum.

Her face lights up. I explain the backstory, and there is so much love and gratitude in her response. She immediately puts it on and refuses to take it off for the rest of the day, proudly showing it to every doctor and nurse that comes to her bedside. They aren't quite sure what to make of it. When I return the next day, she still has the cap on her head. On Sunday, race day, she insists we watch the Bahrain Grand Prix together. So I set up an iPad alongside her beige hospital dinner. Hamilton wins the race after a thrilling late battle against Max Verstappen. As he crosses the line, Mum pats her cap and says: "I've got to fight like Lewis!" By profession, I have to remain neutral, but I'll freely admit: My God, I'm glad Hamilton won today.

Days turn into weeks and, gradually, months. Mum goes from the hospital to a hospice, where she is made comfortable. I live out of a suitcase in her flat and visit her every day, completing a Covid-19 test each time—my nostrils get far too adjusted to those swabs for my liking. We do all we can to make the most of the time we have left together. Some of it is the kind of practical planning you never really want to consider but sadly must. Thankfully, the memories that linger are the hours we spend looking at old photo albums, recalling her life from before I was born or the holidays she took in her youth. So often, she's eager to keep talking about F1, finding out the latest gossip I'd been hearing, even asking to time my visits so that we can watch the races together. The cap sits by her bedside all the while. Her love for the sport serves as a distraction from the reality that, try as we might, we cannot escape.

Four months after that day in the hospital with the cap, I get the phone call I never wanted to receive. After her condition worsened in the space of a few weeks, and just a couple of hours after my final visit, Mum has passed away.

All grief is different. But all grief hurts. It's something that never leaves you. You just learn to live with and work through it. And in the immediate aftermath of Mum's passing—and I guess as I'm doing it in these pages—I turned to words as a form of comprehending it all. Once I'd informed her immediate friends and those nearest to us of the news, I put together some public thoughts to share.

I write about Mum's love and pride for me, her only son and, after being told she may not be able to have kids, her "little miracle," something she called me right to the end. I write about those days at the small race tracks nearest to home, Brands Hatch and Lydden Hill, where we'd watch the cars going around, with nothing to worry about except who was winning and what the next race was. I sum up the indelible impact Mum had on so many people, the support she'd given me throughout my career, the unconditional and unwavering love and pride, the tears she shed upon seeing my work in print for the first time, or when she saw me off to my first race.

The next day, as I try to restore some semblance of normality to my life and wrap my head around all that had happened, my phone buzzes. The messages of condolence have been rolling in from friends and family.

But the last person I expect to hear from is one of Mum's favorite drivers: Charles Leclerc.

"Hey, Luke, I just saw your post," he writes. "I'm sending you all my strength to go through this difficult time. I can unfortunately relate to this, and I hope your family and yourself are okay. See you soon."

It is a small gesture that would've taken him barely a couple of minutes to complete. Yet it is one that meant the world; an empathy and understanding you wouldn't associate with those competing in such a cutthroat, competitive sport like F1.

At the darkest, hardest of times, it serves as a reminder of the underlying humanity that exists within the sport.

■ ■ ■

One way of coping with loss is to keep memories alive. Even seemingly small actions take on a great deal of significance. Starting in 2020, Pierre Gasly began to make the same pilgrimage to the Raidillon corner at Spa each year to pay tribute to Hubert, his fallen friend.

Gasly and Hubert had gotten to know each other in their early racing days, both rising through the French karting ranks with dreams of reaching F1. They knew the odds were firmly stacked against them—only twenty drivers at a time race in F1, after all—but both were determined to give everything to try to make it happen, egging each other on with every race they entered together, every gym session they completed. Gasly revered Hubert as being the quickest driver he knew; high praise from a youngster whose success secured him a place in the prestigious Red Bull academy. As Gasly stepped up to F1 in 2017 and his stock kept rising and rising, going from Toro Rosso, its junior F1 team, to the senior Red Bull team after Daniel Ricciardo's departure for the 2019 season, he was hopeful Hubert would also make the leap to F1 in the next few years and allow them to realize their joint dream.

Weeks before going to Spa, Gasly's dream stalled. Just twelve races into the 2019 campaign, Red Bull decided to demote him to Toro Rosso due to a lack of performance. He'd struggled to match Max Verstappen's results across the garage despite having the same car at his disposal. When Verstappen lapped Gasly at the Hungarian Grand Prix, Red Bull felt it had to take action.

It was a difficult decision to accept, even for someone as matter-of-fact as Gasly. It was a big career setback. He had a couple of weeks off in the summer break to wrap his head around things before the first race back at Spa, during which he leaned on those closest to him for support. A message from Hubert offered some comfort. "Prove them wrong," Hubert wrote to Gasly weeks before his death. "You're going to show them you deserve your seat in a top team and prove them wrong."

The words fueled Gasly, especially as he came to terms with what had happened to his career, and after the tragic events of Spa, he held them dear as part of his friend's memory. At the penultimate race of the season in Brazil, while still processing all that had happened in the three months prior, Gasly scored his first F1 podium in dramatic fashion. He beat Lewis Hamilton in a last lap drag race to the line to finish second, a result far beyond the expected ceiling for Toro Rosso. It served as a message to the F1 world and to those who'd doubted that Gasly remained capable of competing at the front.

The following year, an even stronger message would be delivered. One week after F1's return to Spa, understandably an emotional weekend for so many, but particularly for Gasly, the paddock made its way to Monza, on the outskirts of Milan in Italy. Gasly's team, by then known as AlphaTauri, was scoring points but rarely bothering the leading teams like Mercedes and Red Bull. A best result of seventh so far in the season didn't foreshadow anything too special from Gasly at what had become his adoptive home race since moving to Milan. He thought the highlight would be sleeping in his own bed, a rarity for F1 drivers to savor on a race weekend.

How wrong he was. After a midrace red flag forced the race to be paused, Gasly's decision to pit early had inadvertently vaulted him from tenth to third place for the restart. He overtook Lance Stroll for second before moving into the lead when Hamilton, the championship leader, received a penalty. The final twenty-five laps felt like a lifetime, particularly with the orange McLaren of Carlos Sainz Jr. filling his mirrors, weaving back and forth to try and pick up a slipstream. But Gasly soaked up the pressure and kept his cool, crossing the line for a famous, unexpected victory. In a sport dominated by the same handful of teams winning all the races, Gasly and AlphaTauri had achieved a popular upset.

Gasly quickly descended into delirium on the radio, celebrating with barely comprehensible yells. He returned to the pit lane and got out of his car, punching the air and hugging his mechanics, who came to greet him, all of them still unsure what had happened. The usual podium procedures then followed, giving a sense of order and calm for Gasly as he received the winner's trophy—it sits next to his TV at home in Milan to this day; he makes a point of looking at it while drinking his morning coffee—and then heard the notes of the French national anthem play out.

Hubert was particularly close at mind in this moment. He and Gasly had held that dream of making it to F1, of winning races, of hearing the anthem play for them. Now, Gasly was realizing it.

Once the formal celebrations had ended and the other two drivers had disappeared from the podium, Gasly was left alone to sit on the top step, head in his hands with red, white, and green confetti littered around him, taking in the magnitude of what he'd just achieved. He'd won a grand prix. He'd won for France. He'd won for Anthoine.

He'd proved them wrong.

By 2023, there was an extra degree of significance to Gasly's Raidillon pilgrimage: He'd joined Alpine, formerly Renault, whose academy members included Hubert. It meant Gasly was now working with many people who had known Hubert, seeing the same kind of potential that Gasly once saw in his friend all those years ago in karting.

Ahead of his move to Alpine, Gasly explained to me how he saw success with the team as another way to pay tribute to Hubert. "We always had this common dream of making it to Formula 1, me and Anthoine," Gasly said. "He had his dream to perform with Alpine. If it's something I can achieve and remember Anthoine even more within my life, that would be amazing."

Before the 2023 race at Spa, four years on from Hubert's death and the first time Gasly would race at the track as an Alpine driver, he started to think of a way to pay further tribute to his great friend. Something to bring the paddock together.

Gasly settled on a track run. Once F1, F2, F3, and any other series have finished their running for the day at the circuit, then the literal running is allowed to begin. The track is declared "open," allowing any paddock member to go out and run the circuit. It's proved to be a popular way for F1's traveling circus to stay fit. Plans were made for Thursday at Spa once all the media commitments and weekend preparations had been completed. Gasly called the event "Running for Anthoine."

Four weeks before the Spa weekend, the upcoming track run took on even more meaning. While F1 was in Austria in the middle of June, a young Dutch driver named Dilano van 't Hoff was killed at Spa during a Formula Regional race (a level below F3) in an accident just a few hundred yards from where Hubert had crashed. Wet conditions meant the cars threw up a lot of spray from their rear wheels, reducing visibility. Similar to Hubert's accident, van 't Hoff's car slowed after a crash and was hit by oncoming cars. He was only eighteen years old.

It shocked the motorsport world and only served to reopen the debate around safety standards at Spa. All drivers know their profession carries a high degree of risk. It has from the moment they first sat in a go-kart as a child. But another death at Spa served as a major wake-up call.

"That corner needs to be looked at and changed because we've lost two young talents in five years—it needs to be changed," said

Lance Stroll, the Aston Martin driver. "Every time we go through there we put our lives on the line. Even if it's dry and someone loses the car it's a blind corner, hit the wall, car comes out, 300-plus kilometers per hour, you're toast." Lewis Hamilton called it "devastating" that motorsport had lost two young lives at the same track in such a short space of time. "You're coming over a hill, you can't see, particularly in the bad weather conditions, and this has happened now twice," said Hamilton. "We definitely need to take a step."

"We all cherish Spa because of the track that it is," added Toto Wolff, the Mercedes team principal. "But is there something that we need to look at?"

There is that recognition and acceptance of the dangers run when taking part in these races; that to race on the most spectacular tracks, to get the thrills that only come when racing at the very limit, it'll be impossible to totally eradicate the risks involved. Steps can nevertheless be taken. In the wake of Hubert's death, Spa reviewed the changes it could make to try to improve safety standards, particularly through the complex of corners near to where Hubert had been killed. Officials moved the barriers back to create more space, and also laid down gravel to reduce the speeds of the cars should they lose control and go off the circuit.

Safety is a never-ending pursuit for the whole of F1 and something the drivers are constantly in discussion with the sport's leaders over improving. They say they don't make race tracks like Spa anymore, and there's a reason for that. Newly built circuits are more likely to feature plenty of run-off area—the space on the outside of a corner—meaning that if any cars go off, they have more room to slow down and less risk of bouncing off a barrier back toward the other cars. It's far safer but also less exciting for the drivers.

■ ■ ■

It is the day of the track run. As the rain keeps falling from the thick, foggy skies, the main straight at Spa slowly fills up with bodies crowding under umbrellas to try and stay dry. From the top of a flatbed truck, Alpine team members hand out T-shirts with RACING FOR ANTHOINE written on the front next to his logo, a star, which we put over our running gear. The buzz of conversation peters out as Gasly emerges on top of the truck and grabs a microphone.

"It was important for me to organize it, just to remember a great friend of ours—two great friends of ours, amazing drivers that we lost, Anthoine and Dilano," Gasly says, his voice catching.

"I think it's important just for us as a community and a sport, as a big motorsport family together, to remember these two amazing talents. It's a very special place, a very emotional place, and I just really appreciate you getting all together."

He pauses. "I really hope we never have to lose any of us in the future."

Applause ripples through the crowd. Gasly hands the microphone to one of his teammates, hops down from the truck, and takes his position at the front of the group on the start line. With a nod, he sets off, flanked by many of his Alpine teammates and with a bunch of flowers in his hand.

As a group, we follow Gasly's footsteps, going up the small incline to the first hairpin corner, La Source, before heading down the hill before the dramatic rise of Eau Rouge that leads through to Raidillon. In their cars, the drivers will take the right-hand, uphill corner before then turning left as they reach the crest at 180 mph. Even with the changes made in the wake of Hubert's accident, there's a bottleneck feel for the drivers as they thread the needle, knowing every millisecond of lap time matters. Today, it's a more leisurely speed.

Reaching Raidillon, Gasly pauses and waits as the rest of the crowd catches up. Not all are running; some opted to walk, while others even took scooters. But once everyone is in place, Gasly takes a breath, looks at the flowers in his hands, and slowly walks toward the barrier alone.

The track falls silent, the pitter-patter of the rain the only gentle background noise. Gasly crouches down, lays the flowers, and takes a couple of minutes to honor his friend. It's a powerful moment. On a handwritten note poking out of the flowers, Gasly has written in thick, silver ink: *I'll prove them wrong!*

His tribute paid, Gasly stands back and returns to supportive embraces and back-pats from his Alpine teammates. Many of his fellow F1 drivers, including Esteban Ocon, Charles Leclerc, and Zhou Guanyu, all of whom raced Hubert at points in their career, also take time to pay their respects, as do officials and drivers who knew him in F2. Five bunches of flowers are left standing against the barrier.

The group slowly picks up speed into another light jog, only to come to a pause just a few hundred yards later at the part of the track where van 't Hoff lost his life. His family are the first to lay flowers, soon followed by teammates from the Dutch MP Motorsport team he raced for. Arms around shoulders comfort the mournful faces, tears being wiped away. In the hardest of times, it offers solace to the van 't Hoff family, who later thank Gasly and the F1 paddock for turning out to pay their respects.

The track run then resumes. There's still over three miles of the track to go, starting with the long Kemmel Straight before the downhill sweeps, the smell of the pine forest hanging in the air. One by one, we all finish our laps, congratulating one another as we cross the line. For Gasly and the paddock at large, it's been a run to remember.

The remainder of the race weekend at Spa thankfully passes by without any major incidents or crashes, the worst being some wheel-to-wheel bumping at the first corner. Even as torrential rain impacts Saturday's running, the drivers come away exhilarated by racing on such an iconic race circuit on Sunday. A victory for Max Verstappen, who is half-Belgian and also cheered on by tens of thousands of Dutch supporters who crossed the border for the weekend, leaves many fans going home happy.

Racing drivers will always be committed to doing what they do best: racing. Performing at the highest level, where every millisecond matters, risk and danger cannot be on their minds.

"It's not something I ever think of," said Lewis Hamilton when he was asked about any safety concerns racing at Spa. "I think as a driver, it's not something that you can ever really let into your mind."

Gasly admitted to having "contradictory" feelings about racing at Spa. "I've had the worst emotions of my life here," he said. "At the same time, it's one of my favorite tracks. I love this track, I love racing this track. But I'll never forget what I felt going down these stairs when my parents told me the news. It's obviously tough. But I accept the sport that we do, and it's things you've got to live with. It's life, as sad as it can be, you need to accept and move on.

"I'm happier with organizing this sort of event. It might be a small thing for people, but it's a lot for me and meaningful."

And if you gave any driver the choice between racing or not racing, they would choose to race, every time without fail. It's their nature, the one that has been hardwired and honed from such a young age to always be flat out and push to the limit. It's not to be mistaken for recklessness at all; simply that their competitive mindsets must be matched by the unrelenting commitment to keep racing safe.

6]

Track Runner

Up the thirty-yard incline into the tight turn-one hairpin, grandstand to the right and the giant American flag flapping in the wind straight ahead. Slowly turn in, clipping the apex before the downhill swoop through turn two, which swings to the right, gravity making acceleration that bit easier. Ensure you're in the middle of the track to thread the needle of the "esses" coming up, the succession of left- and right-hand kinks.

No, these are not the thoughts of a Formula 1 driver starting a hot lap. It's me, going at a much, *much* slower speed, as I navigate the early part of a track run at the Circuit of the Americas in Austin, Texas, the host of the United States Grand Prix each October.

An F1 track is the perfect place to go for a run. Yes, there are elevation changes, but for the most part, it's a wide, open expanse of space that is largely flat, without the risk of bumping into people going in different directions like at a local park or running on the roads.

From a more F1-specific point of view, it's also a chance to get a deeper understanding and appreciation of the legendary circuits that F1 visits in its world tour each year. Watching on TV at home (or from the media center, where journalists are stationed for a race weekend), you don't get the same kind of view of the inclines, the tightness of certain corners, the challenges that drivers face at incredible speeds behind the wheels of their cars.

To create an F1 track is no easy feat, whether you're doing so with the limitations of a major city center or have an open patch of land that gives you endless options. You can pour hundreds of millions of dollars into a project, only for it to upset the locals due to the noise or disruption. The drivers might grumble if they find a lack of excitement from driving the track, be it due to limited overtaking opportunities or the design of the corners not giving them enough of a thrill. The quality of the asphalt might not be up to the job. (For me, the humble runner, I just want something flat—so thank you Montreal and Silverstone!) A number of factors need to come together to make a good F1 circuit, particularly when so many of the "classic" older tracks seem to have the right ingredients despite dating back to the 1920s. Sometimes, simplicity can be king.

As I continue on my lap around the Circuit of the Americas, known by its acronym of COTA, I start to understand what makes this track so special. I've been lucky enough to be in the passenger seat of a Mercedes supercar, driven by George Russell, for a lap of the track before. But at my own pace, giving myself time to properly take in the twists and turns of the circuit, it's increasingly obvious why drivers love this track so much.

How does somewhere like COTA go from an empty wasteland to one of the finest tracks in all of motorsport? It's no easy task— but sometimes, like the run to turn one, you have to embrace the uphill struggle.

■ ■ ■

It was never Bobby Epstein's plan to own a race track.

Had things gone the way he planned, his 649-acre site called Wandering Creek to the southeast of Austin, the state capital of Texas, would have turned into space for six hundred homes and offered him a decent return on his first real estate investment. Instead it became home to one of the greatest circuits in all of motorsport.

Twenty years after he purchased the land, we're sitting in his office overlooking the finish line at COTA. Glass windows offer views going down the main straight, of the uphill incline at the first corner, and over the imposing grandstands that are sold out year after year.

Epstein's office is like a potted history of the formation of the United States Grand Prix at COTA. It features pictures from classic moments of the races through the years and some of the most famous cars to have raced there. Music posters for the acts who have played at the track, including Taylor Swift and the Rolling Stones, line the hallway. There's a foosball table with a bottle of F1 podium champagne—sorry, sparkling wine—poking out from between the miniature players.

The top of the boardroom table, where Epstein invites me to sit, is a blown-up aerial shot of COTA and all the land surrounding the track. In 2022, the track recorded a total attendance of 440,000 over the three-day race weekend (Friday through Sunday), which F1 reported to be a record at the time. It has since been surpassed by Silverstone, but the hopes are it can be the first track to break the half a million mark.

As Epstein points to the landmarks around the circuit, he takes me back to the mid-2000s, when he bought what was then barren ranch land. He had been working in the bonds market and looked at investing in real estate. An Austinite, he became aware of a plot of land up for sale just beyond the airport. His plan was to create more affordable housing as Austin faced steady population growth of around 4 percent per year. But resistance from people living in the surrounding area and city officials was fierce. Some opponents claimed a pond dug by a farmer for some cows was actually an environmental water feature that had to be preserved. It meant his plans kept being delayed and delayed until 2008 and the Great Recession.

"They did it long enough that the housing market eventually collapsed," Epstein explains. "Now I'm sitting out here with this really ugly land, the shittiest land you can find, wondering what to do." With the market at a low, Epstein had no choice but to sit and wait.

By chance, the person from whom he'd bought the land ended up having dinner with an investor called Tavo Hellmund, who was working to bring an F1 race to Texas. Epstein recalls thinking it was "a pretty crazy idea" at the time. F1's repeated attempts to establish a race in the United States had failed, simply because it struggled to stir up the same kind of interest as IndyCar or NASCAR, the two major American racing series—a far cry from where the sport is today in the US. A race at the Indianapolis Motor Speedway, home to the Indianapolis 500, between 2000 and 2007 failed to capture American fans, causing the grand prix to fall off the calendar.

Epstein was encouraged to talk to Hellmund. "If you help him write a business plan and help him maybe raise the money for it, you can maybe get rid of your land into the deal, and be all done with your property thing, and walk away," the former landowner told Epstein, who agreed to investigate the project. He soon became a key player, believing it could do a lot for the city of Austin and that there might be some money at the end of it. "We did a lot more for Austin than we did for profit for a while. . . ."

Some "chaos," to quote Epstein, over the leadership of the project—legal disputes led to Hellmund's exit after a settlement—meant that Epstein became the primary backer and main promoter for the project, putting him in contact with Bernie Ecclestone, F1's chief executive and commercial boss up until 2017. Ecclestone was desperate to get a race off the ground again in the United States, knowing the importance of the world's biggest sporting market to F1. He told Epstein to get in touch with Hermann Tilke, a renowned track designer who has put together the majority of the F1 tracks to join the calendar in the last twenty-five years. Tilke had created circuits in Malaysia, Bahrain, Turkey, China, and Abu Dhabi, and now had a chance to create something new on empty farmland in Texas.

There were two primary goals for COTA: to make amazing

views for the fans coming to the track and to make it one of the most challenging and exciting tracks for drivers on the F1 calendar.

The first of those stemmed from Epstein's own handful of experiences watching F1 in person, when all he'd seen was the car zooming past in a blur and no actual sporting action. Offering fans that limited vantage point made it hard for them to get excited about what was happening or being there for *the* moment in a race. "It's like being at a golf tournament and being at the right hole at the right time when the guy hit the shot that everybody is going to talk about," Epstein says. "Your chances of actually seeing something happen on a flat circuit are tough." Epstein wanted this to have as many hills as possible so that fans could see a number of corners from a single vantage point, giving them a better chance of witnessing overtakes.

This desire naturally lent itself to achieving the second objective: making a thrilling race track for the drivers. Many of the older F1 tracks like Spa and Suzuka made great use of the natural topography in the surrounding area, creating elevation changes for the drivers and more exciting corners, the satisfaction heightened by the curvature of the land as downforce fights gravity. But as increasing numbers of modern circuits are situated on completely flat land, it became difficult for the designers to get overly creative.

When the original clockwise track layout was presented to Epstein, Tilke had a suggestion. To the east of Epstein's site, there was a plot of cheap land with a hill—the same one that I'd been slowly jogging up the previous day. "They said, 'If you can get that piece of property, we can design something that hasn't been done before,'" Epstein recalls. "'We've been able to model it on the computer, but no one's given us any hills to work with. Since Spa, there hasn't been a hill like this available.'" Tilke envisioned it could become a landmark for the first corner, totally transforming the track layout.

"We bought the land and flipped the direction around, and that's how turn one happened. It wasn't in the original plans. Credit to Tilke for pushing and recognizing it. They take a lot of heat for doing the best you can on a flat piece of ground that someone hands you, to make the best set of squiggly lines. When you actually let them get to choose the palate, they can paint something that is really quite fantastic."

Epstein also encouraged Tilke to take inspiration from some of the great tracks already on the F1 calendar. It's something I felt when running it: how the esses in the first sector at COTA were similar to the high-speed section at Silverstone; or the long back straight leading into a tight, twisting string of corners seen at Hockenheim in Germany, slowing the cars down right in front of the grandstand; or the flat-out chain of right-hand kinks in the last sector of the race track, a wider version of the famed turn eight, in Turkey—the latter two both designed by Tilke.

"There's no shame in saying someone has done something that's really great, so let's borrow some of those elements and add our own to it," says Epstein. "And given what we spent, if we didn't get one of the greatest tracks in the world, we would have been real idiots." Estimates put the cost of building COTA at over $300 million.

Even with a masterpiece of a track layout, there were still some challenging hurdles to overcome. Simply shifting the dirt to carve out the circuit was a big ask, effectively turning the site into a giant sandpit. Over two hundred trucks were used to move the sand around and help form the undulations, as well as remove some of the poorer dirt. Epstein points out of his window to the parking lot to the south of the circuit on a slope that gently rises, and asks if I'd spotted the hill. "That's all the fill from under the track!" he says, laughing. Turns out moving it elsewhere was cheaper than getting it cleared away.

The bigger issue for COTA as it aimed to host its first grand prix in 2012 was that its money had dried up as government officials got cold feet over supplying state funding. It meant construction of the track practically came to a halt, putting the future of the race and the project in serious doubt. Around this time, a separate F1 race proposal around the streets of New Jersey was being discussed and was seen as a rival to Austin. It meant COTA had to keep the wheels turning somehow or risk losing its place as the future home of F1 in the United States. "We didn't want everyone to know what problems we were having behind the scenes," Epstein says. "We didn't want New Jersey to know we had stopped."

The only entrance to the circuit was a road that now runs north to south, parallel to the main straight. Any time some news reporters would come and do an update on COTA and its perceived struggles, Epstein was eager to ensure it looked like construction was still ticking along. So again, he got creative.

"We got rid of the construction company, and we hired two people," he says. "One guy with the biggest bulldozer he could find, and one guy who was a spotter. And whenever someone pulled up to take pictures of it, they would say: 'Cue the bulldozer!' And the guy would start going right through the middle, throwing up dirt and making it look like construction is happening. And then the stories showed construction was still going on. It 100 percent stopped for a good five weeks. And nobody in the press reported it because every time they'd come by, they'd see the bulldozer!"

When COTA did secure the funding it needed to fully resume construction, there was a new feathery hurdle to overcome when heavy rain hit the area. "Some rare ducks were nesting in the water in the sandpit after it rained," Epstein recalls, his voice a mix of amused and bemused. "The local authorities said, 'The ducks are nesting so close to the runways that they are in danger from the flight pattern for the planes from the airport,' so they closed the sandpit, and we had to pump it out and abandon it." Squabbling between the city and county officials gave time for workers to get the water pumped away and for the ducks to migrate, meaning construction could finally push ahead.

The asphalt was laid and the pit buildings completed a couple of months before the inaugural race, allowing for the track to be declared open after a long, arduous journey through the nine years since Epstein had bought the land. Mario Andretti, the most recent American to win a world championship in 1978, completed some celebratory inauguration laps on the track, and with all of F1's and the FIA's approvals, the Circuit of the Americas hosted the United States Grand Prix in October 2012—and quickly won rave reviews. "The day after the first race, I know a German paper wrote: 'Tilke's masterpiece,'" Epstein proudly recalls. "I thought that was really great."

F1 is now booming in the United States with three races on the calendar, adding events in Miami and Las Vegas in 2022 and 2023. Yet Austin is the one regarded as the true "racer's race," making it one of the best-loved events on the F1 calendar, up there with the likes of the British Grand Prix at Silverstone and the Australian Grand Prix in Melbourne. Austin is one of my favorite cities on the F1 calendar. It has an amazing live music scene—the race is usually a week after the Austin City Limits music festival and will hold concerts that are free for ticket holders, with acts including the Killers, Green Day, and Ed Sheeran in the past decade—and incredible food, particularly if you're into true Texas BBQ. The "Keep Austin Weird" slogan of the city is truly embraced by F1. Daniel Ricciardo turned up at the track one year riding a horse. Cowboy hats and boots become normal paddock attire. The only person I've met who didn't like Austin was a German billionaire who said it was "a bit quiet." I responded by talking up the ten-dollar pizza I'd found on South Congress and where to get the best beer, which generated a pitiful smile in response.

But what has truly made Austin such a hit in F1 isn't the city or the cheap pizza but the track itself. Every year, drivers relish the opportunity to throw their cars around the hills and sweeping turns, knowing it makes for some of the best racing of the year. In the seasons that have been dominated by a single driver or team, like we've seen at times from Max Verstappen and Lewis Hamilton in the past ten years, the nature of the circuit makes it perfect for overtaking action and a thrill over a single lap, meaning it is always an exciting race. For the drivers, it gives a reward few other circuits do in the same way.

"This is one of my favorite tracks," said Hamilton, a five-time winner at COTA. "Often when they build new circuits, they're not really like the classics. But this was a classic from the get-go. It's one that enables us to have great races."

COTA also achieved its goal of being one of the fan-friendliest races on the F1 calendar. Epstein points me to a grandstand from which you can see ten turns from one spot that offers views of 80 percent of the track, something few other circuits can offer. Perhaps greater than the hundreds of thousands of people who attend the race each year is the emphasis to make the United States Grand Prix accessible to fans, keeping tickets at a relatively affordable price of around three hundred dollars—you can buy COTA tickets at Costco, believe it or not—while many of the other events spiral toward four figures for the same kind of experience. It's little surprise there's a rush of people running when the gates open each race day morning to get a prime spot on the hill at turn one. If you want a race on an epic F1 track in the heartland of America, this is the one for you.

It's been a long journey for COTA and never one Epstein expected to go the way it did. But he takes pride in how things turned out and the circuit's reputation, especially at a time when, as Hamilton noted, more and more tracks lack the character of "Tilke's masterpiece."

"We got a chance to build the greatest modern track," Epstein says. "That is how we wanted to be billed. And I hope we are the greatest modern track. I think over time, people will come to appreciate the differences of COTA versus the attention-grabbing street races that maybe are equally good for the brand, but I don't think the sport.

"I think we'll be proven to be a track for the ages rather than for the time being."

...

Much as Bobby Epstein never set out to own an F1 track, Hermann Tilke never set out to enjoy an enormously successful career designing them. Had things gone the way he'd dreamed as a teenager, he might have been the one racing on all of the great circuits around the world.

"Since I was eighteen, I was racing," Tilke, now seventy, told me from his office in Germany. He'd spend weekends taking his mother's Volkswagen Scirocco to enter local events, gradually building his way up to bigger races for road-style touring cars. When the architecture and engineering firm that he worked for wouldn't give him enough vacation days to go racing, he decided to create his own company that could help turn his hobby into his profession, starting at his kitchen table.

"I wanted to do something in my business, engineering and architecture," Tilke said. "So it started with small projects. At the time, it was very small, like the changing of a service road area or small refurbishment at the Nürburgring [an iconic track in Germany]. But then people said after a while, 'He's an expert in race tracks!' That's how it happened."

In the late 1990s, Tilke came into contact with Bernie Ecclestone, who was starting to oversee F1's global expansion beyond the calendar's typical European confines—nowadays, the F1 calendar is spread across five of the world's seven continents—and was looking at building some new circuits in countries like Malaysia,

China, and Bahrain, who wanted to tap into the tourism and prestige boost a grand prix could offer. Tilke had been working on the redevelopment of the F1 track in Spielberg, Austria, now known as the Red Bull Ring, and traveled to Barcelona to show Ecclestone his plans. "He looked at the drawings, and he said, 'Hmm, what you did here is shit!'" Tilke recalled with a chuckle. "I said, 'Okay . . .' I thought it was the last track I would do for him!"

How wrong he was. When Ecclestone went to the Nürburgring in Germany, he marveled at the design of the giant new Mercedes grandstand overlooking the first corner, a two-tier, curved structure offering fans outstanding views of the track that stands as a great landmark to this day. He asked the track officials who was responsible and was told it was a young engineer who just so happened to be at the circuit. "Then he saw me, and he recognized it was the same guy who did the track in Austria!" Tilke said. "Bernie said, 'Yeah, this is very good, very good. I may have some other projects for you.'"

Under Ecclestone, those "other projects" would extend to eleven brand-new F1 tracks, ranging from purpose-built circuits like COTA in Austin or the Sepang International Circuit in Malaysia to new street courses in Singapore and Baku, Azerbaijan. If you needed an F1 track to be built, Tilke was your man. It's a reputation that has extended through to F1's post-Ecclestone era under Liberty Media. Two of F1's new, high-speed street tracks—in Jeddah, Saudi Arabia, and in Las Vegas—were also the work of Tilke and his group, which has grown to a team of more than 150 engineers. Not bad for a company borne out of frustration over the lack of free time to go racing himself.

It has also become a family business. Hermann's son, Carsten, became a project manager upon completing his doctorate in engineering and was appointed managing director in 2017. He works closely with his father on all of the ongoing race track projects. They attend around half the F1 races each season together, and spend much more time traveling to and from the circuits that are being constructed all around the world.

Carsten identified the Sepang International Circuit in Kuala Lumpur, Malaysia, as being one of the big turning points for track design. The circuit itself, which is sadly no longer on the F1 calendar, is wide and offers plenty of overtaking opportunities between the sweeping high-speed corners that made it one of the best-loved among the drivers. Yet it was in the design of the buildings around the track that Tilke's engineers were told to get creative and make something outstanding.

"It was not only a functional race track," said Carsten. "All the tracks before were functional, just for the purpose of racing. But the Prime Minister of Malaysia said, 'I want to have a landmark. I want to have something where people remember we are in Malaysia when they see the track.' And, so it was not only the track anymore, it was also about the buildings, and the connections between the buildings and the track and the architecture." The landmark Hermann and his team settled upon was a gigantic grandstand designed to look like a hibiscus flower, the national flower of Malaysia, with a roof that resembled the petals stretching out. The structure quickly became iconic both within F1 and all of Malaysia when it held its first grand prix in 1999. The grandstand even made its way onto Malaysian currency when it was imprinted on the twenty-five-ringgit coin, worth around five dollars.

At all the F1 tracks that Tilke designed with his team in the following years, they quickly found a landmark to make it shine. In Bahrain, there is the massive race control tower—the one the Gulf Air plane flies around before each race—which has also graced banknotes. Shanghai has an enormous main grandstand structure that towers above the cars down on the grid. Tracks like Istanbul Park in Turkey and COTA, with its famous turn-one hill, became more renowned for the challenging circuit layout. All of Tilke's tracks ended up with a "calling card" that made it unmistakably one of his. "Sometimes it's difficult, it's a flat area," said Hermann. "But we try to do something, try to bring in some sort of landmark to the design, especially at the F1 tracks."

■ ■ ■

The process to design an F1 track is not as simple as creating the best layout possible for racing. It's rare for a project like COTA to come along, where the organizers issue few stipulations and can let the engineers' and architects' creativity run wild. "People often think we have a white sheet of paper, and we start and we have all the flexibility we want, but that's not the case," Carsten explained. He noted how a lot hinges on the purpose of the track, whether it wants to host only national-level racing or go all the way up to F1, as well as whether it will stage motorbike racing, which requires additional safety measures and careful placement of barriers to protect those on two wheels instead of four. Then there are the geographical and physical constraints, such as the number of hills, as seen with COTA, or the quality of the land. "It's a combination of many different factors," said Carsten. "But of course, we want to create an exciting track for racing."

With COTA, one point on which the Tilkes and Epstein were aligned was the importance of a great fan experience. "Our philosophy is that we want to bring the people as close as possible," said Carsten. "It's so they can feel the speeds of the cars. If you're too far away, you miss the speed." For fans, so much of the thrill of watching F1 live comes from that visceral feeling. The track designers have their role to play in that.

It takes time to settle on a track layout. The Tilkes will lean on their experience and past designs to know what does and does not work, liaising with the track owners and the promoters of the race to agree on an initial layout. They can then build a computer model for use in a simulator, allowing drivers to give their feedback on the virtual layout. The Tilkes can then make alterations where appropriate, as well as talking to F1's own track-design team to get a final layout before starting construction.

As impressive as the buildings and architectural feats at some of the Tilke-built tracks may be, the underlying fact is they must remain functional and good for racing. It makes the input of the drivers important. "We ask the drivers, and they come to us and say what are the good and the bad points," said Hermann. "You learn every time when you discuss it with the drivers."

Designs have not gone without criticism. The amount of overtaking seen in F1 races, typically the barometer for whether a race has been good or not, relies on variables including the design of the cars, the competitive difference between teams, the quality and age of the tires, and the weather (and, of course, how brave a driver is feeling). The track layout also plays a role, meaning when there's minimal action, it can be a point of contention for drivers, teams, and fans. The Yas Marina Circuit in Abu Dhabi, which was designed by Tilke and debuted in 2009, was altered ahead of the 2021 race in a bid to make it better for overtaking by removing some of the slower-speed corners, something that proved effective and led to an improvement in the quality of racing.

■ ■ ■

One major shift in the design of F1 tracks over the past ten years has been the increase in the number of street circuits on the calendar. Back when I started reporting on F1 in 2013, there were only four street or street-style tracks on the calendar. As of 2026, with the addition of a new event race in Madrid, Spain, there will be nine street races. It's all part of the push to get to the heart of the world's biggest cities, one that has proven to be an effective way to make a splash and bring a Super Bowl–style vibe to attractive locations. Singapore became F1's first night race in 2008, starting at 8 p.m. local time under floodlights with a course around the Marina Bay area of the city. In the last decade, F1 has established new street races in Azerbaijan, Saudi Arabia, and, most recently, Las Vegas, which incorporates the famous Strip into its layout. Whether you love, fear, or loathe Las Vegas, seeing the cars kicking up sparks beneath all the neon signs as they zoom past the famous landmarks at 200 mph is quite the sight.

Their addition often comes at the cost of most "traditional" track designs that are typically better for overtaking and racing, given there is only so much space on the F1 calendar, capped at twenty-five races. Street tracks typically prove difficult for overtaking because drivers have to race at far slower speeds around tighter corners, meaning they need to be much quicker than the car ahead to realistically make an overtake. Monaco was famously described by three-time world champion Nelson Piquet Sr. as like "riding a bicycle around your living room," and although some of the newer circuits aren't quite that extreme, layouts are often still constrained by wherever the roads go.

"It's very different to design," said Hermann. "In a street circuit, you are very limited for the alignment of the track: You have your houses there, and you cannot knock down a house! So you have to go around and make it very interesting, and it very much depends on details. But on the other hand, you can still be creative."

Pulling off the Las Vegas street race was proof of that. Closing down the Strip for three consecutive nights one week before Thanksgiving is no easy feat, let alone doing so and still designing a race track that is good for F1. When the track made its debut in 2023, it ended up being one of the best races of the season with ninety-nine overtakes, including a dramatic last-lap pass by Charles Leclerc on Sergio Pérez at the end of the Strip. The goal for the race organizers was to ensure F1 was in the middle of Vegas, incorporating the landmarks like the Strip and the Sphere, which lit up the sky throughout the race. The Tilkes helped make it happen.

Hermann anticipated the shift toward street circuits will continue in F1. "The permanent circuits are still there, but there are more and more street circuits in the cities because Formula 1 wants to go to the people," he said, believing the atmosphere is better at street tracks as a result.

"It's important to have the right mixture," added Carsten. "If we only have street circuits, people will get bored of street circuits. But if you have a mixture of permanent tracks, of old tracks, of new tracks, of city tracks, I think for me, this is the best, this different combination so with over twenty races, there is a big variety."

Hermann Tilke's job has changed significantly since starting the company out of his home in 1983, going from service roads at German tracks to the Las Vegas Strip. Yet there is still an underlying love for motorsport, and an excitement over F1's future—and what the next great track might be.

"It was my passion, racing," he said. "This is how it all happened."

■ ■ ■

F1's calendar may be growing increasingly congested with new, shiny street tracks, but if you talk to the drivers, most of them will agree that the old ones are still their favorites.

Four of the seven tracks that were on the original F1 calendar in 1950 are still in use for grand prix racing: Silverstone in the UK, Monaco, Spa in Belgium, and Monza in Italy. Monza holds the record for the most grands prix, hosting F1 every year since the start of the world championship with the exception of 1980. All four of these tracks are held in high regard by F1 drivers past and present, not only due to their rich history, but also the challenge they pose: Silverstone's high-speed corners that push the drivers' neck strength to the limit; Spa's fearsome challenge through the middle of the Ardennes forest; Monza's long straights that require bravery slowing down for the corners from 220 mph; and Monaco's tight, technical layout that punishes anything but the greatest precision.

None of these tracks were built in an era when F1 had anything like the kind of safety standards it boasts today. Upgrades have been made over time to make them safer, particularly as the cars have grown faster and faster, yet there remains an old-school vibe about the classic tracks that even the greatest new-builds struggle to emulate.

F1 drivers are honest about how risk and danger contribute to that. Many of the newer circuits will have more asphalt on the outside of corners, meaning if they brake a bit too late or enter a corner slightly too quickly, they'll lose time but then easily rejoin the track. On the older tracks, grass and gravel remain the deterrents, meaning if they dip a wheel too far off the circuit, it could result in a crash.

"Any historic track where there's a bit more risk, it's a bit more old school," said Oscar Piastri, who made his F1 debut in 2023 with McLaren. "They remind me a bit of when I was coming through the junior ranks on some of the British circuits, where there are a lot of consequences [for mistakes]. It bites you a bit harder. When it does bite, it's never fun, but it adds that element of risk and excitement."

Suzuka, located around three hours outside of Tokyo on the bullet train, hosts the Japanese Grand Prix each year and ticks all the boxes for F1 drivers. It opened in 1962 as Honda's test track after being built at the behest of its founder and was upgraded to start hosting F1 races from 1987 onward. It's the only figure eight track on the calendar, a bridge in the final third of the track taking it over the cars passing below, and has some of the most challenging corners on the calendar. The sweeping esses in the first sector test the limits of not only the drivers' skills but the downforce of the cars beneath them. After all, they're designed to be driven at high speed. Suzuka has only two slow speed sections—a hairpin and a chicane—and, more importantly, the track also provides the undulations that so often make for a great F1 layout. Watching a driver complete a lap at speed around Suzuka is to see their skills being tested to the limit.

"It's actually my favorite circuit of the year," Alex Albon said. "You can really drive the corners and really feel what it's like to drive a Formula 1 car. It sounds silly to say, but a [street] track like Singapore, you don't really feel like you're driving a Formula 1 car. Whereas here just the speed, because it's so tight, so narrow, there's grass either side, the immersion in speed, the feeling of speed is a bit more. It's very special."

Lando Norris agreed with Albon's assessment. "It's one of the ones I look forward to the most every season, probably up there with one of my favorites, too," he said. "You experience what a Formula 1 car is capable of. The whole experience of driving here is always a lot of fun."

But he also moved to note the importance of risk in adding to that enjoyment and excitement. "The room for error is pretty small," Norris said. "It's not changed much over the years, which I think is one of the best things about it. You've got that element of risk, which I think is always genuine. You're always a bit afraid of running too wide, things like that, because you know if you put a wheel half a meter too wide, it's game over. It definitely brings a few more nerves while putting a lap together and driving."

The other thing Suzuka boasts that few of the newer tracks can in the same way is the history. It was one of the earliest F1 tracks in Asia to become a mainstay on the calendar and settled four championships in its first five years hosting F1. This included Ayrton Senna and Alain Prost's infamous showdown in 1989, when Prost crashed into his McLaren teammate and bitter rival. Senna would later be disqualified after controversially being deemed to have rejoined the track unsafely after the incident, giving Prost the championship. One year later, again at Suzuka, Senna and Prost (who by then had left for Ferrari) crashed at the first corner, this time giving Senna the championship. No rivalry in the sport's history, either before or since, has proved so explosive. It quickly put Suzuka into F1 folklore, only adding to the legend that makes it so appealing to drivers racing there in the modern day.

"It's one of the favorites, I think, for all the drivers for sure, because of its figure of eight," said Hamilton. "It's that historic circuit where you saw Ayrton and Alain racing on many years ago. It is an incredible track to drive on and such a beautiful country as well."

This kind of history is something that cannot be built into a track overnight, no matter the magic Tilke and his team can weave. Some of F1's "newer" tracks only hold on to that term loosely now, considering the likes of Bahrain and Shanghai have celebrated twenty years since their first grands prix. Some of the new street tracks like Baku and Jeddah have staged crazy, incident-packed races that also won praise from fans. Daniel Ricciardo won from tenth place on the grid in Baku in 2017, overtaking three cars in one corner en route to victory, while the Verstappen/Hamilton rivalry flared massively at the first race in Jeddah in 2021, the pair colliding on the track at one stage. Maybe we'll consider them to be "classic" tracks someday.

It's inevitable there will be concern among the fans about the direction in which the calendar is heading, dropping more of the old-school circuits in favor of new street events. When F1 announced last year it would be relocating the Spanish Grand Prix from Barcelona, which has a permanent track on the outskirts of the city, to a new street track in Madrid, it sparked some outcry. Although Barcelona rarely made for good racing and was widely panned as being one of the worst tracks on the calendar, it felt like another shift away from the roots upon which the sport was built. As Hamilton put it: "We've got to make sure we hold on to those pillars of what this sport is."

It's a balance F1 needs to strike carefully, respecting its history, those "pillars," and racing on the best possible tracks while also recognizing the commercial boom that comes courtesy of racing in the heart of city centers.

■ ■ ■

A few days after I speak with the Tilkes, I'm in Abu Dhabi for the final race of the season, and my final track run of the year. Except there's one tiny issue: There's a supercar auction taking place in the middle of the circuit.

F1's glitziest events tend to attract a level of VIP and wealth that is difficult to comprehend (like German billionaires not enjoying Austin), and Abu Dhabi is high on that list. Regardless of if there is a championship showdown at the end of the year that hypes up the sporting spectacle, the Yas Marina Circuit becomes *the* place to be seen as the harbor fills up with yachts and people get ready to splash the cash. Among the top items are a McLaren F1 car from 2006, a mangled Lamborghini Countach used in the *The Wolf of Wall Street*, and even a Porsche 911 car still in its original protective film with just six miles on the clock. All will pull up north of one million dollars. Oh, and for the kids, mini motorized cars are going for $15,000.

As the auctioneer talks into the microphone and presents the next car up for sale, a few people turn heads at the sight of me limbering up at the side of the straight, before hitting go on my watch and setting off into the distance. (Yes, I could have started beyond the auction floor, but do you know how annoying an incomplete track run map would look on Strava?)

Since chatting to the Tilkes, I've started looking at tracks differently. Abu Dhabi is unique as it has a pit exit road that actually goes underneath the track, popping out on the left-hand side at turn three for cars to rejoin the circuit. There's a tall control tower overlooking the first corner, which has a gradual climb going through the opening three corners. It's nothing quite as extreme as COTA, Spa, or Suzuka, but at least gives a bit of character to a track built on a man-made island. It remains one of the most modern facilities on the F1 calendar, fifteen years after its debut.

I push on through the rest of the lap, looking at the giant grandstands either side of me, then coming toward the marina, where yachts are moored, blasting music as the parties begin (no doubt some celebrating their latest supercar purchase). I pass underneath the W Hotel that is at the center of the track, lights flashing on its exterior, which looks like scales on a fish, and come through the final couple of corners to cross the line, dipping to the side of the track to avoid interrupting the auction, which is still in full swing. A new PB, and a lot of sweat in the humid Abu Dhabi night.

After completing my cool-down stretches, I go for a wander among the supercars and the sheer wealth on the main straight, awestruck by the cars. Amid the runner's high, I'm also feeling smug about ticking off twenty track runs for the season, only missing Las Vegas and Brazil from the full schedule.

The chance to run the tracks is one of the most unexpected perks of working in the sport. It's not something I even contemplated when I started out, barely doing any exercise. Now I can say that I've run two marathons, in London and Chicago, in part thanks to training on F1 tracks, which has also given me a greater appreciation for where we go racing every other weekend. Although it's not been without a few mishaps along the way.

I said earlier that an F1 track was, in many ways, a perfect place to go for a run, given it's a wide, open expanse, and how once all the cars are finished for the day, it's open for the paddock to use. Sometimes, that's not quite true.

Take Monaco, for example. Once the on-track action is complete, the police are pretty quick to reopen about two-thirds of the track to road traffic, albeit at slow speeds. It meant I was able to run along the open roads of the track, waving my paddock pass to get through anywhere shut off to pedestrians, still continuously looking over my shoulder for nearing traffic shuttling the rich and famous from point to point, lest they have to walk themselves. But by the time you get to the final third of the track, the bit near the harbor, the bars and restaurants that line the circuit are not only open, but spilling out onto the track itself. Determined to complete my lap, I weaved through the crowd of a couple hundred people sipping their beers and Aperol spritzes to the thump of dance music. A bit of a challenge.

The same thing happened in COTA the day before I spoke to Epstein. The track always hosts concerts as part of the race weekend, but no one had told me these take place on a stage next to the back straight, making the track itself effectively the "pit" for the show. After going around the hairpin, I saw a massive crowd of people looking up toward the stage that was flashing with lights as Adam Lambert and Queen prepared to start their set. Again, I tried to find a path through the crowd of gig-goers. One guy yelled that I nearly knocked a beer from his hand. Another (rightly) found it funny to go: "Dude, you're missing the show!" Still, I made it through. At the end of the lap, I was greeted by a group of stunt dogs who were just finishing up their rehearsal for a prerace show on Sunday, all wearing coats with dog-related puns such as "Max Fur-stappen" and "Sergio Paw-rez." Truly the best end to a track run ever.

One thing that stood out to me over the season of running the F1 calendar was, like the drivers had said, how the old tracks did feel that bit more special. A run is a run, yes, but tracks like Baku or Jeddah, as impressive as they are for the feats of engineering, just didn't give the same kind of satisfaction or feel that the likes of Silverstone, Spa, or Monza do. It's a different experience. These iconic tracks are the pillars of our sport, the roots that keep us connected to its incredible history. And they are true joys to run. It's a deep privilege that I try not to take for granted.

My favorite track run of the year was Suzuka, for many of the same reasons listed by the drivers earlier. It was tracing the same patches of track that once staged landmark moments in F1's history. I headed out long after sundown, the track only illuminated by the lights of the pit lane and the Ferris wheel slowly circulating. Qualifying ended more than three hours ago, and there had been no reason for the fans to stick around, yet they remained in their seats in the grandstand. It was quite a sight as I ran through the final chicane and began the downhill drop to the main straight, seeing the glow sticks and flags still being waved in case they got a glimpse of their favorite driver chatting to a mechanic in the pit lane; they simply loved being there. It's the kind of dedication you don't get at many of the newer, city-based F1 tracks; a true appreciation of the history and significance of the place.

Because just as F1 is nothing without the great circuits that have hosted so many historic moments through the past seventy-five years, it is also nothing without the people who are its heartbeat and keep it going: the fans.

Fantastic Fans

Wandering along one of the many canals in Amsterdam with a cup of coffee and a croissant has to be one of the most civilized ways to start my working day.

It's late August and F1's summer break is over, meaning there's a "back to school" vibe for the Dutch Grand Prix at Zandvoort, named after the small town on the North Sea coast of the Netherlands. A month apart is a considerable amount of time by the F1 paddock's standards, and most of us have used the break to take some much-earned holiday in the throes of a busy season. I've already got my small talk nailed down: "Go anywhere nice?" "The break never feels long enough, does it?"

I walk past beautiful townhouses lined with flowers in full bloom and people sitting outside cafés on street corners sipping their espressos and smoking cigarettes. It's an early start, before 8 a.m., but already many are heading in the same direction as me, making the trip to Zandvoort via Amsterdam Centraal station.

And the vast majority of them are going there to see one person: Max Verstappen.

Verstappen's emergence onto the F1 scene as a once-in-a-generation talent is an astonishing story. Red Bull saw him as a rough diamond with a remarkable raw, natural speed who simply needed to iron out mistakes and the occasional crash in the early years of his F1 career as a teenager. He quickly learned, and from that point on, there was never any doubt he was going to become one of the greatest of all time—a belief that has since been fully justified. After winning championships in record-breaking style through recent years, Verstappen trails only Lewis Hamilton and Michael Schumacher for race wins.

Verstappen's success wasn't just a big story in F1 circles. It captured the imagination of the entirety of the Netherlands. For a sports-mad country that had little history of producing notable F1 drivers—the only other Dutch driver to score a podium in F1 is Max's father, Jos, who raced in the 1990s and early 2000s—it quickly latched on to the mania surrounding its great new talent. Verstappen is half-Belgian, and grew up just across the Dutch border in Belgium, but always raced under the Dutch flag. The "orange army," the name used to describe the droves of Dutch sports fans who adorn bright orange whatever sport they follow, typically soccer, quickly heralded Verstappen as being their next sporting icon.

This means when you attend the Dutch Grand Prix, you are very much on Verstappen territory, something made clear even on the walk to the train station. Wherever you look, fans are wearing either orange shirts or Red Bull merchandise. Other tracks typically have a mixture of team support, ranging from Ferrari's red to the black and silver of Mercedes to the papaya of McLaren. Here? It's all Max.

After crossing the paths for the cyclists and trams that make Amsterdam a far cry from the fumes and noise of other national capitals, I make it to the train station and buy my ticket to Zandvoort, a journey that takes around thirty minutes. Dozens of fans and I are funneled along to the ticket barriers, my white shirt and black slacks making me an outlier in the sea of orange and the odd spot of navy, the color of Red Bull. One man a few feet in front of me has Verstappen's logo, a mash-up of the letters M and V, tattooed on the back of his neck. I wince thinking how painful that would've been to get done. The more I look, the more tattoos I see, be it of Verstappen's race number, thirty-three—he uses number one when he is the world champion—or of the lion logo that adorns the top of Verstappen's helmet, which I spot on another man's bare shoulder.

On the platform, every information board reads: MAX EXPRESS. Yes, even the trains are renamed after Verstappen today. Like him, they are quick and efficient, one leaving every five minutes from Amsterdam and going direct to Zandvoort.

I take a seat on the Max Express and watch as it quickly fills up with fans. The race doesn't start for another seven hours, but they're keen to get into the track early. A group of twenty-somethings, three men and one woman, take the seats adjacent to me, and quickly fish a box of beer out of a backpack. It'll be the first of many today.

The Max Express jolts to life and pulls out of the station as people are still moving to take their seats. A family passes through, parents and kids all wearing identical orange bucket hats. A group of lads on a bachelor party, each with a can of beer in hand, have matching checkered flag T-shirts reading: THE LAST RIDE! DESTINATION: WEDDING. One teenager is playing the unofficial anthem of the Verstappen fans, a parody song called "Super Max!" by Pitstop Boys—the lyrics are literally: "*Max, Max, Max, Super Max, Max!*" over and over again set to a dance beat—out loud from his phone, enlivening the mood on the train for so early in the morning. Sports can be incredibly polarizing at times, yet there's a strong sense of community here. Even the handful of fans not decked out in Verstappen gear are getting in the spirit of things. As people file past him in the aisle to move down the train, one man in a Ferrari shirt starts making a "*neowww, neowww!*" sound, mimicking the F1 cars. An actual car sound is then played over the loudspeakers as the train pulls into Zandvoort.

We get off at the other end to the smell of sea air, the first sign we're only a stone's throw from the Dutch shoreline. Helpful guides wearing checkered flag jackets stand at the end of the platform, calling out instructions through megaphones as the crowd slowly mills toward the race track entrances.

Zandvoort hosted the Dutch Grand Prix most years between 1952 and 1985 before the track seemingly became a relic of F1's past. It was deemed too small a facility for F1, meaning it was reserved for national championships and junior categories no higher than Formula 3. A town of seventeen thousand people, Zandvoort was chiefly a resort for people looking for sun and sandy beaches on weekend breaks or holidays, not a motor race.

That was before Max happened. All the tracks around Europe soon became engulfed in Max mania as tens of thousands of Dutch fans traveled from race to race, turning the grandstands bright orange. Red Bull's home race in Austria and the Belgian Grand Prix at Spa became the most frequent sites of pilgrimage for Verstappen's followers, yet there was a craving for a race of their own.

It proved to be the perfect time for F1 to return to Zandvoort. It ticked the box of Liberty Media's "destination city" requirement, its proximity to Amsterdam making it accessible for fans no matter from where in the world they traveled. You're actually not allowed to use cars to attend the Dutch Grand Prix, leaving attendees to use trains or, as is the norm through so much of the Netherlands, a bicycle, making it one of the most environmentally friendly events on the calendar. The funding was secured for Zandvoort to undergo a significant upgrade so that it would be ready for F1, including the creation of three banked corner sections for a bowl-like feel in places. The last corner is thirty-two degrees steep (difficult to run on!), giving the circuit characteristics that made it unique in F1. Like Austin's turn one hill, Zandvoort had its calling card. The race eventually returned to the calendar in 2021—the season Verstappen won his first world title—after the Covid-19 pandemic set plans back a year and was an immediate hit. Each year since has been a sellout crowd of more than three hundred thousand fans per weekend, which ends with the vast majority going home happy. At the time of writing, the race has always been won by Verstappen, his victories heralded by explosions of orange flares and flags as he crosses the line.

There was little grumbling or concern from Zandvoort as a community about bringing F1 back, something that is clear on the walk to the track. On the main street from the train station, the houses and apartment buildings have gotten fully into the spirit of the event, draping Dutch flags from their windows. Children wearing oversize Verstappen shirts that reach to their ankles have buckets filled with soft drinks that they're selling for a euro each. When the rain starts coming down, they run out of their houses clutching as many ponchos as their arms can hold, trying to take advantage of any fan's poor planning. As the sand dunes of the coastline start to come into sight nearing the track, so does the sheer number of Dutch fans piling into the circuit for the day and filling up the grandstands. Tens of thousands at the track, and millions more back at home, will watch expectantly.

Verstappen takes it all in his stride. Even with the lengthy list of extra commitments for his home race weekend, be it marketing appearances or fan meet and greets, he's appreciative of the support. At no point does it become too much to distract him from the job at hand. "It's just great," Verstappen says when I ask him ahead of the race in the press conference about the pressure, fittingly accompanied by a snap of cameras the moment he flashes a smile. "Nobody ten years ago even thought about a grand prix here. For me, it's just amazing to be here."

He does his job and sends them home happy. Even when a late storm leads to the race being suspended with eight laps remaining, threatening to quite literally rain on Verstappen's parade, he hangs on to his lead upon the resumption, doing enough to clinch victory. The fans, still wearing their ponchos, go wild when he crosses the line as dance music blares out to celebrate yet another Dutch success on home soil.

Verstappen's team boss, Christian Horner, can't quite believe how Max—still in his mid-twenties at this point—copes with the spotlight. "You guys have seen all the pressure and expectation that Max is under from 100,000 Dutchies here," he says. "A lot would have cracked under that pressure today. He kept his composure and delivered, as he's done so many times.

"The race is on the calendar for one reason, which is Max, and the effect that he's had. When you come here and feel the atmosphere, it's a phenomenal event."

To have sparked such a fanatical support speaks volumes about Verstappen's impact on F1's fanbase. He's not especially prolific when it comes to doing things that might strike a chord with younger fans. You won't find him posting memes or making Tik-Toks. "I'm a bit more old school in that," Verstappen admits. "I wish social media never existed." To some, that's part of his appeal, that he's always considered himself to be a straightforward person who simply wants to go racing and live his life away from the race track, not concerning himself with life on a handheld screen.

On the walk back to Zandvoort train station, retracing the same steps from the morning, now just a little soggier after the rain shower, the fans remain in a jubilant mood. The verandas in front of the buildings on the residential streets have been given over to tipsy karaoke sessions. One of the singers goes up to people walking past to sing along to his garbled rendition of "Sweet

Caroline," getting a surprising amount of participation at the required moments. On the Max Express back to Amsterdam, the carriage is filled with faces that are damp, a bit sunburned, but all smiling.

This is the power F1 drivers can have. The success of one driver took a country from not really caring about a sport to investing in its own race and having its own distinctive fan club, turning grandstands bright orange. In less than ten years, Verstappen has turned the Dutch into some of the biggest F1 fans in the world.

It's far from the first example of a driver's or team's success being a deep source of national pride. You can find that right at the start of F1's story with its most famous, successful team.

■ ■ ■

Ferrari has woven itself into Italian culture from its origins in the 1930s, when Enzo Ferrari first set about building cars and going racing. As of February 2024, a net worth of $75 billion shows the commercial behemoth the company has become, but its significance goes far beyond such a lofty valuation. Ferrari cars are intrinsically linked with the highest levels of culture and society, meaning when you think of the world's greatest, most exciting cars, one of them will likely be a bright red Ferrari. Even if you don't know the names of the car models, you'll definitely know the importance of the Ferrari logo, the black prancing horse against the yellow badge.

Racing in F1 was always part of Ferrari's identity and actually played a role in red becoming its hallmark color. In the earliest days of grand prix racing, prior to the formation of the world championship in 1950, all cars entered to a race were required to race in a designated national color, a far cry from the colorful schemes and sponsor-heavy designs we see today. Cars from Great Britain were green, cars from Germany were white—and the Italian cars were red, making it Ferrari's color.

Ferrari was there from the first race at Silverstone in May 1950, making it the only team to have raced in every F1 season. It quickly established itself as a successful team on track but also had an air of mystique and magic that no other team could capture, in no small part down to its fans. Ferrari was the first F1 team to really capture a fanbase, who became known as the *tifosi*, the Italian word for *fans*. While it is used throughout Italian sports, it has become synonymous with the Ferrari fanbase. The literal meaning of the word is "those who are infected with typhus"—and when Ferrari succeeds at Monza, its home turf on the outskirts of Milan, it's a fever and fervor that rapidly spreads. As sporting religions go within Italy, Ferrari's success is as significant as that of the Azzurri, the national soccer team. Victory or defeat of either is front-page news, rarely resigned to the sporting sections.

Verstappen's orange grandstands have nothing on Monza. Hours before the cars go out on-track to start practice for the Italian Grand Prix each year in early September, the seats will be filled with fans wearing Ferrari red, bringing homemade banners and giant flags celebrating the rich history of their team. The 2023 race, taking place in a season of Verstappen and Red Bull domination, does not dampen the support, which, in some cases, is made a religious affair. One fan with a paddock pass regularly graces Monza as a pope, wearing papal regalia covered in Ferrari logos, and waits by the garage entrance to bless the Ferrari team members and wish them luck. One banner in the grandstands replaced the face of Jesus with that of Charles Leclerc, one of Ferrari's F1 drivers, on an image of Christ Pantocrator. The banner next to it has the face of Carlos Sainz Jr., then Leclerc's Ferrari teammate, on a ketchup bottle, his name offering a punny play on "Heinz Tomato Ketchup." Even outside of the track, fans without tickets will line the roads entering the circuit to lend their support, waiting for the drivers and the team members.

"Driving for Ferrari, we've got support everywhere," said Leclerc. "But when we come to Italy, it's on a different level." The creativity and noise are unmatched.

Race day at Monza is always the biggest moment of Ferrari's season. Today, the stakes are even greater. Sainz starts from pole position at Monza and with Leclerc third, the pair split by Verstappen, whose Red Bull team has won every race so far this season; there's hope Ferrari could score a popular home win. The qualifying result had Ferrari fans celebrating outside the hotel of the drivers until 1 a.m. As appreciated as their support may have been, the impact it had on the drivers' sleep was likely less welcome.

Shortly before the race begins and the grid starts to form, I always make a point to get as close as I can to the *tifosi* for the moment the Ferrari cars are wheeled to their starting positions at Monza. As Sainz's car is pushed through the crowd of bodies, the sound is remarkable: a cacophony of chants, cheers, and air horns blaring. Both Sainz and Leclerc get out of their cars, give a brief wave to the crowd, and then do their best to get into the zone ahead of lights out. Avoiding the distraction of the noise must be impossible. Spirits are roused further with a booming rendition of the Italian national anthem, "Il Canto degli Italiani," the final note of which is accompanied by a flyby of airplanes that form streaks of red, white, and green for the Italian flag in the sky down the length of the starting grid. The crowd whoops and cheers in delight. This is Italy's day. Will it be Ferrari's day?

When the lights go out, the grandstands explode with noise as the *tifosi* will the Ferrari cars down the main straight to the first corner. Sainz stays ahead of Verstappen as the pair pull away at the front, Leclerc doing his best to keep up with them. Leclerc's second Ferrari win came at Monza in 2019, something he regards as one of the greatest moments of his career. Today, it might be his team-mate's turn.

Verstappen ultimately proves too strong. Sainz's Ferrari car, while quick, burns through the rubber on its tires trying to keep the Red Bull behind. After fourteen laps, Verstappen can apply the brakes a little later going into the first corner, his car shooting ahead of Sainz. Italian hearts all around the track sink. They know the race is lost. The cheers, still loud, become a little less impassioned as the stakes lower.

By the end of the race, the *tifosi* is back in full voice, albeit for the wrong reasons. Sainz has by now dropped to third and is under pressure from Leclerc, who looks quicker. The two cars are separated by mere inches as they near speeds of 220 mph at the end of the straights. Neither driver is willing to back down, yet both know the consequences of contact that could put them both out the race. It would be plastered on the front of all the Italian newspapers tomorrow. The unforgiving home media would ask how Ferrari could throw away a podium finish because it couldn't control its drivers. Did they not know what this meant to Italy? To the *tifosi* in the grandstands? Teammates crashing into each other is a worst-case scenario but does occasionally happen. It would be the ultimate letdown for it to happen here. Every moment they get close at braking for each corner, the Ferrari fans yell out, both in support and in protest. It's too much, even for a fanbase so seasoned in heartbreak.

Sainz and Leclerc keep it clean, just about, to come home third and fourth. Even if Sainz couldn't win, he'll be leaving as the hero of the *tifosi* today. In most circuits the podium is part of the main pit building, meaning those standing in the pit lane get closest to the celebrations and sprays of sparkling wine. At Monza? It's the fans who get that privilege. The podium is suspended partially over the main straight, with a walkway leading the drivers over the pit lane. Once the cars are all back in the pits after the race has finished, the track underneath is then opened up for the fans to congregate under the podium. Tens of thousands of people spill through the gates, running to get as close to the celebrations as possible. Regardless of the result, a giant Ferrari flag will be unfurled in the middle. Today they get to celebrate third, but it's a moment that Sainz, standing on his first Monza podium, will never forget. "P3 in Monza in front of the *tifosi* is as good as it can get, at least for this weekend," Sainz says.

Leclerc admits he had the fans in mind when fighting against Sainz. "We know how important it is for the *tifosi* to have one red car, whoever it is, on the podium," he says. "The guys on the pit wall perhaps had one heart attack or two, the *tifosi* probably, too."

"But for me," Leclerc adds, "this is Formula 1. This is what it should be all the time." He's not wrong. The highs and lows are part of being a fan of any team, but when you're following Ferrari, the swings are that much greater. They live for this kind of drama.

■ ■ ■

Sitting in traffic leaving Monza at the end of a busy, hot race weekend is a rite of passage in F1. The roads around the track are always congested. Unlike Zandvoort, there is no speedy train to take us to and from the circuit every day, nor can you get around via bicycle easily. Every fan who has attended a grand prix will know the long waits creeping out of parking lots at the end of a day of racing. The same goes for those of us trying to get away after a long day of work. As the sun begins to drop behind the trees, I'm sitting in the passenger seat of a friend's car, making minimal progress as fans outpace us walking down the sidewalks on either side of the road. From behind, the blare of a siren tells us to move over and make some space, blue lights flashing in the rearview mirror.

A police car pulls past, closely followed by two Ferrari road cars, the sight of which quickly turns the heads of the walking fans. The penny drops as they quickly realize Ferrari's F1 drivers, Leclerc and Sainz, the very same drivers they've spent the past three days cheering on, are behind the wheels of their respective cars.

The fans immediately break out into a sprint. Along either side of our car, we hear the *thud-thud-thud* of feet hitting the pavement, willing to catch up with the cars and to see their heroes. The fans fumble for their phones to get a picture, for Sharpies to maybe get an autograph. The slow-moving pace of the traffic means neither Leclerc nor Sainz can get very far, prompting both to briefly but kindly oblige those who make it to their windows for a picture or a couple of kind words. They're gestures that take seconds, but for the fans in red, they are memories that will last them a lifetime.

At the end of the season, Ferrari's team principal, Fred Vasseur, cannot shake the impact the *tifosi* had on him at Monza. It had been his first season at the helm of Ferrari, a position that comes with immense responsibility. A string of poor results can put you at risk of losing your job. Losing the support of the Italian media is one thing. Losing the fans will see you on your way out even faster. As a first year goes, he's done a pretty good job, all things considered.

"At Ferrari, what is different is that the pressure is coming more from the outside, it is coming more from the *tifosi*," Vasseur says. "But this was positive, and I was very surprised with this. Monza was the beginning of the good part of the season for us. We arrived in Monza not really in good shape, but the *tifosi* were outside when we arrived on Wednesday and were very, very supportive. You had guys without tickets waiting for the drivers, positive, always supportive, and this is giving you mega energy.

"It was a very good feeling for me that all the weekend in Monza, and the podium . . ." Vasseur puffs out his cheeks dramatically, and smiles. "I did Monza perhaps forty times in my life, and this was by far the best one."

That's the power of the *tifosi*.

■ ■ ■

The makeup of the F1 fanbase has changed significantly in recent years. If you thought of your stereotypical F1 fan twenty-five years ago, you'd likely have pictured a middle-aged white man. He might be balding and was likely to be a "car guy" who grew up in an era when safety standards were far looser in F1, adding to the sport's danger. Despite the low quality of the majority of races, when the immature technology of the cars compared to modern standards meant far fewer cars would even make it to the finish line—at Monaco in 1996, only four cars finished the race—it all felt *better back then*.

Bernie Ecclestone, F1's one-time ringmaster who oversaw the sport well into his late eighties and paved the way for its global expansion, famously claimed he did not need to worry about appealing to young fans because they didn't have the income to buy a Rolex, one of F1's major sponsors. He also saw zero value in social media websites like Twitter or YouTube, believing they were a fad not worth his time because they could not be directly monetized. Incredibly, he once banned the drivers and teams themselves from posting content from the paddock on social media, believing it could infringe on broadcast rights. It caused Lewis Hamilton to once land in hot water with F1 because he posted a video on Snapchat. "I'm not interested in tweeting, Facebook, or whatever this nonsense is," Ecclestone said in an interview with *Campaign* magazine, the quote coming to define his final years at the helm. "I tried to find out but in any case I'm too old fashioned. I couldn't see any value in it. I don't know what the so-called young generation of today really wants."

Therein lay the issue. While the hardened *tifosi* would still sell out Monza and the serious fan support never really went away, F1 struggled to properly capture young audiences at a time when social media was starting to boom through the late 2000s and into the 2010s. Other leagues and series were making significant ground while F1 stood still. The bosses of F1 were focused on making as much money as possible for its shareholders. It led to some lucrative TV deals to stuff the coffers, many of which put broadcasts on pay channels across Europe—having cable wasn't the norm as it is in America—which meant it was less likely people would simply stumble across F1 and have their interest captured, like I did watching that rainy Brazil race in 2005. You couldn't watch F1 without setting out to do so in the first place.

It could not be further from the modern-day F1 we now know. When Liberty Media took over F1 in 2017 and ousted Ecclestone, it doubled down on trying to capture the attention of younger fans by taking a new approach toward social media, actively working to promote the sport across its channels and latch on to viral trends. It had to catch up with other sports that had realized there was enormous value in those platforms to grow a fanbase long ago. The Netflix series *Drive to Survive* was the most obvious example of that formula working. It was an immediate hit from its debut in 2019, opening the sport up to a totally new demographic of fans, those who might not sit down to watch an entire F1 race but were curious to learn about the drivers and, crucially, the personalities in a sport so often hidden in smoke and mirrors. Finding F1 on TV or Netflix made it a gateway for so many.

It helped fuel a significant change in F1's fanbase beyond the Verstappen fans or Ferrari's *tifosi*. Now there was a way to connect with every single driver on the grid not merely based on how they performed on-track or the number of trophies they won but because of *who they were*. People came to love Daniel Ricciardo for his personality and quirkiness, or ex–Haas boss Guenther Steiner for his foul language and spectacular turn of phrase. Fans started to invest in the people, not just the racing.

Drive to Survive was a particular success through the onset of the Covid-19 pandemic, which coincided with the release of its third season, when people were cooped up at home and had little else to do but try to complete Netflix. It meant by the time the world was starting to rediscover some semblance of normality, the interest in F1 had surged. Races became sellout events, particularly through the 2021 season, when Verstappen and Lewis Hamilton went head-to-head in one of the most dramatic championship fights in recent history.

And it wasn't the same fans as before who were coming through the gate. In a survey conducted by Motorsport Network in 2021, the average age of F1 fans was found to have fallen by four years from thirty-six to thirty-two since 2017. In that same four-year period, the number of female fans had almost doubled from 10 percent to 18.3 percent. Almost a third of fans had been following F1 for five years or less, a sign of *Drive to Survive* having a deep influence. This was especially true in the United States, where half of the fans who took part in the survey said they'd only started watching in the past five years.

The change in F1's fanbase has not been without its problems, unfortunately. The nature of "gatekeeping" seen in any sport rings especially true in F1 because of just how quickly things have shifted.

Criticism of *Drive to Survive* fans on social media or in website comment sections is depressingly frequent, as though the sport expanding to the next generation of people hungry and excited to follow F1 is a bad thing, simply because they're doing so through different platforms.

F1's fandom shift goes far beyond the raw statistics. Walking around the fan areas at F1 races, there is far more diversity and young people making up the crowds than there was even when I started working in F1 around twelve years ago, and greater numbers of families with small children, pointing to encouraging signs for the sport's future. Starting that fandom young can be a way to make them fans for life. While the home races for the likes of Verstappen and Ferrari will be dominated by their merchandise creating seas of orange or red, across the majority of events, there is a remarkable spread of driver support visible in the grandstand. Drivers like Lewis Hamilton and Lando Norris certainly have a level of popularity others on the grid may not match, yet that doesn't mean the rest go unsupported. From seeing fans in customized Zhou Guanyu ice hockey shirts on a train platform in Japan to a group wearing matching Esteban Ocon tees reading ESTIE BESTIE in Australia, it's evident that, more than ever, F1 fans are fans of the drivers—every one of them.

The scale of the transformation is not lost on the drivers. All of them have seen their followings skyrocket in the past five years, becoming known names even outside the F1 world. If you'd stopped someone on the street ten years ago and asked them to name an F1 driver, if you were lucky, they'd have told you about Lewis Hamilton. Now, the grid is filled with drivers who have become celebrities in their own right.

"All of our profiles have grown in the last few years, in particular since *Drive to Survive*," said Ricciardo, who has graced the sofas of *Jimmy Kimmel Live!* and *The Late Show* in recent years. "Me with my personality, and also just having some fun with the sport, that probably got a little bigger as well because of that." He's maintained his focus is on racing, even if fans may not always realize it. "It's funny, sometimes people come up to me like: 'You were great in that season!' and I'm like: 'Racing season, or *Drive to Survive* season?' Maybe we're not all viewed as race car drivers. It's part of it. I think we're all building profiles and a bit of a brand, but it's not anything that's taken away from the racing side of it."

McLaren F1 driver Lando Norris has been one of the most prolific drivers when it comes to engaging with the new influx of young fans. Even before he reached F1 in 2019, Norris was in tune with what fans wanted to see on social media, embracing memes and bringing a fresh energy to the grid. He would regularly stream himself playing video games on Twitch, particularly through lockdown, and even set up his own gaming brand, Quadrant. It's little surprise that in the Motorsport Network surveys, Norris ranked as the most popular driver among the younger demographics. His home grand prix at Silverstone tends to be one of the most Norris-heavy fan events. A couple of years ago while leaving the track, I came across a group of fans chanting, to the tune of *Hey Jude*: "*La, la, la, la la la laaaa, la la la laaaa, LANDOOOO!*" thrusting their beers toward the sky to toast his podium finish. Still in his mid-twenties and a race winner, Norris is going to be a fan favorite for a long time to come.

F1 drivers have become more conscious and savvy about the way they engage with fans away from racing, knowing the benefits it can have for their personal brands. The same is true for the teams. They can't solely rely on their racing prowess and the simple fact they are one of ten F1 teams to capture the attention of fans and sponsors, the latter being particularly important to fund their racing. Now more than ever, they need to make a real effort to connect with fans.

When Red Bull decided to rebrand its sister F1 team, Alpha-Tauri, for 2024, it saw an opportunity to step up those efforts. It struck two major sponsorship deals with Visa and Cash App, meaning AlphaTauri's name became "Visa Cash App RB," something the team itself admitted was a mouthful. Away from its naming conundrum, it wanted to reach an audience outside of racing. The team's new identity was revealed during Super Bowl week in Las Vegas with a concert from Kendrick Lamar, helping the event reach far beyond the traditional motorsport publications that would ordinarily carry coverage.

"We believe it's important to be aiming at that whole new, younger audience, which we are reaching now through the social media," said Peter Bayer, the team's CEO. "It's about racing, obviously. We want to be very serious and focus on the racing. But at the same time, we want this team to be fun, to have some entertainment. We want to democratize the sport by connecting with fans who cannot come to the race track because maybe it's unaffordable or sold out, by having events in the city center, for example. We have ideas for the US events, for example, which will again feature big music content. And so it's that combination of on-track performance combined with off-track entertainment and that Red Bull spirit, which is what we want to give to the fans."

Bayer's point about wanting to "democratize" F1 is an important one. For so long, the sport has been regarded as highly exclusive, something only reinforced by attitudes such as Ecclestone's that it was a world for people who could afford a Rolex. Ticket prices have always been high—the first grand prix I ever attended was the first I went to as a journalist, at Silverstone in 2013—but the digital age has helped break down some of the barriers.

It's something Rob Bloom, Aston Martin's chief marketing officer, wanted to put at the heart of the team's efforts toward fan engagement. The Aston Martin name may be well known within the automotive world, famously being the brand of car driven by James Bond, yet its links to F1 are less historic. Besides a few races through 1959 and 1960, it wasn't until 2021 that Aston Martin properly raced in F1 after Lawrence Stroll bought shares in the car company and rebranded his Racing Point team, meaning it had a blank canvas from which to build its identity within the sport.

"Aston Martin is an inherently exclusive and luxury brand, and sport is inherently *inclusive*," Bloom explained. "So we've created what we described as an 'inclusive exclusive' brand. Fan engagement has been front of mind and the core belief from which we built our entire brand positioning and marketing strategy from day one. It's been such an amazing opportunity, to build a new brand from scratch."

Bloom was especially eager to focus on the human stories within the sport, particularly from the point of view of the team. "The sport has always been an amazing technology showcase, it's the pinnacle of innovation," he said. "But what where it was struggling was to connect on a more human level with fans. *Drive to Survive* has been exceptional to really bring the sport to life through a powerful platform, but not directly linked to one of the teams."

The buy-in of the drivers has helped with this. Bloom met Norris when he was working at McLaren, and said Norris was "really a catalyst" for changing how drivers approached social media. At Aston Martin, Bloom works with the oldest driver of the grid, Fernando Alonso, someone few would expect to be so engaged with platforms like TikTok. Instead, Alonso has embraced the fun side of it when working with the team. In the spring of 2023, there was a rumor on social media that Alonso could be dating the newly single Taylor Swift, despite the two having never met. Around the same time, a sped-up version of her song "Karma" was trending on TikTok. Alonso used the audio and simply posted a video of himself winking, delighting fans who saw him buying into the meme of the moment. "It's so important that all drivers engage. For younger drivers, it's more native, but the more long-standing drivers on the grid recognize that's how they remain relevant and put their personalities across," Bloom said.

It's for that reason Bloom thought F1 has not only become more accessible than ever before, but also more human than ever, and is a break with the previous waves of the sport becoming too technical-focused or lost in the racing.

"*Drive to Survive* has set a new direction for storytelling in the sport and accelerated that direction," he said. "It's effective in bringing new fans in, giving a brilliant insight. It's not something we now want to wheel back from."

■ ■ ■

It's not only the drivers and teams who have revolutionized the way fans can access F1. The fans themselves have also changed the game.

I met Sarah, Tiggy, and Chesa, hosts of the F1 podcast *Paddock Project*, at the Austrian Grand Prix, which is not a race where I'd been expecting to chat with a trio of New Yorkers. The track is in one of the most remote locations on the calendar, taking place in Spielberg, a small town in the heart of the Styrian mountain range, and is nearly three hours away from Vienna and an hour from the closest city, Graz. The grandstands were largely made up of fans camping for the weekend, a lot of whom made the journey from the Netherlands to support Verstappen at Red Bull's home track. But the trio made the trip over for their latest F1 experience, wanting to see what a European race is like.

Paddock Project is an F1 podcast that has not only been a great success for Sarah, Tiggy, and Chesa but is also symbolic of the change within F1's fanbase over the past five years.

Coming from an Italian family, Chesa was a longtime Ferrari fan, while Sarah and Tiggy considered themselves to be more "new age" F1 fans who came to the sport through *Drive to Survive*. "As a lot of new people who get into F1 realize, there is just no limit to how much you can get into it and where you can go with it," explained Sarah. "We were all just talking about F1 all the time amongst ourselves, and separately really liked podcasts. We noticed that there just wasn't kind of 'us' out there that we could listen to and we felt like there really was a space for that.

"We just figured we'd give it a try. We ordered mics on Amazon and it was very homemade. We thought maybe five people would listen to it."

Paddock Project has established a sizable listener base since it was launched in 2022, initially known as *F1r the Girls* and grown to more than one hundred thousand followers on Instagram. The trio have interviewed F1 drivers including Oscar Piastri, Sergio Pérez, and Yuki Tsunoda, but they often talk to less-profiled people behind the scenes, particularly women in key roles within the sport. "I think our audience is hungry for behind-the-scenes knowledge, whether it's the technical side of the car or the business or logistics, or sustainability," said Tiggy. "People want to learn about the sport in a way that wasn't necessarily true before. It's just more exposed, now there are so many more women in high-profile roles, and there seems to be more interest in interviewing people behind the scenes."

Importantly, *Paddock Project* has grown into something far more than a podcast. It's a community. They have a booming Discord channel that gives fans—mainly women—the chance to chat about the latest F1 news, gossip, and races, all in a welcoming, safe space. "One thing we heard so often from women, whether it was in the Discord or DMs, is that they don't have anybody in their day-to-day lives to talk to about F1," said Tiggy. "But they've really found this community online and through platforms like ours. It's just been really amazing to be a part of building that."

That sense of community is ingrained in American sporting culture. If you go to a football game or a baseball match, you'll see families, friends, and groups taking part in tailgating or sharing experiences. F1's international appeal makes that harder, as does the European-centric timings that mean most races have to be watched over breakfast. *Paddock Project* took their community-building project a step further by starting some group watchalongs in New York, allowing fans who'd met through their channels to do so in person and watch the grands prix together. "A bunch of girls met each other on the first one and became friends, then came along to the second one altogether, and that to me is the coolest thing," said Chesa. "In the States, when you're in your twenties, sports is a big reason for people to get together. Imagine if you want to do that for F1? You don't have people who are all going to get together at a bar. So the more we can do to give people a sense of belonging and legitimacy to their fandom of their sport is pretty special."

One of the standout statistics they shared is that around 90 percent of their podcast listeners are women. From my experience in F1 media, it's pretty much the inverse of the normal audience makeup, speaking to the shift they are helping to encourage. They also produced a line of merchandise that played on the "Saturdays are for the boys" meme, creating T-shirts, caps, and hoodies that read: SUNDAYS ARE F1R THE GIRLS.

The live watchalongs have achieved exactly what Chesa thought had proved so tricky for the sport. Getting over fifty Americans watching F1 together in a bar in New York on a Sunday afternoon would've been unheard of ten years ago, even more so with mainly female attendees. "We're for everyone," said Chesa. "People were DMing us like, 'Would you guys mind if my boyfriend or my husband came along?' It's like, of course, you're not ruining the sanctity of sisterhood! It's so funny. We always have some tailing boyfriends." Again, an inverse of what would've previously been seen as a typical F1 fan dynamic.

The increasing diversity of the F1 fanbase has, sadly, exposed some ugly attitudes among existing fans that go beyond the gate-keeping backlash to *Drive to Survive*. At the 2022 Austrian Grand Prix, a number of female fans reported incidents with men over the race weekend, including catcalling and the use of racist and homophobic slurs. Sebastian Vettel, F1's four-time world champion, called for lifetime bans for the offenders. "If people have a good time and drink too much that's okay, but it doesn't justify or excuse wrong behavior," he said. "We race as one, and the fans are a part of that." F1 responded by saying it would be discussing with the race organizers what happened and launched a campaign focused on fan inclusivity, as well as taking steps for the following year's race, such as increased security and limits on how much alcohol could be taken into the track, to prevent a repeat.

It made me curious to learn more about Sarah, Tiggy, and Chesa's experience in Austria, and why they'd picked to attend the race in the first place given the issues the previous year. They'd been keen to experience a European F1 race, and a former engineer recommended they check out Austria, given the picturesque setting and the amazing grandstand views. "We were definitely very aware of what had happened the year prior and the experience for female fans at that race," said Tiggy. "We'd never been to a European race, and that one seemed, as far as atmospheres go, something so different that we could not get in the US. We wanted to see what it was like as women, given all the press from the year before.

"It was a very fun trip. We definitely felt like fish out of water. At the same time, we did not feel disrespected. We very much felt like

F1 fans. Everybody was serious about the racing. We got some looks, but they were very welcoming." The whole race was deemed a success, going by without any issues among the fans in the grand-stands.

Sarah said the men to women ratio among the fans in Austria was 90:10—Chesa jumped in with "if that!"—but loved the fan experience at a more traditional racing venue, away from the hospitality and corporate events in Miami or Las Vegas. "That's one of my favorite things about F1, too, how with twenty-three or twenty-four races, you can get a different experience at so many races," she said. "There's really a place in the sport and need for both: These really classic racing-focused races, where it's serious fans, every-one's there for the racing, it's no frills, and at the same time there is space for these races like Vegas and Miami that are really over-the-top, but they get a lot of news coverage and they generate new interest in the sport. I've loved getting to experience those different types of races." They're keen for future trips to include more "classic" race tracks like Budapest, Silverstone, and Spa to experience even more fan cultures.

The female shift within F1's fanbase is something that will only continue, in no small part thanks to groups such as *Paddock Project* who've helped change perspectives and barriers in what has typically been a male-dominated sport. But there's also the hope that, over time, there won't be the same kind of gap to make up.

"I'm so grateful for the community we've built and the space we've had to create and to fill a niche that hasn't existed," said Tiggy. "But I would love for us not to be 'for the girls' in fifteen years because we really are for everybody. There's definitely a need for that now, to serve female fans and shed light on the women behind the sport and all of that. But I would love for that not to be such, like, a special, unique thing."

Sarah added: "To be a woman liking the sport should not be a novelty."

There's a long, long way to go, but the shifts within F1's fandom in the past ten years point to an exciting future for the sport. The electric atmospheres of Zandvoort and Monza provide the heart, passion, and history that is impossible to replicate. Yet the sport is also becoming younger, more diverse, and, crucially, more inclusive—something that matters not only to the fans, but to the drivers and teams, too.

8]

"Stick to Sports"

A gloomy, drizzly July day, allegedly in the height of British summer, on an industrial estate in Greenwich, London, a stone's throw from the River Thames, would not strike you as an obvious place to witness the oncoming change within F1.

The location has me questioning it, too. I double-check my Google Map directions to make sure I've definitely got the correct place, only to turn a corner and see a sign for the TeamSport indoor go-karting center entrance. Yes, this is the right spot. Walking up the stairs, I can already hear the squeal of tires and the whirr of engines as the first races of the day are underway.

It's not your typical session at the go-kart track. What makes today different is that, of the thirty children out on the track, there's not a single boy.

It's a far cry from the usual composition of a racing grid, even down in go-kart racing, which is the lowest and most accessible level of motorsport. Anybody can turn up at a go-kart track and take part in an arrive-and-drive session. Still, it is rare for there to be more than a handful of girls among the dozens of boys that might be taking part in a kids' event. The further you go up the racing ladder, those numbers thin out more and more. Racing, for so long, has been a "boy thing."

There's a fresh buzz and energy in the air around the circuit that is different to what I normally feel walking into an F1 track on the morning of a race, where an undercurrent of competitiveness always exists. Because today isn't about trying to beat the track record or even win races. It's about offering these girls a first taste of go-karting and showing that this sport is accessible to all.

Among the onlookers stands Susie Wolff, who was once a racing driver herself. She knows that as a woman in motorsport, an industry dominated by men in almost every single area, whether it's driving, design, or engineering, the odds are stacked against you from the start.

It's something Wolff set about changing. In 2023, F1 launched an all-woman racing series called F1 Academy, cofounded by Wolff, who serves as its managing director. The championship is intended to help give young women an entryway into single-seater racing with the hope of putting them on the path toward F1. The series uses Formula 4 cars and features on the undercard of F1 race weekends alongside other junior categories such as Formula 2 and Formula 3. Today's event in Greenwich is part of F1 Academy's

Discover Your Drive scheme, which wants to get more and more young girls into racing by offering a first taste of go-karting.

As I watch by the side of the circuit, I can see the confidence building with each lap that is completed, the karts getting that little bit closer to the barriers on each side of the circuit as they carry more and more speed. Anytime there's a brush of the wall or a spin, there's no frustration, only calls of encouragement from the side of the track, where dozens of parents and friends are watching excitedly, giving claps, cheers, and raised thumbs to the blurs of white race suits and helmets as they zoom past.

Once the on-track action is complete, the girls reunite with their family and friends, smiles beaming from the thrill of the experience. They're all desperate to speak to Wolff, asking moms and dads to take photos and fish out Sharpies for a signature on their new F1 Academy caps. Wolff is more than happy to oblige.

"You know, I look at all of you, and it literally feels like yesterday I was putting on a racing helmet for the first time," Wolff tells the crowd before her. One girl, no older than seven or eight, asks what her favorite thing about racing is. "It's the speed, it's the adrenaline, it's the competition," Wolff says. "It's pushing yourself out of your comfort zone. Sometimes it is scary. Sometimes doing scary things make you progress, make you develop as a person, as a racing driver. There will be tough days. But I'm so looking forward to seeing you and all the other girls being nurtured, to progress through the sport."

"I know how few women are participating at all the different levels," she said in a later interview. "You need to figure out how we're going to change long-term."

But what is F1 doing to assist the kind of shifts that can make it a more open, accessible, and inclusive sport? And how much is it really changing?

■ ■ ■

Wolff, who was entered to four practice sessions with Williams as part of her development role at the team, was the sixth and most recent woman to partake in an F1 grand prix weekend when she ended a twenty-two-year gap since Giovanna Amati's failed attempt to qualify for the 1992 Brazilian Grand Prix. Just two women have actually taken part in a race, the last being Lella Lombardi in 1976. Lombardi is also the only woman to have recorded an F1 points finish, scoring half a point for finishing sixth in the shortened Spanish Grand Prix of 1975. It's now been over ten years since Wolff's last F1 practice appearance.

In the history of F1, over nine hundred drivers have taken part in a grand prix weekend. Out of those nine hundred drivers, only six have been women, a ratio of 0.67 percent.

It's a staggering statistic, and one that on the face of things does not make sense. Motorsport should be accessible regardless of gender, given so much is usually down to the capabilities and qualities of the car. Yet the physiological differences between men and women mean there will always be an inherent advantage for men when it comes to handling the g-forces and physicality at the highest levels of racing. Many cars in junior categories lack power steering, which also gives an advantage to those better able to deal with the additional physicality while working the steering wheel. Tatiana Calderón, who reached F2 and tested an F1 car for Alfa Romeo in 2018 and 2019, once told me it was easier to drive an F1 car than an F2 car, which lacks power steering, for that reason. As of 2024, even F1's rule book uses only "he," "his," and "him" as the pronouns, not the inclusive "they," although plans are in place for this to change. It is still little wonder to regularly hear from young women in racing who, when they first got interested in motorsport as children, thought F1 was only for men.

When Wolff called time on her racing career in 2015, having spent much of it racing for Mercedes in DTM, a German touring car series, she dedicated the next chapter of her career to taking down many of the barriers she faced. She started by founding Dare to Be Different, a scheme intended to help more young women pursue careers in motorsport that was eventually absorbed by the FIA, before moving into team management by becoming the boss of the Venturi Formula E team—the first and, thus far, only woman to hold that role in the electric championship's short history—in 2018. By the time Wolff left her role and sold her shares in the team in the summer of 2022, she wasn't sure where to go next. "I really felt I had said everything there was to say about women in motorsport," Wolff said. "I felt I had, or tried to at least, give back to the sport with Dare to Be Different. And it was time for me to move on because . . . I was like a broken record. I just couldn't talk about women in motorsport anymore."

Yet the world was changing. Women's sport was having its moment, enjoying surging audiences and buzzing interest across soccer, basketball, and tennis. F1 was also experiencing a rapid rise in its female audience and fanbase. All these factors played a big part in why F1 Academy exists, Wolff said, because it left her compelled to try to aid the push for change within motorsport. A separate all-women's racing championship, called W Series, was launched in 2019 to much fanfare for its mission of helping to level the playing field in motorsport but only lasted three years after hitting financial struggles. With the commercial and operational might of F1 itself backing it, F1 Academy aimed to be something more stable that could help Wolff on the mission she knew she needed to be part of.

"I was initially quite reluctant until I realized: This is actually a once-in-a-lifetime chance from the very top of the sport, with a lot of investment," Wolff recalled. "And if I wasn't going to do it, who was? I didn't want to regret having this opportunity and not at least trying to make impactful change because there hasn't been enough change. The world is a different place now, and those at the top of the sport and the more commercially-minded realized that we have to do something."

Fifteen women were entered to F1 Academy's first season in 2023, all in cars run and supported by established junior teams already racing across F2, F3, and F4. F1 also helped by covering €150,000 ($162,000) of the costs for the race seat, meaning drivers only had to bring the same amount to fund the full season; still a sizable amount, but not nearly as big a hurdle as it would ordinarily be.

Wolff said she's not a believer in segregating men and women on the track, but believes the concept of F1 Academy can "be the rocket fuel to progression for these young drivers. Because trying to raise sponsorship is tough. With the momentum that we're giving them, the exposure that we're giving them, I hope that will make it easier to go out and raise that money to move further up the sport." The series is already succeeding in bringing in new sponsors that previously would not have shown much interest in motorsport. Charlotte Tilbury, the British beauty brand, became a partner of the series in 2024 and even sponsored one of the cars, complete with a paint scheme covered in the company's "hot lips" logo holding lipstick, something that had never been seen before on an international race car.

The added funding has been a game-changer for the young women racing in F1 Academy. "I haven't had this opportunity before, so it's amazing to have it now," said Hamda Al Qubaisi, an Emirati driver who finished third in the first season of F1 Academy. "They're really helping girls progress in the sport. It's something we were always wishing for in my early years in racing. It's good to finally have it."

F1 Academy is already helping women progress up the racing ladder. Spanish driver Marta García won the inaugural F1 Academy season at the age of twenty-two, with her success leading to a fully funded seat in Formula Regional, a category between F4 and F3, for the 2024 season—progression that would have been much harder to make without F1 Academy's support. The 2023 runner-up, Léna Bühler, also made the same step, marking a promising start for the series, which as of 2024 had input from all ten F1 teams, each with a nominated car and driver in F1 Academy. To see these women in the same Ferrari or Red Bull race suits that Lewis Hamilton or Max Verstappen wear is a powerful image; after all, if you can see it, you can be it.

"We can be role models for girls who want to get into the sport," said Al Qubaisi, who signed to Red Bull's young driver program. "The grid is really tough. All the girls are really fast, and they're progressing really well. It shows the girls coming through that we can be in the sport and we can succeed. Being role models for them, it's an amazing feeling." García agreed, pointing to the shift she's already seeing. "We're seeing more women racing," she said. "Everything is going in the right direction for women in motorsport."

The numbers support this perception of an uptick in the levels of female participation. According to Wolff, in the initial rollout of the partnership between F1 Academy, Motorsport UK (the national governing body), and TeamSport karting, the number of young women trying to qualify for the British championships almost quadrupled from eighteen to sixty-five. "We're trying to create an environment which is welcoming for an eight-year-old to come to a go-kart track for the very first time," Wolff said. "We need to create the pipeline because otherwise in three years, you're just going to see the same drivers racing year after year because there won't be the next generation."

It will take time for the growth in female participation at lower levels to translate to the higher professional ranks of racing, but Wolff felt by the end of 2025, it will be possible to see if F1 Academy is helping women advance up the ladder should more follow the path set by García and Bühler in the first season. In 2024, there was only one woman, Sophia Flörsch, racing in F3, and none racing in F2. The goal is to sow the seeds that will increase those numbers in the future and break through the glass ceiling to have a woman race in F1 again.

One of the most prolific female drivers in recent years has been

Jamie Chadwick. She was the champion in all three seasons of W Series before moving across to the American racing ladder, taking part in the Indy NXT championship in 2023 and 2024, becoming the series' first female race winner in fourteen years, as well as being part of the Williams young driver program. Back when Chadwick started out karting as a hobby with her older brother, she said she was "blissfully unaware" of the challenges that women faced to make it in racing. Looking back, she realized that's because there wasn't a clear direction. "I never really thought there was an opportunity to be a driver," Chadwick said. "I never believed that was going to be my career path. I didn't know the next steps or anything like that."

Chadwick made the move into more serious levels of racing around the time that Wolff was testing for Williams, making her an important role model and source of advice. Chadwick found her email address and sent her some questions—Chadwick told me she recently found that email and was "a bit cringed out" by her message—while she was racing in Ginetta Juniors, a first step in car racing. To Chadwick's delight, Wolff emailed her straight back. "I was very fortunate to have role models like that," Chadwick said. "Of course we want to create even more role models for the next generation."

Being to other young women what Wolff was to her is something Chadwick is embracing. She launched her own go-kart racing initiative to help young girls take up arrive-and-drive sessions at tracks in the same way she did at the age of twelve. Chadwick established her own karting championship and offered mentorship through the year to the girls racing, as well as some financial support for the winner. Similar to Wolff's efforts with F1 Academy, Chadwick wants to open up opportunities to those who may not previously have considered a career in motorsport or known it was even possible.

Chadwick agreed the grassroots focus is what will grow participation for women in motorsport, believing it will eventually create a larger pool at the F2 and F3 levels—something that, allied with the surge in support and interest from F1 teams in women on the junior ladder, could open the door to the highest level. "I would like to think, potentially, we could be within ten years of seeing a woman drive in Formula 1," Chadwick said. "I wouldn't bet on it, but I'd like to think we're in a position where there's so much desire, so much support now, even from the F1 teams, that we're in a different place to what I've experienced in previous years."

Wolff was adamant F1 Academy is about far more than fulfilling quotas or ticking boxes, or even ending the long wait for a woman to race once again in F1. "It's changing perceptions," she said. "The fastest-growing fan demographic for F1 is young women. So what we stand for is much more than being a race series, we're a movement. We're out here to show this huge global fanbase of Formula 1 that this sport actually wants to become more diverse and give opportunities to women. The data will be hard to quantify because it will look like a lot of effort for small wins. But it can be something much wider."

That wider shift applies both on and off the race track. At one media session in early 2024, Lewis Hamilton beamed when he saw the entire front row was made up of female journalists, happily saying he thought it to be the most diverse press call he'd seen through his F1 career. More women are also appearing on the pit wall, where each team places its senior engineers and strategists, who make the decisions that can win or lose races. Figures such as Bernie Collins, Ruth Buscombe, and Hannah Schmitz have broken up the male-dominated pit walls in recent years, all working in senior strategic positions. Collins and Buscombe both have race victories to their name, while Schmitz played a role in Red Bull's domination of the early 2020s as a principal strategy engineer, making calls to help Max Verstappen and Sergio Pérez win races that led to championship success.

Yet there is still a long, long way for F1 to go when it comes to gender equality. Walking up and down the paddock, you can tell it's still a male-dominated world (something felt far more acutely, of course, by my female counterparts). The number of women in senior engineering or technical roles, while growing, remains a handful per team at best. There hasn't been a woman at the helm of the day-to-day running of an F1 team since Claire Williams stepped down as the deputy team principal of Williams when the family sold the team in 2020. On average, less than 10 percent of a team's staff are female. The same is true in the media; the majority of my colleagues I spend weekends working alongside are men, with usually only one or two women standing in the group of fifteen to twenty in the written-media bullpen after a race waiting to speak to the drivers.

The topic was put into the spotlight in early 2024 by a couple of events. In February, a female complainant brought allegations of inappropriate behavior against Red Bull's team principal, Christian Horner. Horner strenuously denied the allegations, and the grievance was dismissed following an investigation overseen by a King's Counsel barrister. An appeal of the ruling was dismissed five months later. Yet it only served to reignite the debate surrounding the standing of women within F1, particularly when messages purported to be sent by Horner to the complainant were leaked to the media, and after the complainant was suspended with pay due to the findings of the investigation. Horner refused to comment on the messages, while F1's regulator, the FIA, showed zero sign of getting involved, claiming it was an internal company matter.

The FIA's own president, Mohammed Ben Sulayem, faced criticism around the same time after his organization briefly launched an investigation into a claim there could be a conflict of interest between Susie Wolff, who works for F1 itself as the managing director of F1 Academy, and her husband, Mercedes team boss Toto Wolff. The move sparked an angry backlash from the other nine F1 teams, who all denied raising any concerns with the governing body, making it unclear from where the suggestion emerged. The FIA closed the investigation just two days later without giving further information beyond saying it was satisfied by F1's processes, and offered no comment or apology to Wolff. She responded by saying it was "disheartening that my integrity is being called into question in such a manner" due to her relationship with her husband, and said the move "seems to be rooted in intimidatory and misogynistic behavior," prompting her to pursue a criminal case in the French courts, given the FIA is based in Paris. In the previous year, comments that Ben Sulayem wrote in the early 2000s emerged where he stated that he did not like "women who are smarter than men, for they are not in truth." These were found on an archived version of his blog, but the FIA responded by saying it did not reflect Ben Sulayem's views and claimed he had a strong record promoting women within motorsport. Ben Sulayem did appoint the first female CEO of the FIA, Natalie Robyn, in 2022, only for her to leave by mutual consent eighteen months later.

The events of early 2024 left many women in the paddock feeling an unease and frustration about the commitment of the community to promote and support gender equality. For many, it summed up why there had been so many barriers and hurdles for them to overcome in their bid to make careers in F1. Experiences vary from person to person, but there's no denying that although F1 is changing and we are seeing a gradual shift, there is still a necessity for the continued effort to remove outdated attitudes and mentalities from the sport.

It is why figures like Wolff and Chadwick remain so important to the future of F1. The sport needs to be welcoming to all; it needs to prove that if you are a woman, you're entitled to a place at the table just as much as any man. As we see increasing numbers of women come into F1 roles, be it on or off the track, that is something that must be ingrained in the thinking of every single member of the paddock. The "boys' club" mentality of the past cannot be allowed to survive.

Watching on at the go-kart track in Greenwich, it is clear how the tide is starting to turn. The girls speeding past me will go home riding the adrenaline high of their first karting experiences, surely begging their parents to go again. It could be what spurs them on to a career in racing, be it as drivers, engineers, or the myriad of other roles in this sport. Simply encouraging those dreams or proving they are possible only furthers the efforts to assist the change our sport so sorely needs—something that goes for all areas of inclusion.

■ ■ ■

At the end of the 2019 season in Abu Dhabi, as is tradition, Mercedes brought every member of its on-site F1 team together for a team photo. The two silver cars were placed in front of the hundred-strong team that formed three long rows for the wide-angle shot. Everyone was wearing their team uniform of crisp, white shirts and black trousers. Think of your classic school class photo, just with F1 cars. Team principal Toto Wolff sat in the middle, while the team's drivers, Lewis Hamilton and Valtteri Bottas, each perched on a tire of their cars in their race suits. The team had won fifteen races en route to both championships, making this a photo many would remember to mark the success of that year.

But when Hamilton was scrolling through Instagram a few days later and saw the picture had been posted, he started to zoom in on the faces of his teammates.

Almost every face in the photo was white.

The lack of diversity was nothing new for Hamilton. From the moment he'd first stepped into a go-kart as a child, he was often the only Black driver out on the track. The trend continued as he made his way up the professional ranks, eventually reaching F1 in 2007 and making history: There hadn't been a Black F1 driver before Hamilton. An American, Willy T. Ribbs, became the first Black driver to test an F1 car when he drove a Brabham car in

1986, and the first Black driver to qualify for the Indianapolis 500 in 1991, but he never raced in F1. Hamilton was a history-maker, yet it was not the spark that brought about wider change, clearly illustrated when looking at the photo twelve years later. What he spotted in that photo was how the underrepresentation stretched off-track as well as on-track, making it an issue the industry as a whole had to tackle.

The photo led to conversations between Hamilton and his Mercedes team about what they could do to become more diverse and inclusive. The chats only accelerated in 2020 when, in the wake of the killing of George Floyd in Minneapolis, protests around the world and the growth of the Black Lives Matter movement put racial equality increasingly in the spotlight. Paul Mills, Mercedes's chief people officer at the time, recalled the "genius" way in which Hamilton addressed the issues. "He came at it from a learning perspective," Mills said. "It wasn't a judgment thing of, 'You're not good enough and you're not trying hard enough.' It was about learning, that we've got to learn about this topic and learn about inclusion and learn about unconscious bias and all the barriers in society."

The conversations prompted Mercedes to take a visible stand by changing its car color from its traditional silver, first used back in 1934, to an all-black design ahead of the delayed start to the F1 season in July of 2020, as well as carrying slogans reading END RACISM on the car. Hamilton also raced with a revised helmet design for the season including the message BLACK LIVES MATTER on the top around the raised-fist "black power" symbol.

They were big steps, but Mills knew the commitment to change had to run far deeper than a new paint scheme on the car. *What was going to be the action that sat behind the symbol?* Mills recalled thinking. "Otherwise you're in danger of putting a token gesture into the world and not really following it up with any actions. It was really exciting, but also quite scary at the time, because you know with teams, companies, organizations being accused of being too woke, you're entering a lot of judgment and politics and opinions. We had to be authentic about it."

At the time, just 3 percent of the Mercedes F1 workforce came from ethnic minorities and only 12 percent were women. Discussions with Hamilton helped the team better understand the challenges facing those from underrepresented backgrounds within F1 and the motorsport industry as a whole. Mercedes reached out to organizations such as the Association for Black and Minority Ethnic Engineers and the Sutton Trust, a charity focusing on social mobility, to establish relationships and learn best practices. To Mills, it became a "genuine, authentic challenge for us to try and make some changes to the diversity of our team."

Underpinning all of Mercedes's efforts was a desire to find the best talent that would make it stronger. Think about it: If you are widening the talent pool by appealing to whole groups of young people that typically would not have considered a career in engineering or STEM subjects, then you are automatically going to have a broader realm from which to find the most talented students and allow more stars to come through. During his research and work on leadership and culture within a team, Mills found that the "diversity topic was actually a performance topic" for that reason. Beyond the morals involved, it could actually make Mercedes a better team.

"By accessing talent pools that previously had never considered working in F1, never mind Mercedes, that was performance," Mills said. "But also inside the organization, there was a deeper understanding of these issues and these topics. They develop conclusions, help psychological safety, create more innovation, and encourage creativity in your organization. There was a strong performance rationale for the program." The results from Mercedes have been positive. From 2020 to 2025, it surpassed its yearly target of 25 percent of new hires coming from underrepresented backgrounds. The workforce is now 12 percent ethnic minorities, and the proportion of women has increased to 17 percent.

That uptick goes beyond the raw statistics; it can be felt within the team as well. Anca Raines, who took over from Mills as Mercedes's chief people officer in 2024, told me about arranging a photo of all the women in the team for International Women's Day in the race bays, where the cars are built and serviced in the factory. Shortly before the photo call, every woman in the office got up from their desks and descended on the race bays en masse. "It was hilarious!" Raines said with a laugh. "All these women got up and were walking through the office, and you can see all the male engineers thinking, *What on earth is happening!?*" She said that some staff members at Mercedes told her there was a time when the female workforce simply stood around a single car in the main reception area. "Now, it was a sea of women walking through the office and taking over one of the race bays," Raines said. "It's a very visible change in that sense."

Raines thought her own move into F1 with Mercedes also spoke to the increasing levels of accessibility, never previously believing it was an "obvious path" to take. "Speaking frankly from afar, it feels quite male," she said of F1. "You have to come from a certain background, and the only way in is through engineering, and I would have never thought about it." She highlighted the openness and generosity shown by Mercedes in support of creating an inclusive, welcoming, and, ultimately, high-performance environment. "You feel like you could belong, and you do feel like you are being invited in," she said. "I think that's quite special."

It left Raines feeling "hugely encouraged" by the direction Mercedes is going with its diversity campaigns as she prepared to take over from Mills. "I genuinely believe diversity and inclusion are not just topics that the 'woke' group can just poke at," she said. "They're genuine drivers for performance and for innovation because different mindsets, different backgrounds will add something different to the conversation, and it's worth continuing to invest."

To Hamilton, the work is not yet done. He thought the Mercedes team photo at the end of the 2023 season, four years on from the one that brought home the issue to him, showed it had "not moved anywhere near as much as it should have." But he also felt that Mercedes was "ahead of every other team in that respect," and he was "immensely proud" of the work he'd done in his time there. Upon agreeing to his blockbuster move to Ferrari for the 2025 season, Hamilton made discussions with the manufacturer's president, John Elkann, about its own diversity initiatives a priority, saying the team had "a lot of work to do." He's remained vocal on the matter with high-ranking figures throughout F1. "There still is a huge amount of work to do within the whole sport."

Hamilton supports this with his own real, meaningful action, investing not only his time but also his money to help the cause. In 2020, he helped found the Hamilton Commission with the Royal Academy of Engineering to complete a thorough investigation and study into the lack of representation for Black people within motorsport. Its findings were published in July 2021 and estimated that less than 1 percent of those working in F1 were from Black backgrounds. Interviews conducted across the industry tackled the core issues contributing to the lack of representation in the sport, as well as the lack of monitoring and underlying attitudes—such as a belief in "color and gender blindness" and claims of meritocracy that externalized the issue, per the report—and also addressed the racism that many had faced. Hamilton has been open about racist abuse he has experienced through his career. In only his second season, at the Spanish Grand Prix in 2008, Hamilton and his family were targets of racist abuse from fans. As recently as 2021, Nelson Piquet Sr., the three-time world champion, used a racial slur in reference to Hamilton in a Brazilian TV interview. Hamilton responded publicly by saying it was "more than language. These archaic mindsets need to change and have no place in our sport. I've been surrounded by these attitudes and targeted my whole life. There has been plenty of time to learn. Time has come for action."

Off the back of the Hamilton Commission's report, Hamilton founded his own charity, Mission 44 (in a nod to his race number), to help improve representation within motorsport, pledging £20 million of his personal wealth to get it up and running. Mission 44 works with organizations to provide grants that can assist these efforts within STEM subjects and through the motorsport industry. Hamilton is directly engaged in Mission 44's projects, including bringing kids from underrepresented backgrounds at local schools into the F1 paddock, such as in Austin, where Hamilton was part of an event that saw fifty young women and nonbinary people get a chance to talk to him about F1 and STEM careers before experiencing some F1 at the track. It was a rare chance to get up close to the cars and see what a garage looks like, and hopefully inspired them to pursue a career that could lead them to F1. "It makes me really proud," Hamilton said. "It's really cool to be in a position to open up the door for these kids, to see what is possible, and spark interest and create dreams that they perhaps never thought was possible. I'm excited for the future."

Just as with the initiatives to get more young women into racing, for Hamilton, improving diversity and representation all starts at the grassroots. He has real excitement about the work being done at the lowest levels. And when it comes to defining what his F1 legacy will be when he eventually hangs up his helmet, this is what he wants to be remembered for, not all the trophies, records, and wins.

"It's more important for me."

■ ■ ■

F1's push for inclusion is something that could appear to sit at odds with some of the countries in which it races, where there is a lack of equal social rights for certain communities.

While putting on his race helmet and climbing into his car before the start of practice for the Qatar Grand Prix in 2021, Hamilton noticed he felt more nervous than usual. This was a process he'd been through thousands of times in his racing career, one he could probably do with his eyes shut, yet this felt different. Yes, the stakes were higher in Qatar from a competitive standpoint, given it was the third-to-last race of the season and his fierce fight against Max Verstappen for the world championship was raging on. That wasn't why he felt nervous.

As he peeled out of the garage when the session started, the TV cameras picked up that his purple helmet design, one he'd been using since the start of the 2020 season, had changed slightly. On the top and sides of the helmet was a rainbow pride flag in support of the LGBTQ+ community. The messages WE STAND TOGETHER and LOVE IS LOVE were also written on the back of the helmet as part of the design.

"I was very proud to do it," Hamilton reflected two years later, when F1 returned to Qatar. "It was also nerve-racking, because I didn't know how the country would react."

Qatar is one of three countries on the F1 calendar where homosexuality is criminalized and punishable with the death penalty, the other two being Saudi Arabia and the United Arab Emirates, of which Abu Dhabi is part. In 2021, these three countries hosted the final three rounds of the season. Hamilton carried the rainbow flag on his helmet for all three races and has continued to use it at certain races since then.

When Hamilton first raced with the pride flag on his helmet in Qatar, he said it was important for him to support the community on a global scale to highlight the need for change, saying sports are "duty bound to raise awareness" for the issues in the countries in which they race. "These places need scrutiny," Hamilton said. "It needs the media to speak about these things. Equal rights is a serious issue."

The rate of F1's expansion through its history, but particularly in the past twenty-five years, has led it to race in countries with big question marks hanging over their human rights records. We live in an era when "sports washing," a term used to criticize countries that bring in major international sporting events as a way to distract or divert attention away from poor human and social rights records, is discussed with increasing levels of frequency. The counterpoint is that by racing in these countries, greater scrutiny of such issues follows, sparking important discussion and assisting change. It's a similar line that a lot of international sports facing the same questions and criticism throw out. So how real is that change?

F1 has long served as a way for countries to boost their prestige on an international level by attracting the eyes of the sporting world for a week. Bahrain was the first country in the Middle East to host F1 from 2004, followed by Abu Dhabi in 2009. More new projects emerged across Asia in Singapore (2008–present), South Korea (2010–2013), and India (2011–2013), before Russia (2014–2021) and Azerbaijan (2016–present) also hosted F1 events for the first time. The Russian Grand Prix was held in Sochi, which staged the Winter Olympics in 2014, and was the main legacy project of the city. As a result, it had significant interest from Russia's president, Vladimir Putin, who even presented the winner's trophy on the podium in the first couple of races before its contract was terminated in 2022 following the invasion of Ukraine.

The sports washing debate was thrust into the spotlight for F1 toward the end of 2021, when the sport expanded from two to four races in the Middle East by adding Qatar and Saudi Arabia to the calendar. Qatar secured the hosting rights for the 2022 FIFA World Cup back in 2010, the biggest sporting event for the region at the time. It set the tone for the mass growth of major sporting events in the area, particularly in nearby Saudi Arabia, which has leaned heavily on sport as part of its Vision 2030, overseen by the Crown Prince, Mohammed bin Salman, known as MBS. The Saudi government has paid for soccer, tennis, and boxing events, claiming it is all part of its efforts to diversify the nation's economy and reduce its dependency on oil and gas. Saudi Arabia will get its turn at hosting the World Cup in 2034. For both countries, F1 plays a part in their long-term sporting vision. Saudi Arabia's F1 contract runs through to 2030, and it plans to move the race from the existing track in Jeddah and design a new, state-of-the-art track and facility in Qiddiya. The proposed track includes a twenty-story-high incline to the first corner that looks like something out of Rainbow Road in Mario Kart. Qatar's contract runs through to 2032, but again, there's little doubt F1 will be there beyond that point. Both are among the highest fee-payers to stage F1 events, with sums in the region of $50 million a year.

F1 quickly faced criticism when it became the latest sport to expand into Saudi Arabia. Ahead of Saudi Arabia's first race in December 2021, Amnesty International issued a statement warning that the F1 race could not "deflect attention" from Saudi Arabia's "dismal" human rights record, including the increase in executions of those on death row and the repression faced by activists who were critical of the authorities and the government, as well as the murder of the *Washington Post* journalist Jamal Khashoggi in 2018.

Felix Jakens, Amnesty International UK's head of campaigns, said in 2022 that the Saudi Arabia F1 race was "sports washing, plain and simple," and called on figures involved in the race to speak up about human rights concerns.

Figures such as Hamilton did exactly that. He admitted at the first race in 2021 he was not entirely comfortable racing in Saudi Arabia and has regularly spoken of the need for those in power to show they are making positive changes. Wearing the helmet with the pride flag on the top was a big step to show his support for the LGBTQ+ community, a show of solidarity that others made with their own gestures. Walking on the starting grid for that first race in 2021, I remember seeing a female mechanic wearing a rainbow bandana to keep her hair out of her eyes while servicing the car, as well as a number of TV presenters who wore rainbow shoelaces. Tiny gestures, but important stands.

Martin Whitaker, the CEO of the Saudi Motorsport Company, which oversees the running of the grand prix in Jeddah, felt F1 has "done a lot to change perceptions" of Saudi Arabia. "I think people came here wondering what to expect because they'd probably heard stories, and, once they actually got here, they realized they'd perhaps got the wrong angle on the story," said Whitaker. "I think they realized that Saudi is a place which is rich in culture, the hospitality here is quite extraordinary." He noted the difference in culture between the Middle East and the Western world. "People have to understand that it's a different culture in this part of the world," said Whitaker. "We're not going to push the culture of the Middle East down the throats of the drivers. But at the same time, they're not going to push their culture down the throats of the Saudis."

Whitaker also felt F1 was already leaving a positive impact in Saudi Arabia, particularly through the opportunities it was creating in the region. Over 40 percent of the staff at the Saudi Motorsport Company are women, while a number of go-kart tracks are also being opened across the country in a bid to get more children into motorsport. "We're creating jobs for young people here," said Whitaker. "And frankly speaking, no matter where you come from around the world, nobody is going to criticize somebody for trying to improve the lives of young people and to give them job prospects and opportunities. I think motorsport has done that pretty well."

In 2024, F1 Academy hosted the opening race of its second season in Jeddah, supporting the F1 race. Six years earlier, women had only just received the right to obtain a driver's license in Saudi Arabia. Now, there was an all-women's championship on the race track, including one Saudi driver, Reema Juffali. A number of the women racing also took part in a local school event ahead of the race, meeting local children in the hope of inspiring them to pursue future careers in motorsport. "The awareness, interest, and knowledge that they now have of Formula 1 is quite extraordinary compared to where it was in 2021, when it was completely new then," said Whitaker. "We've moved on an awful lot. Our community activities are strong here. I think the sport has done a lot to change those perceptions."

Talking to people on the ground in Saudi Arabia, there is definitely a feeling their prospects have brightened and there is an excitement for the future. Upon landing in Jeddah for the F1 race last year, I was met off the plane by a young woman called Tala and her male colleague Younis, who assisted me at immigration and in finding a taxi to my hotel, both showing a warmness and kindness in welcoming me to their country. They felt enormous excitement about F1 coming to Jeddah, seeing it as another step in the ongoing evolution within their country. "It's been a huge change," said Younis, "even just having you guys coming here for F1." He put a lot of that down to MBS and his "vision" for the future of the country.

But the sports washing debate is up for discussion whenever F1 returns to the kingdom, with Hamilton regularly talking about social issues. Ahead of the 2023 race, a few of us were able to discuss the subject during a small media session with Saudi Arabia's minister for sport, Prince Abdulaziz bin Turki Al Faisal. Al Faisal said the drivers could "speak freely" and share their opinions, but he wanted judgments to be made on the action the country is taking. "We know that we have a lot of work to do, not just as a sporting point, but as a country, and we are doing that," he said. "Hopefully we'll prove to [Hamilton] that we are developing in that area . . . and see how we can develop together and towards the future." When the sports washing criticism laid against the F1 race was put to Al Faisal, he responded by pointing to the increased levels of interest in motorsport. "Most of the families, their kids are here watching, and they want to leave here, get in a car, and start to race," Al Faisal said. He claimed a similar thing happened when boxing prize fights came to Saudi Arabia, sparking a large rise in the number of boxing gyms that opened, while there was also a surge in interest around soccer when stars such as Cristiano Ronaldo and Neymar joined the national league, earning unimaginable salaries. "That's why we host these events, because it helps us develop our youth and our programs and deliver on what they want.

They have seen it all over the world, and they ask why can't we have it in our cities and so on.

"These are the benefits that we really see on the ground, that when maybe a lot of people that speculate about it, they don't talk about these things. This for us is the benefit for the people."

What is critical for F1 is that it does not shy away from tackling these big issues, for they are so much greater than racing, greater than our own little "world." As a paddock and a community, we need to continue to talk about it every time we go to countries where equal rights are such a pressing issue. Yes, it may become a broken record, discussing the same issues and topics over and over. I can see that some of the drivers are uneasy facing such questions, simply noting they are "here to race" and that it's not their choice where F1 holds its races. Asked about the topic following the 2024 race in Saudi Arabia, Max Verstappen said he felt it was "important that sport is sport, [and] politics are politics," and that "we are not going to change the world at the end of the day as a sport, but we try to share positive values." He added that he thought there had been some "really nice positive changes" in Saudi Arabia since F1's first visit. Ferrari's Charles Leclerc thought the entire grid could act as a source of inspiration to younger generations. "We need to keep going to those countries in order to hopefully open minds, and for them to have a better future and also to inspire young people in order to follow their dream," he said.

Others put faith in the sport's leadership to ensure a positive legacy is left where it goes racing. "We put our trust in Formula 1 to help with these decisions," said George Russell, who serves as a director for the Grand Prix Drivers' Association, essentially the union for the grid. "It's important that we do see change, and I think change is happening. It obviously doesn't happen overnight. It's a very important topic with many places we go to, but I think Formula 1 and sport generally can have a really positive impact for the local culture and issues that that they're facing. I hope we're here for the right reasons."

But so long as there remains a need for change, and so long as social rights are lacking where F1 goes racing, it remains an important conversation to have to maintain the commitment to improve inclusion. Otherwise, sports washing is doing its job entirely. This is why the likes of Hamilton are so important for F1. The platform that comes with the sport means it can be used for good.

When we returned to Qatar in 2023, two years after he first raced with that rainbow helmet, I asked Hamilton about what more F1 can do as a sport to raise awareness of the issues in the countries where we race. He paused and rubbed his forehead, searching for the right words. "It's a really difficult question, with so many facets," he said. What followed was a typically thoughtful, well-reasoned answer.

"One thousand percent, every single person could be doing more," he said. "I think it's always well and good raising awareness for things, but it's more about the work that's done in the background, the conversations that you continue to have. It's just such a big machine to shift as well. It's not only people here, it's a whole country that's very young—particularly in this part of the world. It's taken the West a long, long time to get to where they are. All we can do is be positive when we come to these places and do take the opportunity, so that's why I continue to wear the flag here.

"It's amazing when I do meet people who are incredibly grateful for utilizing a platform for something like that, where they perhaps didn't feel included."

As we work to make the sport more diverse and inclusive for all, Hamilton's voice and presence remain vital to encouraging that and keeping it at the forefront of our minds. Whenever he does opt to retire, F1 will be a far poorer place for his absence.

By that point, the growing momentum within our sport will hopefully have led to an even more visible shift within the paddock. Pit walls, garages, and media pens should reflect the newly diverse fanbase and be more representative of society as a whole. And, more importantly, so should the drivers in the cars. Until such a point, we cannot "stick to sports" and simply accept things are the way they are, as much as that may be scoffed at, labeled woke or politically correct.

We'll always love F1 for its spectacular on-track action, the thrill and the buzz of the drivers battling at high speeds. It is what compelled us at the very start and is what thousands of people each year spend their lives traveling around the world in support of making happen. But now is a time when the F1 community as a whole needs to unite and work together to make good on the ambition of being a force for good in a rapidly changing world.

9

The Race for Change

Perhaps the most unique aspect of Formula 1 is how global it is.

No other sporting series can claim to be as international as F1, racing in twenty-one different countries across five continents each year. No other sporting series has such a massive amount of freight that has to travel, either. For a football or soccer game, the stadiums are all roughly the same, meaning so long as the players and their necessities are in the right place, the game can go ahead. F1 relies on much more and has a far bigger group following its schedule that ranges from the drivers and engineers to those working in hospitality and the media. With thousands of people venturing from race to race, it's no wonder F1 has a reputation for being a "traveling circus." (I do often wonder if that makes us the clowns. . . .)

The opportunity to travel the world and be part of that circus was always an element of F1's appeal to me. From seeing the sunshine in Australia or the scenery in Japan from my living room, to the glitz of Monaco or the lights of Singapore, they all seemed like exotic places one could only dream of going to someday. Nothing else got close. It wasn't like watching other sports, where stadiums all largely look the same. The world tour that was ingrained in F1's identity was also what made it so magical. The chance to go to all these races and incredible cities is not something I ever take for granted. I didn't travel much as a kid—the third flight I ever took was to Singapore in my first year on the F1 beat—so to have now been to so many stops on the F1 calendar, and even farther afield, is a true privilege.

To make F1's traveling circus function requires significant levels of planning to a meticulous degree to ensure that everyone and, just as important, everything is in the right place at the right time. Be it navigating back-to-back races that are continents away, or getting all the freight through the tricky customs requirements in some of the countries where F1 goes racing, it's a monumental effort just to get the paddock in and out of town to make a grand prix happen.

Nowhere is the sheer amount of people and freight that need to travel between races more apparent than during "packdown," which takes place in the hours after the race. It's not dissimilar to having to dodge the cars, mechanics, and VIPs on the Formula 1 starting grid, only this time, there are giant freight boxes and forklift trucks to avoid as I weave through the paddock to head to my postrace interviews with the drivers and team principals. It's organized chaos to a T.

Before the race even finishes and the drivers hop out of their cars, the race to the next grand prix begins. Teams will quickly set about packing up all their equipment into the freight boxes that are then sent via air, road, or sea to another race, often taking place just one week later. Some of the freight stays regionalized—one "set" of gear may be used for China, then kept on a freight ship until Singapore, reducing the need for added travel back and forth. Packdown turns the area between the garages and the team hospitality buildings into a maze of vehicles, equipment, and parts. All of the garage gear and the tools used to put the cars together must be carefully packed away, along with the cars themselves. The tires are taken down to Pirelli, which supplies the entire grid, to inspect, wash down, and then recycle before bringing a fresh batch to the next race. Then there's the hospitality units. In some cases these are enormous glass structures used to host guests and be a home away from home for the drivers and the team members over the weekend, which then have to be rapidly deconstructed after the race before being loaded into trucks and going to another track. Everything inside, including basics such as chairs and tables, needs to be packed up and sent on its way.

As I go about my postrace duties at the track, talking to the drivers and seeking out team bosses to chat with, I'll watch as team members don fluorescent T-shirts intended to make them easier to spot, particularly as night falls after a race, and pitch in at the end of a long race weekend. Drivers, now showered after a grueling race, do the rounds to thank their crews before heading off to the airport or into the night to celebrate. Team principals wheel through with their suitcases, fearing they may have cut it too fine with their flight bookings to get back to the office. To work in F1 is to become fluent in airport codes, mileage programs, and airline lounges.

At the end of each year, I use a flight tracking app to tally how much I've traveled. Take a rough guess now: twenty-four races per season, how much flying does that add up to?

It's something I'm not even precisely sure of myself as I put in the information. The app pauses for a few seconds to crunch all the numbers and routes, then draws a map with all the flight paths from the season just gone. It looks like a spider with dozens of legs, all originating from London and stretching right across the globe, from Las Vegas on the far left of the map right across to Tokyo on the right, diving as far south as Melbourne.

Then comes the data, which makes for less pretty reading. Over the year, I've spent 263 hours—or 11 days—in the air across 46 flights. I wince at the thought of adding on time at airports and other transit. It's just over 118,000 miles, which is nearly 5 times around the Earth. It's halfway to the moon.

And still not a single upgrade. Thanks, British Airways.

All that travel has an inevitable impact on the environment, something made all too clear by the numbers detailing my carbon footprint. The emissions from all my flights come to a total of 23.3 tons of CO_2, which is about the weight of sixteen medium-sized road cars. On average, each person emits around 4.5 tons of CO_2 per year. A search through an online converter tells me that my flying footprint is equivalent to making 202,000 cups of coffee—I don't drink quite that much—or over 3,000 meat-based meals.

It's a staggering amount, and that's just me, let alone those who top my numbers. You need to multiply it by the thousands of people who crisscross the globe to make each F1 event happen. Then factor in all the freight that has been packed down so carefully after each race. Then add on the emissions from the factories running back at base. And, of course, the actual cars themselves on the race track will push that number up a little more.

It is why as the world grapples with the ongoing climate crisis, F1, like all sports, must adapt, particularly as the severity of the changes to the environment start to have a material effect on where and how we go racing. For F1, which has high-octane cars and extensive international travel as a central part of its image, that's a challenge that is much sharper and harder to tackle than in other sports.

■ ■ ■

It was while taking one of those forty-six flights that the brunt of the climate crisis's impact on F1 hit home for me.

Emilia-Romagna is one of the most picturesque and culturally rich regions of Italy. Its capital, Bologna, is known as the "fat" for its remarkable food culture; the "red" for the colors of the roofs in the center of the city and, in the past century, its left-leaning politics; and the "learned" for its educational prowess as home to the oldest university in the world, dating back to 1088. Dotted throughout the region are smaller cities and towns, many of which have rich cultural roots from the Italian Renaissance, such Parma or Modena. Others are known for their industry, particularly when it comes to cars and motorsport. Ferrari's home, Maranello, is about forty-five minutes outside of Bologna, while the RB F1 team is also based out of the smaller town of Faenza. Between the two, you will find the town of Imola, which also lends its name to the race track next to the Santerno river, which hosts the Emilia-Romagna Grand Prix.

Traveling to Italy in late spring sounds idyllic. A few years ago, I made the most of an extra day in Bologna before heading to Imola for the grand prix weekend, spending a morning sipping espressos on the Piazza Maggiore in the center of the city, watching the world go by before roaming around the beautiful Catholic churches, seeing the medieval towers, Garisenda and Asinelli—the former of which, like its Pisa counterpart, has started to lean—and sampling the finest pasta, burrata, and parmigiano I could get my hands on. Booking an early-morning flight from Gatwick for the race in May 2023, I'd planned again to make the most of my one day off before going to the track.

Boarding the flight, I knew it was going to be the last time I'd see the sun for a few days. In the lead-up to the race weekend, heavy rain had been falling in the region. A hot summer had caused the ground to harden, meaning when six months of rain fell in the space of just thirty-six hours in the days leading up to our arrival in Italy, localized flooding had started to cause serious problems for the people living and working in the area.

It was only when we broke through the clouds on our descent into Bologna that the extent of the flooding and the damage it was causing became starkly apparent. Not a single town we passed over was unaffected. Major roadways were no longer identifiable, taken over by brown rivers that had long burst their banks and now ran eight feet deep in the middle of towns, submerging the bottom levels of the buildings.

Around me on the plane, people wearing F1 merchandise started to worry: What if the grand prix didn't happen? The money they'd saved up to make it to Imola, was it about to go to waste? Would it be possible for them to make it to their hotels? Would the hotels even still be there?

Upon landing, I made it to the lobby of my nearby hotel, where a message soon arrived confirming the Emilia-Romagna Grand Prix would be canceled. The river next to the track had burst its banks and flooded the lower part of the F1 paddock, forcing the team members who had gotten to the circuit early to set up all the equipment they'd packed down just eight days earlier in Miami to evacuate. For the safety of everyone involved, it simply wasn't possible to even contemplate going motor racing. This was, in many cases, literally a matter of life or death. The focus for the people in the surrounding areas had to be on the recovery effort once the worst of the rain and flooding stopped, not hosting a major international sporting event. The flooding resulted in seventeen deaths, and over fifty thousand people were displaced as it ruined businesses, homes, and lives.

One F1 driver who was directly affected by the flooding was Yuki Tsunoda. Hailing from Japan, Tsunoda had made the small town of Faenza his home to be close to his team, AlphaTauri, now known as RB. On a weekend when he was expecting to race at Imola and be fighting for points against the other drivers, Tsunoda was instead in the streets of Faenza helping with the cleanup effort, shoveling mud and debris out of ground floor homes and shops after the water levels subsided and the extent of the destruction became clear. A far cry from typical F1 life, and unlike anything that Tsunoda had ever seen before.

"I saw it maybe on TV, and I never expected horrible things could actually happen in front of me," Tsunoda said a week later, when F1 returned to action in Monaco. "But suddenly it happened, I was just so scared."

It was the first time an F1 race had been canceled due to a natural phenomenon such as a flood. In previous years, some races had been cut short due to heavy rain. The Belgian Grand Prix in 2021 lasted just two laps behind the safety car before being called off. The Japanese Grand Prix used to take place around typhoon season, causing qualifying to be postponed until the Sunday morning on three occasions, most recently in 2019, due to the risk in the region. Never had a grand prix been called off altogether before a driver or car had made it onto the circuit due to a climatic occurrence. As much as it may have been outside of the sport's control, it was a stark display of just how the environmental issues facing the world are increasingly relevant to F1's calendar.

Another wake-up call arrived less than six months later, this time affecting every single driver on the grid as they struggled with extreme heat during the Qatar Grand Prix. Drivers are used to getting hot while racing, given the extreme physical exertion while wearing fireproof overalls and a carbon fiber race helmet, all while sitting directly in front of an engine revving at 15,000 rpm. Doing so in countries with high ambient temperatures and energy-sapping levels of humidity, such as Saudi Arabia or Singapore, makes the challenge even greater. What happened in Qatar took it to another level.

The first running of the Qatar Grand Prix took place in November 2021, and the springtime events in Bahrain and Saudi Arabia never take place any later than mid-April in order to avoid the hottest months in the region. In 2023, the Qatar race was scheduled for early October, prior to the "winter" dip in temperature, because of a reluctance from the organizers to run the race too close to Abu Dhabi, the other end-of-year race in the region and a local political rival.

Daytime temperatures in Qatar were upward of 105 degrees Fahrenheit, and although it cooled to "only" 90 degrees Fahrenheit for the race at 8 p.m., inside the cockpit, it reached almost 120 degrees Fahrenheit. Roaming the grid before the race, I could feel beads of sweat forming on my back, wearing only a T-shirt and jeans; nothing compared to the mechanics in their full-body overalls, a few of whom would occasionally make use of the leaf blowers intended to cool the cars on the grid to blow some cold air into their faces. The smoke coming off the dry ice being kept near the cars quickly evaporated in the heat; the drivers wore cooling vests over their torsos, placed towels filled with ice around their necks, and took on as much fluid as they possibly could.

It was not enough to prepare them for the race. A tire safety concern meant all teams were required to make at least three pit stops, meaning they did not need to worry about burning through their rubber too quickly, and could therefore push flat out instead of going slower to extend tire life. Qatar is also one of the highest-speed tracks on the calendar with few slow corners, which meant the toll on their bodies was far greater than normal. And that's before accounting for the heat. It was a dangerous combination of factors.

During the race, Williams driver Logan Sargeant was forced to pull out because he was feeling so unwell after battling sickness before the race even started. His teammate, Alex Albon, required help getting out of his cockpit at the end of the race, as did Aston Martin's Lance Stroll, with both drivers being taken to the medical center for a checkup by the circuit doctors. Even Max Verstappen, the race winner, sat slumped in the corner of the aptly named "cool-down room" before going onto the podium, asking the organizers jokingly if anyone had a wheelchair.

As I emerged from my air-conditioned media center to go and speak to the drivers after the race, the extent of their physical exertion was impossible to miss. Tsunoda's fringe was speckled with salt from his sweat. He'd tried to get more cool air into his helmet by opening his visor, only for that to blow sand into his eyes. Esteban Ocon, looking somewhat pale, admitted he'd vomited in his cockpit just fifteen laps into the fifty-seven-lap race, at which point he thought: *Shit, this is going to be a long race.* Stroll revealed he was struggling with his vision going through the high-speed corners in the closing stages. Every single driver had a similar story as they passed through the media bullpen, each one sipping furiously from the straw poking out of their drink bottles. The exception was George Russell, who, remarkably, turned up wearing a sweater. It was because he'd jumped straight into an ice bath immediately after finishing to cool off. "I was close to fainting in that race," he said. "The cockpit was over fifty degrees Celsius. You've got your fire-

proofs on, race suit on, the physicality of the car. . . . It's just crazy."
There was no amount of physical preparation that could have made
it easier for the drivers to endure the heat in Qatar. These are some
of the fittest athletes in the world, well-accustomed to handling difficult driving conditions. "It has nothing to do with training," said
Verstappen after the race. "Some of the guys who were struggling
today, they are extremely fit, probably even fitter than me."

It sparked calls for change from drivers after finding the limit
of their physical capabilities. "It's sad we had to find out this way,"
said Lando Norris. "It's a pretty dangerous thing to have going
on." The FIA introduced some minor rule changes for the future,
allowing the installation of a cooling "slot" into the cars—which
F1 teams, paranoid and obsessively focused on the performance
of the car, previously rejected, fearing it might be used as an aerodynamic device—and promised to look at other solutions to help
drivers deal with extreme heat, like investigating the use of cooling vests in the car. The FIA did also point out that no future
Qatar races were scheduled for October, instead shifting to November, when the temperatures would be cooler and a repeat
occurrence could be avoided.

It did not dilute the overarching issue coming out of Qatar: Extreme heat is starting to impact F1 races in a way that it has not in
the past. To think that high temperatures are specific only to a single race or a result of poor scheduling would be folly. There's a reason that races in central Europe in the height of summer, such as in
Austria or Hungary, are starting to become more challenging for
drivers than they were fifteen or twenty years ago. Or why the
lengths drivers must now go to in order to prepare for the toughest

of races are getting increasingly drastic. For some of the hottest grands prix on the calendar, such as Singapore, they'll go as far as placing exercise bikes inside a sauna to complete a workout and try to adjust to exerting themselves in extreme levels of heat. As the world continues to heat up, and more races become impacted by high ambient temperatures, what are now considered extreme levels of conditioning for drivers may increasingly become the norm.

■ ■ ■

Qatar and Imola brought the severity of the climate crisis right to F1's doorstep, serving as a wake-up call that the time for change arrived long ago and increasingly tough questions need to be asked about how the sport operates, starting with the composition of its calendar.

Because right now "there is not a single race track that's not in trouble."

That's the view of Dr. Maddy Orr, who laments the fact that she is always the "bad news girl" when it comes to conversations like the one we are having. Yet as a researcher focused on sport and climate change who has analyzed leagues, teams, and series ranging from skiing to football to motor racing, she has become an expert in her field and one of the most authoritative voices when it comes to the existential challenges facing sport.

As we chat over Zoom, I joke how my travel schedule at the start of the new season highlights why F1 is so different than other sports. I'm talking to her from my hotel room in Bahrain, and in the next couple of months I'll be going to Saudi Arabia, back to the

UK, then all the way to Australia, up to Japan, and then home again. I've committed to only going home once in the seven-week spell to save myself some time on planes, which I can style out as doing a little something for the environment, too. A lot of other paddock members are doing the same.

Fitting twenty-four races into a fifty-two-week calendar may sound straightforward, but it is anything but for the officials who are entrusted with piecing the schedule together given the date demands or restrictions of the host countries. Qatar was proof you can't host races in the Middle East any later than the end of March, nor really any sooner than the end of October due to the heat. The opposite is true for races such as Montreal in Canada, which can't go any earlier than June due to fears it might snow. Much of the European season needs to take place from late spring to early autumn due to the cold of the winter. That's before you start to consider the demands of some races having to be on the same weekend every single year—in some cases, the prime minister of a country has intervened to say no to a move—and the geopolitical considerations that might make it tricky to run some races on back-to-bck weekends, particularly in the Middle East. Designing a calendar that makes the most amount of sense geographically is a long way from the reality of what actually works both logistically and politically.

It means we do end up with some strange calendar sequencing or race pairings. Traveling directly from Azerbaijan to Miami in 2023 did not feel like F1's best bit of scheduling, nor was the end-of-season trip from Las Vegas to Abu Dhabi later that year. Efforts have been made in recent years to rationalize the calendar more.

From 2024, Japan was brought to the start of the season to create a sequence with Australia and China. After some convincing by F1, Qatar also moved to the end of the season to pair up with Abu Dhabi, albeit after Las Vegas one week earlier, to create a run of three races in three weeks to end the season.

But Orr feels more must be done with the scheduling of races, particularly to avoid the climatic issues that challenge their safe running, meaning the calendar could look very different in years to come.

"Formula 1, in order to survive into the future, is going to have to drop the current assumptions around the calendar," she says. "If they do that, there is, at some point during the year, a safe time to race in just about any place. It's not that I want to say you can never race in Saudi Arabia or you can never go to Singapore—that's not the case. We are going to reach a point where there are times in the calendar that just have to be blacked out."

Orr believes the window for F1's more vulnerable events is only going to get narrower as temperatures continue to rise and circuits face greater environmental challenges. As part of the Sport Ecology Group, Orr was commissioned to complete a review of every track on the calendar in not just F1, but in other series, including Indy-Car, Formula E, and Extreme E. Every single circuit came back with some kind of threat, most of which were related to heat.

It goes beyond what the drivers deal with in the cockpit. It also impacts the operations of all the mechanics and team members, particularly those in close proximity to the car, at a time when they need to perform at their highest levels. Even the slightest mistake in a pit stop can prove costly, not only from a performance standpoint, as cars pull in for service at speed. The mechanics are working in built-up areas wearing full protective fire gear that reduces heat transfer—again, by design—and often do so off the back of long flights while adjusting to new time zones and conditions. "You're dehydrated and tired, you're a bit discombobulated, and then you're introducing heat, which is a perfect cocktail really for disaster," says Orr. "We're fortunate that we haven't seen more issues with heat already. And this will be probably the big issue moving forward."

One concern Orr has in all elite sports, not just F1, is the "sense of high performance and kind of 'eliteness' being associated with a degree of macho behavior." Essentially, the idea of pushing through and beyond the limit of what's physically tolerable all because of their commitment to a result. "People in elite sports, particularly on the men's side, play through all kinds of injuries and ailments," she says. "Drivers will continue driving even though they're overheating, even though in some cases concentration is dipping." That was true in the Qatar race, with Esteban Ocon's words in particular sticking with me when he was asked about pulling out after he started vomiting. "It's not an option, retiring," he said with total certainty. "I was never going to do that. You need to kill me to retire."

It adds to the need for strict protocols and monitoring to be in place when it comes to racing with high levels of heat. Orr says it's not due to a lack of trust around athletes, stressing it's not their fault that they overheat; all the training in the world or workouts in saunas can't prepare their bodies for the most extreme of conditions. But the risk of losing concentration when driving at high speed next to other cars on the track or when coming into a pit stop and being near pit crew members means they cannot afford a slip. "In football, if one player is having a bad game, they get a bit dizzy or nauseous, maybe they get a bit of cramping and lose concentration, no one except that player is at risk," she says. "In motorsport, the stakes are that much higher, and so the response needs to be that much tighter. If a guy on your pit crew who is responsible for screwing the tire on correctly is off for that one second because they're experiencing heat illness, you could crash. We don't have room for that."

Although that scenario has not yet occurred, Orr feels the risk is only going to increase "unless there is a heat policy that would call a race off completely above a certain temperature threshold—which I doubt they're going to want to do because that will put a lot of places off the map. They're going to have to figure that out." In response to what happened in Qatar, the FIA said there was "broad intention" to write a heat or humidity threshold into the regulations at which point action would be taken, but as of the time of writing, this has yet to be formalized.

Flooding also remains a serious concern for a number of races that are near bodies of water. The events of Imola did not come as a surprise to Orr and her colleagues, given it was in an at-risk zone, and there are others that fall into the same scope; she makes mention of Miami, Singapore, and Montreal. Although the circuits themselves are not so much of a concern, the nearby area is, particularly when it comes to the transport infrastructure routes to and from the track. "Montreal is a good example of that," says Orr. "You're racing on an island. If that river floods, that's not pretty. The track itself would probably be fine, but all the infrastructure around it is in a flood zone."

It's a fairly bleak picture for the future of F1, particularly when it comes to scheduling. The calendar has expanded by 20 percent in the past fifteen years, making it even harder to strike the right compromise. While more races is great news for F1's income and profits, it does complicate the environmental challenge and the image that the sport portrays. "If F1 continues to be perceived by the public as this high-emitting, high-class touring property, then it will at some point skew towards unjustifiability among the vast majority of the global public as climate change worsens," Orr says. "We're not there. But that could be something that becomes a reality out of perception."

Orr also notes potential reputation issues in relationships between F1 and big oil companies. Shell, ExxonMobil, BP Castrol, and Petronas are all heavily involved in F1, as is Aramco, the Saudi-state-backed oil company. Aramco is a partner of both the Aston Martin team and F1 itself, yet it is regularly named as the world's biggest corporate polluters. Multiple studies have attributed more than 4 percent of global carbon emissions in the past thirty-five years to Aramco. "F1 is going to have to keep its eye on that because that is also going to be a reputation burden in the future if these trends continue, if big oil continues to not be a credible partner on sustainability," Orr says. The counterpoint that F1 itself and the teams working with oil companies as their partners give is that as they explore new initiatives such as sustainable fuels, they need to lean on the biggest companies who have the resources and knowledge to bring about long-lasting change. Yet it's still a big asterisk over F1's environmental efforts.

Orr identifies another area that may pose a challenge to F1 teams' sustainability goals: the limit on spending. Since 2021, in a bid to make F1 more financially sustainable and reduce the gaps between the haves and have-nots on the grid, all ten teams have been subject to a cost cap, which starts at $145 million per year for their race operations. There are exemptions, such as driver salaries and the wages of the three highest-paid employees, yet sustainability does not come under that umbrella. Hypothetically, if a car part could be made more sustainably but would cost more, there'd be no incentive for teams to make that switch if it might eat into their budgets and leave them less money to spend on improving performance. Orr hopes F1 changes its approach in the future to encourage such changes by making sustainability premiums exempt from the cost cap, even if the wealthier teams would be better-placed to pursue these more sustainable avenues. "Smaller teams are going to grumble for sure, because 'Oh, we're giving advantages on sustainability?'" she says. "My answer to that is like . . . yep! The world's on fire!"

It is evident F1 must adapt if it wants to ensure it can keep racing successfully and remain relevant not only within the automotive industry, but as a wider sporting product. Thankfully, this is also a sport that is home to some of the finest technical and engineering minds in the world, something Orr, with some excitement, calls "a huge advantage" for F1. "I have no doubt that F1 is going to figure this out," she says. "It's not about whether they have the capacity or whether they will. I think it's more how fast."

■ ■ ■

In 2019, F1 revealed its first sustainability report and set the target of becoming net carbon zero by 2030—an ambitious goal, yet one that Liberty Media recognized as being critical to the sport's future quite early into its ownership of the series.

It's a mentality change that is a big ask for a sport like F1. If you think of motor racing, you think of the loud engines screeching, kicking out all kinds of fumes from their exhausts, tires burning. It's a visceral, sensory experience, and that has a natural environmental cost. Whenever I talk to people about F1 and the environment, there's understandably a frequent skepticism: Those cars are literally on the track going at speeds of more than 200 mph; how on earth can that be considered sustainable?

The first thing to note is the cars themselves are far from the gas-guzzling image you might have in your mind, contributing only a tiny part to F1's overall emissions. According to F1's 2019 sustainability strategy report, only 0.7 percent of the sport's carbon emissions come courtesy of the hybrid engines and the fuel they burn to go racing and testing over the course of a season. Even the tires used at every single race are taken back by the sport's supplier, Pirelli, and are recycled to generate power for its factories. The actual event operations for a grand prix amount to 7.3 percent of the carbon footprint, meaning the running of a grand prix itself is not the bit of F1 that is so harmful to the environment. It's everything around it to make the race happen.

The biggest contributors to F1's sizable emissions are logistics and, unsurprisingly, travel. The transportation of all the freight for races, including the cars, tires, and equipment used by the teams and the whole paddock, comes to 45 percent of F1's carbon footprint, going across air, sea, and road. Then there's the people, which comes to a further 27.7 percent for all the business travel for the paddock over the entire season. The remaining 19.3 percent of the footprint is the ten teams' factories and facilities.

Since F1 released those figures, the sport has been taking steps to try to reduce its annual carbon footprint. In 2024, it reported that its baseline figure of 256,551 tons of CO_2 from 2018, when the net zero target was set, had already been cut by 13 percent. But the focus cannot be on what has already been achieved, rather on the remainder of the goal: the further 37 percent F1 wants to make up in the following six years.

It's a task that lies with Ellen Jones, who was appointed F1's first head of sustainability in 2022. As I greet her for our chat outside the F1 hospitality unit at the Albert Park Circuit in Melbourne, she's hurriedly typing notes into her phone about things she has spotted around the paddock, identifying bits of gear that could have been left back in the UK instead of traveling to the other side of the world. The necessity of every single piece of equipment that travels to races is now being challenged in order to help the push to the 2030 goal, reducing freight where possible. There have been some big changes already, such as transitioning to 100 percent renewable energy for F1 office buildings, but the travel element is always going to be the biggest hurdle to overcome. "Less than one percent of our carbon footprint is from the cars," Jones says. "What that means though is that all of our other footprint is from operations."

A first step is trying to reduce the number of people on-site for a race. After the onset of the Covid-19 pandemic, F1 was the first international sport to resume, starting its season in July 2020 with a far-reduced on-site operation as limits were imposed on the number of team members and wider personnel that could attend races due to restrictions on travel. It prompted a rethink for how all the teams went racing and how F1 staged an event, placing a greater emphasis on remote operations—think work from home, but make it F1. Similar to how work from home remained in place even as Covid-19 restrictions eased, the same was true in F1, leading to a reduction in the number of people and the amount of freight going to an event. Teams found ways to complete more of their operations back from their factories in areas such as strategy or race management, with the happy byproduct of also cutting costs. "That means fewer people are traveling, and that's amazing, it really supports us," Jones says. "Setting up that new way of working is really critical to show that we can deliver an amazing product and deliver it better."

There's still a huge amount of freight that needs to get from race to race. Jones focuses on three key areas when it comes to bringing about change on the logistical front: the amount that travels; the distance it travels; and the mode in which it travels. Teams have been looking at every single item that goes from race to race. If it has to travel, can it be designed or packed more efficiently? A reduction in the number of freight boxes also means a reduction in the carbon footprint, but so long as the calendar remains so sprawling and, seemingly at times, geographically out of sequence, it'll always be a tricky ask.

That is where the mode of transport that F1 uses to take its circus around the world plays a big role. Teams will often have multiple sets of gear, with some being kept in sea freight for some of the more spread-out, far-flung events that do not require immediate use at the next race, helping cut the amount of air travel required. While some gear needs to be transported to every single race, plane transportation is also going through changes. F1 said its switch from Boeing 747 to 777 freight planes helped reduce emissions by 19 percent. On the road, F1's trucks will complete around 6,000 miles per year throughout the European season, but now do so using biofuels that reduce carbon emissions by 60 percent.

F1 sees alternative fuels as being the key to a more sustainable future both on- and off-track. Although electric vehicle technology continues to develop and increasing numbers of manufacturers commit to only making electric cars in the future, the internal combustion engine is not going to be disappearing anytime soon, making hybrid technology important for the sport's future. "It's great to see that alternative fuels can help drive reductions today, and we can do it across all modes of transit," Jones says, believing the use of sustainable fuels in the cars helps draw a link to its efforts to make the same change in its logistics across air, land, and sea. It also extends to the power supply at the tracks with the generators that are used in the paddock. At the 2023 Austrian Grand Prix, F1 trialed a low-carbon-energy system that was powered by hydrotreated vegetable oil (HVO) and a solar panel farm on the outskirts of the circuit, which was estimated to reduce emissions by 90 percent.

Each grand prix is closely looking at how it stages its event from a sustainability standpoint. From the moment a fan purchases their ticket, race promoters are encouraged to help them make more sustainable choices. This ranges from small steps such as having digital tickets instead of paper ones to only using public transport—Australia and the Netherlands are two successful races in this regard, as fans make use of trams and trains—or adopting schemes such as carpooling or park and ride for more rural events like the Belgian Grand Prix, which is in the middle of the Ardennes forest. "This is a core thing for us to do as a sport," Jones says. "How do we make those operational choices and communicate to fans how they can be part of it?" Each race is scored from one to five on a series of criteria, fostering some healthy competition between events for sustainability bragging rights and, more important, to help share best practices that can be adopted at other races.

That competition extends to the ten teams, all of whom have their own sustainability targets that focus on both goals set out by F1 and more specific internal targets. Together with F1, they have formed a Sustainability Working Group that helps them to discuss their initiatives and find ways to work together. "When it comes to sustainability, shared solutions are better solutions," says Jones. "That recognition and that ability to talk to the teams on a professional level where we all have the same understanding whether it's events, carbon footprint, circular economy, that just helps us move faster." As much as they may want to beat one another on the race track, there's an understanding that the race against climate change is one nobody can afford to lose—although that doesn't mean there isn't pride in being the first to bring an idea to the table that can be adopted by everyone.

Mercedes has already been making big strides with its environmental goals. Alice Ashpitel joined the team as its head of sustainability in 2022, and has felt a "step change" entering the F1 world after previously working in the construction industry. "There is an opportunity to demonstrate that you can go racing at the highest level but travel in a more sustainable way," she said. "I think that was a really key moment for the team and the sport." F1 teams are adept at analyzing vast amounts of data when it comes to gaining performance with their cars, meaning the same thought process could be applied to tracking every single movement of personnel or freight over the course of a season. "That was the big challenge, collecting the data, synthesizing it, and then also going back to the team and saying how we can start to use that data to make more informed decisions," Ashpitel said.

In 2023, Mercedes reported a 21 percent reduction in its F1 air-travel emissions against the previous year, in part due to the uplift in remote operations. Toto Wolff has even occasionally missed races in recent years but still been able to talk directly to the drivers over the radio by pressing a button on his "pit wall" back at the factory. Mercedes has also become the first F1 team to invest in Sustainable Aviation Fuels (SAF), which makes up less than 0.1 percent of all jet fuel but can offer a reduction in emissions by 80 percent. "If we're serious about meeting global targets, that production has got to scale and it's got to scale now because it takes years to build a refinery," said Ashpitel. "That's why we went into our SAF project where we've got an initial volume that we've secured for the next few years. Longer term, we're actually investing in a refinery capacity to help scale that market."

The adoption of more sustainable fuel has also extended to the fleet of black Mercedes trucks that will travel between the European races through the summer months, trialing the use of HVO in 2023.

This helped reduce Mercedes's overall F1 travel emissions by 46 percent. At its factory, the team has procured 100 percent renewable energy since 2019 and 100 percent green gas since 2020, while new buildings under construction are designed to be powered by fully renewable energy sources. Even on a smaller, more personal level, Mercedes is encouraging a reduction in employee emissions by reducing waste in its canteen areas and encouraging greener commuting initiatives such as carpooling, which also has social benefits: Ashpitel said two car-sharers even became friends and signed up for a half-marathon together.

It all serves as justification of Maddy Orr's faith in the F1 mindset to tackle the climate challenge it faces, which Ashpitel relished being part of. "What's exciting is the agility of F1 as a sport and the team recognizing that we're not going to know all of the answers right now," she said. "But as we uncover and see that standards change, we will make sure that we're at the best-practice leading edge. I have confidence the teams in F1 as a whole are fully committed to this, and have the skills and ability to adapt and change as needed." Jones agreed, saying the sustainability challenge stretches to "everything" in F1. "It never ends, because what is leading today is table-stakes tomorrow," she said. "To win in one area is not a success. It has to be that culture change in everyone so sustainability becomes part of who we are."

It's true: F1 does require a culture change, and we are starting to see the early signs of that in motion. Working toward net zero was never going to be an easy task, nor is changing how the sport is perceived from the outside. Orr's description of F1 as being a "high-emitting, high-class touring property" is an incredibly accurate one of what F1 will continue to be if it doesn't change. If F1 fails to adapt quickly enough on its own, extreme weather events, similar to what we saw at Imola or in Qatar, will force it to do so.

The biggest obstacle in all of this remains the calendar. F1 has prided itself on the surge in demand for races since its global boom at the start of the decade, allowing it to push toward its upper-limit of permitted events with a twenty-four-round schedule each season. There are plenty of other countries that are angling to join the calendar, such as Thailand and South Korea. They know what F1 can bring to their cities and how powerful the sport can be. As each race comes up for a contract renewal, there'll be fresh questions asked about whether it's best to continue with the status quo or consider a new location. If the sport is to truly make good on its commitment to the environment and to changing its culture, the environmental and sustainability considerations need to be at the forefront of those decisions.

Rationalizing the calendar to work in better geographic groupings is a target for the current F1 leadership under the series' CEO and president, Stefano Domenicali. It's an unenviable task for Domenicali and his senior staff to try to make a calendar meet the varying demands and restrictions that are in place. As the world continues to heat up and more circuits handle climatic events, those scheduling restrictions are only going to get tighter and more challenging.

That collective effort goes for the drivers, too. As the stars of the sport who have the greatest platforms and reaches of anyone, they, too, need to show their commitment to helping F1 adapt to a rapidly changing climate.

For one driver, that commitment has become a postcareer purpose.

■ ■ ■

Suzuka is one of Sebastian Vettel's favorite race tracks in the world. He's always loved the crazy, passionate fans who don their creative costumes each year. When he was racing, Vettel's most ardent fans in Japan would make the journey to the famed circuit, about three hours outside of Tokyo, to cheer him on. Vettel won the race four times through his vastly successful F1 career, as well as clinching the second of his four world championships at the track in 2011. When he announced his plan to retire from F1 at the end of the 2022 season, Vettel admitted the only condition upon which he might consider a comeback would be if someone needed a replacement driver at Suzuka.

Nine months after his final F1 race in Abu Dhabi, when I last saw him outside a party wearing what he called his "party shirt," a jazzy blue and green number, Vettel is back in the paddock and back at Suzuka. Except he's not racing. He's here for a very different reason.

Bees.

On the apex of the first corner at Suzuka, a turn he would have driven over one thousand times through his F1 career, Vettel stands in jeans and a T-shirt (less jazzy this time) alongside the drivers he once called rivals, friends, and, in some cases, teammates. The entire grid, along with every F1 team boss, is supporting Vettel in his latest venture. A giant banner is unfurled, reading: BUZZIN'

CORNER—complete with a logo of a bee on one side. The curb of the corner at their feet, usually red and white to provide drivers a visual reference when inside the cockpit, has been repainted yellow and black.

Vettel's project is the installation of "bee hotels" on the inside of the first corner at Suzuka. In the patch of grass that was previously overgrown with weeds and plants, a number of wooden structures, designed to resemble the Ise Shrine around an hour south of Suzuka, were installed to promote biodiversity.

"The idea is to make a buzz, create noise, make noise, and create awareness around the topic, and especially the loss and decline of biodiversity," Vettel explains, proudly standing in front of the now-colorful wooden structures. "The bee is a great ambassador with its colors, with the pattern, because everybody has a picture in their heads immediately. We used her to spread the message.

"We also built these huts to create more habitat and space for insects, bees, bugs, butterflies, everything that crawls, and to have some space, mostly for nesting, to hibernate, to find some food. It obviously has a small impact here at the track, but change starts in your head. That's what we're aiming for."

Once the photoshoot is complete, Vettel invites the drivers to come and see the bee hotels, and to help decorate them with a selection of paint cans and brushes. It's social media gold, seeing the drivers produce their "art" (think fourth grade) and write messages in the paint. Vettel takes time to show the drivers how the "hotels" would work, helping Lewis Hamilton, once his championship rival, place pieces of wood and plants inside the hotels, which Vettel explains the insects can use as nests during the winter.

Hamilton comments that he's proud to see Vettel has found such a purpose after F1, going as far as saying he did not know of another driver who had "shown real compassion for the world outside of this little world that we're living in." Vettel later admitted to being overwhelmed by just how supportive the F1 community has been for his scheme, taking time to come and see part of his post-F1 focus in action.

Vettel's passion for the environment grew rapidly through the closing years of his F1 career. He became increasingly aware and interested in the topic, often serving as one of the key spokespeople on the grid. Where other drivers shied away from tackling difficult topics head on, Vettel was unafraid to speak up no matter the topic. It was environmentalism that became his big passion. He started to read up on sustainable farming and food sources, and made big changes to his own way of going about life. Through 2022, his final F1 season, he opted against flying to any of the races in Europe, instead traveling by car, to reduce his emissions. He started wearing a range of T-shirts at races highlighting environmental issues, the most powerful one coming in Miami, saying a potential 2060 race could be the 1ST GRAND PRIX UNDERWATER. ACT NOW OR SWIM LATER. Through his final F1 season, he started to take an interest in sustainable fuel solutions, completing some demonstration laps in a classic Williams F1 car at Silverstone using carbon-neutral fuels through an initiative he calls Race Without Trace. It proved that even old machinery and technology, complete with their screaming V10 engines, could be made sustainable.

Vettel was never afraid to acknowledge F1's environmental

shortcomings. Around a month before announcing his retirement from F1, he appeared on *Question Time*, a leading UK political talk show that features active politicians and occasionally the serving prime ministers. Despite hailing from Germany and living in Switzerland, Vettel spoke eloquently about the UK's political topics, running rings around a future (and short-lived) home secretary, Suella Braverman, and it was on the environment where he really excelled. He went as far as calling himself a hypocrite for highlighting such issues while being part of a sport he agreed had a "gas-guzzling" image.

Vettel isn't sure if environmentalism is now his purpose post-F1, but he does not understate its importance, warning of the catastrophic impact a decline in biodiversity could have on all species. "It's not *my* calling," Vettel said. "It should be all our callings."

"I think we are starting to understand that we do have an impact, whatever way we look at it. The world we know is changing. That's what we should fight for."

And it is also something Vettel felt F1 can fight for. "I think every company, every sports platform, has a responsibility that is growing," he said. "Obviously it's good to set targets, but it's much better to achieve those targets and to see the steps towards that target. The answer is we can all do more."

F1 is conscious of the challenge it faces, but as Vettel said, it is going to be a never-ending battle for the sport, particularly if it retains the elements that make it so compelling. To think of F1 without the humming sounds of loud engines or hopping from country to country would be to think of it without its heart. It's unreasonable to think the sport will snap its fingers and change immediately.

There is reason to be hopeful. The work of Jones, Ashpitel, and their colleagues shows how seriously F1 as a community is taking its sustainability goals. Figures like Vettel speaking up is vital to highlighting these issues on a wider scale. F1 cannot shy away from the existential threat it faces, particularly if it wants to keep its current form. It's about using the best qualities of this sport, for all its issues, to tackle something far greater than any world championship or race win; to use the same mindset that has helped save lives to develop the kind of innovative technology that could help the world to win this fight.

Because this is a race for our future.

10

Checkered Flag

After five hours stuck on the tarmac in Las Vegas, a missed connection in Los Angeles, and a change of route to Dallas, George Russell and Pierre Gasly had time to kill.

It was the middle of the night, and they wouldn't be continuing the onward journey to the final race of the F1 season in Abu Dhabi, one ocean and two continents away, for a little while longer. And they were getting hungry. So they ended up paying a visit to one of America's great culinary institutions: IHOP, short for International House of Pancakes.

"That was an eye-opening experience," Russell says, laughing, a few days later as we sit down for an end-of-season interview in the cool of Mercedes's hospitality unit at the Yas Marina Circuit, over eight thousand miles away from that IHOP. He reveals someone within the traveling entourage had a pack of Uno cards, helping the group whittle away the hours. Being a beacon of health even at the end of a long season, Russell is quick to note he swerved the pancakes on the menu and instead picked an omelet.

"Well, they'll have to rename it 'IHOO,'" I say.

The excruciating silence and blank looks from George, his accompanying PR, and the two other journalists present tell me the joke has quite spectacularly failed to land.

I hastily hit record on my phone and ask a question to start the interview, designed to recap Russell's second season with Mercedes and look at his progression as a future F1 star. He concedes to feeling a little rundown—not because of the IHOP—and apologizes for the occasional pauses to cough.

The journey itself from Las Vegas to Abu Dhabi has been hard for us all to navigate, requiring two or three flights to cover such a long distance in only a couple of days. But it was the demands of the Las Vegas race, F1's first on the Strip, that had really broken everyone. All of the sessions started late at night to minimize disruption for Sin City and provide a stunning visual image of the race—the neon standing out against the night sky. The race started at 10 p.m. on the Saturday night—most races begin around 2 or 3 in the afternoon on a Sunday—while one of the delayed practice sessions didn't finish until 4 a.m. on Friday. It was hard to know when to sleep, when to eat, or even how to consume enough daylight (sunset is around 4 p.m. in Vegas in November). A low moment came when I emerged from the Flamingo casino at 7 a.m. after the race to be blinded by the sunlight, two hundred dollars lighter after my first (and last) foray into gambling in Vegas had lasted about twenty minutes and left me wondering what I was doing with my life. (When I told my American colleagues the next day what happened, they were aghast: "You went *where*?!")

A few days after our interview, Russell's cough has grown much worse. As he walks into the press conference room after the race, which he's finished in third place, the host asks how he is feeling.

"Pretty shit, if I'm being honest with you," Russell replies, summing up the feeling of so many people within the paddock.

In his all-black Mercedes race suit, Russell slumps into the white sofa used for the postrace press conference and sips from his water bottle as the cameras start to roll and the questions begin. His sweat-matted hair serves as proof of his exertion and how much has been taken out of him. Whatever virus he was battling only made the race all the more miserable.

"I was coughing every single lap, but when you're strapped into the car, you can't breathe," Russell says. "You can't take a deep breath in to get the cough out. It was pretty, pretty miserable. I was pleased when I saw that checkered flag."

Abu Dhabi is the twenty-second and final race of the season. Typically, it's a moment of celebration and reflection when teams and drivers can toast their achievements. In Russell's case, his third-place finish helped clinch second place in the Constructors' Championship for Mercedes, beating Ferrari by three points, while McLaren has won the race for fourth ahead of Aston Martin. They're results that are worth millions in prize money to the teams and thousands of dollars in bonuses to the team members. As one friend puts it: "That's my new kitchen paid for."

This year, few are in the mood to toast the end of the season. No one has the energy. The previous year, upon leaving the track after wrapping up my work at midnight, I'd bumped into one F1 driver asking his accompanying group which yacht moored in the harbor had the best party. About ten minutes later, another was being dragged into the W Hotel that serves as the centerpiece of the circuit—the rooms literally overlook the race track—where the relentless thud of dance music from the afterparties would continue until the sun came up. This time around, everyone is happy to check out with little more than a "see you next season."

The Vegas–Abu Dhabi back-to-back has hurt, and the usual end-of-year bugs that tend to do the rounds in the paddock feel worse than ever. "I've got so many mechanics who are ill," Russell explains. "People in the engineers' office are just really struggling with the constant time zone shifts, the body not knowing where you are, eating at different times, staying in different hotels, different environments, different climates.

"I don't think it's sustainable for four thousand people to do twenty-four races a season, especially when you see how geographically it still doesn't make a huge amount of sense."

The question of human sustainability is a rather new one in F1. Only ten years ago in 2015, the calendar had nineteen races and was comfortably finished by the end of November, ensuring there was time for a proper off-season. Ten years prior to that, the season usually wrapped up in October. With the bulk of the races taking place in Europe, the demands of the job were more manageable for everyone working in the paddock.

As F1 grew and added more races to the calendar, forming grueling schedules like going from Las Vegas to Abu Dhabi or, for 2024 and 2025, putting Qatar in between those races for a three-week stretch, the toll it took on people's lives and their mental health, an area that has only become more widely spoken about in F1 circles in recent years, has increased.

It's a far cry from the origins of the sport. The first F1 world championship season in 1950 was only seven races long, running from mid-May to early September; now it's March to December. A sport that was once a pursuit for the wealthy has transformed immeasurably through its history, relentlessly redefining what F1 stands for. It was always about more: higher speeds, quicker lap times, greater extravagance.

But F1 has now reached a point where that constant push for doing things bigger and better has led to questions about what its future may look like. What is it about this sport, now more demanding than ever, that keeps us coming back for more season after season? After going through so much change in its history, where will it take us next? And will our love for F1 still burn so brightly?

■ ■ ■

It should come as zero surprise that drivers love racing.

Reaching F1 is something they—and, for many, their families—dedicated their entire lives to achieving. Whether they were supported by great wealth or had to scrimp and save to keep their dreams going, it became their whole purpose. It means none of them take it for granted upon reaching the pinnacle.

So whenever we talk to F1 drivers about the demands of the

calendar, they're reluctant to complain too much. They'll typically fly first class (assuming they're not on a private jet), get the most comfortable hotels and the kindest schedules, arriving at a track as late as they can before commencing media duties and quickly dashing off after the race while their teams pack up the garages. "We have it best out of every single person in this paddock, the way we travel," said Russell, whose IHOP stopover is probably about as bad as it gets. "We're in a very fortunate position."

Even off the back of a twenty-something race season, many of them will spend their free time driving cars. Max Verstappen has dreams of forming his own racing team someday, believing that sim racing using video game software can become a genuine pathway for young drivers to make it up the ladder. He even has a full racing sim setup in his motor home that travels with him from race to race in Europe. After a day at the race track, he'll jump online to race with some friends, mainly professional sim racers, all sharpening the same skills he's used to win F1 races and world championships. Verstappen also wants to race alongside his father, Jos, in the 24 Hours of Le Mans, the world-famous sportscar race.

Just because Max lives and breathes racing does not mean that he is immune to the tolls of the ever-growing and demanding schedule. "We're way over the limit of races," Verstappen said. "I know I'm still very young, but I also know that I'm not doing this for another ten years." It's not a new criticism; Verstappen has always preferred a calendar of quality over quantity. "This is not sustainable," Verstappen said. "I love racing a lot and I do it a lot, also outside of Formula 1. But at some point you start looking into the quality of life and how much you are away doing a sport that you love. At one point, I'll prefer probably to just be at home and focus on other projects."

Verstappen is only twenty-six when he's saying this. He has literally grown up as part of F1's traveling circus, one of its main acts since debuting at the age of seventeen. Even if he did hang up his helmet at the age of thirty-six, he'd have done twenty seasons in F1 and started close to five hundred races—and would still be several years shy of the age at which some of his fellow drivers have retired. Most will tend to race until their mid- to late 30s before calling it a day. Some will explore other racing series, like IndyCar or Le Mans, as a way to satisfy their competitive cravings. Others might move into punditry or step back from the racing world entirely. To still be racing when you're in your forties, let alone at the highest level, is extremely rare in F1.

Fernando Alonso tore up that script entirely. His life is all about racing. Alonso made his debut back in 2001 at the age of nineteen, and was the youngest F1 champion in history at the time he won his maiden title at twenty-four. He's spent more than half his life racing in F1, largely spent toward the front of the grid, but that hasn't stopped him exploring other racing interests. He's won Le Mans twice, raced at the Indianapolis 500, and even entered the grueling Dakar Rally across the Saudi Arabian desert a few years ago. A weekend without an F1 will sometimes be spent throwing a go-kart around the track he owns in his hometown of Oviedo, Spain. If he could, he'd probably race fifty-two weekends per year behind the wheel. It's a mentality that, to me, puts him up there with the all-time greats.

So it's telling when a driver of his attitude also starts to question the demands of the sport. In Abu Dhabi, he reflected on what had been a very successful first season with Aston Martin. When Sebastian Vettel announced his retirement, the team didn't look for a younger driver to take over; in Alonso, it hired someone *even older* at the age of forty-one and quickly reaped the rewards: Alonso took the team from fighting in the midfield to challenging for podiums immediately, returning him to the front of the pack. He admitted it had made for a more rewarding and enjoyable season—I mean, what drivers don't love winning trophies?—and even after the journey from Las Vegas, he looked fresh and ready to go, not weathered by the length of the season. So I asked him if, at this rate, he thought he could simply keep going and going and going.

"The day that I will stop racing is not because I'll feel unmotivated for driving or I feel slow," Alonso said. "I don't think that time will arrive, in terms of feeling slow, because I have extreme self-confidence in my performance." No kidding. "But it could be with the calendar and the demanding schedule, one day I will feel it is time because there are other things in life. It has been a very demanding season. This type of thing will drain my battery, not the driving."

It's not only the number of races but the length of the season. In 2024, F1 added another two races to the calendar, taking it to a record-breaking twenty-four rounds that started with preseason testing in early February and ended in early December in Abu Dhabi. In 2021, we didn't have the last race of the season until December 12 due to the pressures of the Covid-19 pandemic. Only arriving in Abu Dhabi from the previous race in Saudi Arabia to see a massive Christmas tree in the lobby of the hotel did I realize

I'd done absolutely zero shopping, prompting a hasty Amazon order. On the grid, a few F1 team crew members got into the spirit by wearing Santa hats while going through their final prerace checks on the car—a nice touch, but also a reminder of just how long the season had dragged. The earliest we've finished a campaign in recent years was in 2022, when F1 held the last race in Abu Dhabi on November 20 to avoid clashing with the FIFA World Cup starting in nearby Qatar the same day. Now, it seems December finishes are going to become the norm.

It only adds to the all-consuming nature of the sport, which, as Russell highlighted, takes the greatest toll not on the drivers, but on the team crew working around them. Ahead of the 2025 season, January and February were the only months without any racing, but with most of February being taken up by the F1 car launches and preseason testing before making the long trip to Australia, it's only the latter part of December and January that can be considered "downtime." And most of that is spent hastily making preparations for the new car and the new season. So it never really stops.

There are a couple of fail-safes in place to try to help the F1 paddock cope with the demands of the job. First, the current commercial agreements in place between F1 and the ten teams mandate there can be a maximum of twenty-five races per season. It's a considerable number, yet it at least places an upper limit on how many races can be squeezed into a season (for now at least—there are fears it could edge higher in the future; each extra race brings more money into the F1 coffers). There is also a protected four-week summer break between races in August, at least two weeks of which teams are required to cease all operations, helping to bring a bit of respite in the midst of a busy season. An extra winter shutdown was recently written into the rules, again protecting time when they are not required in the factories. A drawback of these enforced periods is that it does heavily limit what vacation employees can take.

It has led to the start of staff rotation at teams, targeted at keeping people fresh by ensuring they do not do every single race and can share their duties around. Although it is not possible for every single person to do this—for example, a driver will always want the same engineer working with them at races, so important is that relationship—it has at least been a step in the right direction to look after employee well-being.

It's an area that teams are increasingly conscious they must prioritize. In previous eras of F1, the attitude was that you were lucky to be working in the sport, and if you don't want to do the job, complete with all the sacrifices involved, then there's a line of people who would happily do it instead; be grateful or get out. Nowadays, thankfully, there's not only greater tolerance and understanding but actual action within organizations to look after their people.

"We're really working to make sure that well-being is at the cutting edge of any decisions that we make," explained Chris Armstrong, who joined Mercedes as its well-being program manager in 2019. "It's a focus on the whole team, so that's everybody from the front door of the factory, all the way through to the drivers." With over 1,300 team members, Mercedes stands as one of the largest organizations in F1, with varying demands coming with each role.

Besides the 120 or so staff traveling to each race (60 involved with the car operation; the rest spread across other areas such as the driver performance coaches, marketing, communications, hospitality), there's also an extensive build team back at base that work on the cars when they're back at the factory. There's strategists, designers, chefs, cleaners, some working night shifts, some adjusting their schedules to fit with wherever F1 is racing that weekend. It's a lot to take out of people.

Armstrong's program at Mercedes focuses on four key areas: physical, mental, recovery, and social. One of the main cornerstones of its staff support is a free, optional health assessment that all new hires are offered, which over 85 percent of team members have accessed, according to Armstrong. While it can help identify smaller health concerns, such as weight change or slightly raised cholesterol levels, Armstrong said it had also helped identify far greater issues. "One gentleman found out he'd got cancer," he said. "He didn't have a clue, he felt fit and healthy. He was provided with incredible support through the team, but not just through the well-being team, but through his line manager giving him the empowerment to go and get whatever he needed. He was assisted by our performance center to make sure he was fit before he had an operation. And all of a sudden, he was back at work. It's not nice to talk about, but it could have been life-changing."

Mental well-being is also something Mercedes has actively prioritized, right from the top. Toto Wolff, the CEO and team principal, has been open about his own mental health challenges in the past, revealing that he has spent more than five hundred hours in therapy. He is also an investor in a mental health digital platform, Instahelp, and has long vaunted being in touch with one's sensitivities as being a "superpower." It's an example Armstrong felt was vital to inform the wider Mercedes team that, even through the pressures and demands of an F1 season, it's okay not to be okay, and support is there if needed. "It's really important for the team to see that from the top," he said. "It's that authenticity that we have in everything we do as a team. Everything is about leading with real intent of what we want to achieve."

There's the added complexity of success in F1 often being defined by technical aspects that are outside any individual's control. Take the mechanics servicing the car: They can do their jobs to perfection, completing rapid pit stops and ensuring every nut, bolt, and wing on the car is in perfect place, but if the car isn't quick enough, then the result on Sunday might lead to disappointment. "Making sure that as individuals and as a team, certain departments don't hang everything on the outcome of a race weekend has been really important," Armstrong said.

For those racking up the air miles by going to every single race, there's an added focus on ensuring the support they require is in place. When the Covid-19 pandemic hit and restrictions were enforced, Mercedes scrapped room sharing and has maintained that policy ever since, ensuring each member of staff on the road can have privacy at the end of each day, something especially important when making calls to loved ones thousands of miles away. Staff rotation is implemented where possible—even Wolff has skipped the odd race here or there in recent years—and Armstrong is part of a race team well-being working group that meets after each race to discuss how things went for the trackside team, covering everything from the flight options to the quality of the hotel they stayed in. Even things like the food offered at the track and the factory are tailored to ensure every team member has what they need to get through a weekend in the best condition, keeping energy levels up. "All the food we provide is of good quality, that can have such an impact on the ability to work well in the afternoon," Armstrong said. "Our designers can come up with good concepts late in the day because they're still fresh of mind."

Little things, but in an era when the concept of marginal gains has become fashionable across elite sports, they add up. We hear about it most frequently when it comes to what drivers do on the track, yet Armstrong thought it was something best applied across a team, not toward individuals. "Everybody talks about the drivers because that's the super exciting stuff we see on TV," he said. "But actually when it comes down to it, if you've got thirteen hundred people in an organization, there's probably a lot more power in everyone taking a step forward than having two drivers take six hundred fifty steps each."

It was heartening to hear just how things are changing in F1, ensuring that through the challenges of working in the sport, the support is there to make it sustainable. As we finished talking, Armstrong told me about a research paper he'd been reading from the University of Oxford, discussing the practice of using canaries in a coal mine to detect high levels of carbon monoxide.

"What we need to do is to change the environment to make sure that canary not only survives, but thrives," he said. "It's about being more proactive than reactive."

■ ■ ■

Sometimes, we all need to come up for air. Even the drivers. To "live the dream" in F1 requires nothing but total dedication. Staying there often requires the same mentality, making it tricky at times for drivers to properly switch off and find themselves away from the sport. The men and women who work behind the scenes want to try to find a work-life balance around F1, but what about the drivers?

It's something Russell admits he had previously struggled with. Reflecting on his season, he feels one of the biggest steps forward he's made hasn't come on the race track but actually off it. Now firmly established as one of the sport's leading drivers and certain of his future with Mercedes, there's stability. "I finally feel like I've got a home, a base where I see myself for many years to come personally and professionally, a good group of friends and people near where I live," he says. "I've got my family in a good spot as well. It all feels like I'm in a good place. I've probably been enjoying life a bit more this year, doing activities that I've never done."

New things? I ask. Surely as an F1 driver, you get enough of your thrills driving some of the fastest cars in the world? Oh no, not for Russell: "I've been free diving recently, diving into the water without breathing apparatus and swimming down. When I was younger, I was shit scared of the water. I didn't like going under. And now I'm diving tens of yards down. It's something I never thought I would do. I'm finding huge enjoyment and relaxation in doing these new things. Being settled gives me that chance." Importantly, it's breaking the cycle of F1 taking up every single waking thought. "It can't be just racing, racing, racing—you need to disconnect," Russell says. "When I took a holiday, that's when I came back fully refreshed with new ideas, and now feel like I'm back performing better than ever. You need that step away."

Was George guilty of that in the past, only thinking "racing, racing, racing"? "Definitely. This schedule lends itself to that, not just myself as an individual, but for everybody. You go from race to race, on the Monday, Tuesday, and Wednesday, you're talking about the previous race, then you're onto the next race, and you get caught up in the whirlwind of what's happening."

Russell says his Mercedes teammate, Hamilton, gave him inspiration to explore more pursuits. Hamilton has a wealth of interests beyond F1, ranging from music production (appearing under a pseudonym on a Christina Aguilera track, "Pipe," back in 2018) to skydiving and even fashion, establishing his own line with Tommy Hilfiger and becoming an ambassador for Dior Men. Back in 2018, Hamilton arrived at the race in Singapore via New York Fashion Week, sparking questions over his dedication and focus in the midst of a championship fight. He went on to produce one of the best qualifying laps in F1 history and win the race, well and truly putting such suggestions to bed. "What I admire is that he's found a way to disconnect," Russell says of Hamilton. "But when he comes back to the racing, it's 120 percent focus on that job. There's nothing else. Having that escape, it allows you to fully disconnect. But once you're in, you're all in."

Charles Leclerc is a proficient piano player and has started to release his own music. Lando Norris has his own gaming company and clothing line, the latter being something Daniel Ricciardo has also explored, along with his own wine brand. Esteban Ocon adores Marvel comics and movies. Valtteri Bottas has his own coffee and gin companies. While it's still motorsport-related, Max Verstappen's sim racing project is something he sees as a serious post-F1 career. There's a depth and interest for each driver that extends beyond their job. For some of the older drivers on the grid, it's their families: Three of the 2024 grid—Nico Hülkenberg, Kevin Magnussen, and Sergio Pérez—have children. But even for the younger racers who are yet to settle down, they are racing in an era when outside hobbies are encouraged, not disparaged, and can be additive to their F1 success.

Russell tells me his next goal over the winter is to go skiing for the first time, but he'll need Wolff's approval, given the risks involved. Yet the small things have still helped him to detach, even during unexpected detours through Dallas.

"We had a great laugh for the whole flight, going to the IHOP and playing cards," Russell says. "It's really important to help you get over any race weekend, even if you have a successful one. You have so many emotions. It's such a fall back to reality, regardless if you're standing on the top step or you had a disaster."

■ ■ ■

Straddling that line between glory and disaster is ingrained into F1. And no matter how interested the drivers may be in their outside interests, their love for the sport ultimately boils down to the competition: the chance to go wheel-to-wheel, to prove themselves as being the best in the fastest race cars in the world; the fights, the rivalries, the trophies, the fizz that comes at the end of it. They are out-and-out racers, putting their reputations and their bodies on the line all in dedication of this glorious sport.

It's what has defined the evolution of F1 through its history. Today, it stands as a commercial giant that is largely unrecognizable to how it started out. The calendar is three times as long as it once was, spanning the globe and taking its toll on the people who make it happen. The cars reach speeds thought unimaginable back in the 1950s. The money is eye-watering, as is the extravagance that has built up F1's identity. It is now about so much more than merely motor racing. Have we lost our way?

No. Because there is still that love and connection to the roots of the sport for every single person who swipes into the paddock gates at the start of each day and leaves once their work is done, usually long after the sun has gone down (or, for night races, when the sun has come up). Nothing can dilute that passion for racing and competition.

Lando Norris always remembers falling in love with F1 when watching Lewis Hamilton race in the chrome-colored McLaren, back in 2007. Norris was seven years old at the time and never could have dreamed he'd one day not only race against Hamilton, but do so driving for that very same team. There was an innocence in his outlook on the sport. The pure racing spectacle was what ignited his love for F1. "You just watch them go around the track and you see them on the podium," Norris said. "You didn't really get to see anything else of what a Formula 1 driver does. It's hard to imagine when you're a kid, when you're seven years old. . . . 'Ah now he's going home to a nice house with cool cars!'—you don't really think of that.

"I just fell in love with what I saw. I fell in love with driving, the competition, the feeling, of being in control of everything. You feel free because it's just you, you're in control of everything that goes on. You don't really get that in anything else. It's so much more than what you think it will be."

The realization of the dream of reaching F1 does come with elements that take drivers away from their racing roots. "It's a business, so it's got to please the crowd," Norris said. "There's certainly aspects I prefer of Formula 1 when I grew up watching it to now. There wasn't as much media and all these things as there are now." I laughed and promised not to take it personally, but I get his point: The demands on drivers are much greater nowadays. They're so much more than racing drivers. "In a perfect world, I'd just turn up for the race and go home!" Norris said frankly. "That's my dream world. But that's a dream. Every driver is greedy with what they want and what they say. Of course you're here, you're employed by the team, and you've got to deliver for the team."

For Norris's McLaren teammate, Oscar Piastri, a driver at the start of his F1 career, that competition and love also fuels him. "Being blunt, when you get paid good money to drive race cars, and the fastest race cars in the word, that's pretty easy motivation. . . ." Piastri said with a wry smile. "It's pretty easy to love doing that. But I've always enjoyed racing, and the competitive side of things, trying to beat other people. That really hasn't changed from when I was in the junior categories. I'm still attacking things in exactly the same way and trying to improve myself in exactly the same way. I think for me, it would be a bit concerning if that had changed, especially so early! I'm just loving driving the quickest cars in the world, trying to become a world champion."

Being part of something bigger and working as a team is what Lewis Hamilton cites as being such a big source for his passion for F1, one that has kept him in the sport far longer than he anticipated. There was a time when he expected to be done with the sport by the time he was forty. He's just passed that landmark, and shows little sign of slowing down. "It's the team element, the competition," Hamilton said. "It's everyone working to be the best that they can be. It's everyone in a team rowing in the same direction and chasing something that is almost unobtainable, which is perfection, innovation, and winning the world championship—it's such an incredible thing." Hamilton knows all too well just how incredible that thing is, being a seven-time world champion and winning eight Constructors' titles in a row with Mercedes, helping create one of the greatest team dynasties in F1 history.

The competition helps spur all the drivers on. Being so reliant on the quality of the cars at each driver's disposal, F1 does tend to go through cycles of domination. "You've had the Michael Schumacher dominance, my era of dominance . . . it happens all the time," Hamilton said. He was speaking at a time when Red Bull and Max Verstappen were at the height of their powers, enjoying unprecedented levels of success to the point that race results often felt like foregone conclusions. "I'm in awe of what they have done as a team. But it would be great if we were all having a closer battle," Hamilton said. Only a few races later, he'd be back fighting for wins as Red Bull was caught by Ferrari, Mercedes, and McLaren.

Since he debuted eighteen years ago, Hamilton has seen F1 go through dramatic levels of change. He's played a significant part in that, becoming by far the most recognizable and famous driver in its history. No one from the F1 world has hit celebrity status in the same way as him. He takes heart in how F1 has changed for the better. "This sport has grown in so many ways and we are seen and accepted in so many more places than we ever have been, which I think has been a real positive," he said. But he urged F1 to "stay true to our core values, and that's our integrity" in everything it does for the future. "Our fans need to trust us and be able to trust the sport."

As much as the drivers may rightly raise concerns about the expansion of the calendar and the demands placed upon them, or issues within the sport, that core love for F1 always prevails. In some cases, it's a love that is only strengthened by a little bit of time away.

At the end of 2020, Kevin Magnussen thought his F1 career was over. He'd been dropped by Haas after four seasons and was at peace with leaving the sport. He signed a deal to go and race sports cars in the United States, which, thanks to a less demanding schedule, meant he had the chance to move back to his native Denmark and start a family. But when Haas needed a driver on the eve of the 2022 season, they called on Magnussen to make a shock return. He didn't need to think twice about it, accepting the offer before even running it past his wife (who, thankfully, was on board).

Magnussen admitted that the time away and the chance to reflect on F1 from the outside helped change some of his feelings. "In those years before that, maybe I'd lost a little bit of love for Formula 1," he said. "For some people, they come in to Formula 1 after their junior career, and they just get straight into success there. But I didn't. I had six seasons or something before that break, of not winning at all. So, I think I'd maybe fallen out of love a little bit. Then I had that year out, missed it, and came back with a new appreciation for it."

Some time on the sidelines also did Daniel Ricciardo a world of good when it came to reigniting that fire. Once an established front-runner at Red Bull who regularly won races, Ricciardo was without a seat at the end of 2022 after a miserable two-year stint at McLaren, but he had come to terms with being out of F1. He deliberately went away at the end of that season with no interest or desire to train as though he'd be back racing anytime soon; he wanted to see what life outside the sport felt like. Only when that hunger came back naturally did he realize just how much he wanted to return, something he'd realize midway through 2023 when he secured a seat on Red Bull's sister team, AlphaTauri. "Having the time off, it gave me the answer of how much I do love it, how much it means to me," Ricciardo said. "I feel like I got a second chance, a second wind, where it's like, okay, I want to make sure this is my one and only priority, I'm going to put all my energy into this. Because I just don't want to walk away one day and be like, 'could have done more' or, 'that career slipped a little bit out of my fingers.' I'd hate to feel that."

Even in the toughest moments, F1 has a way of rewarding dedication. Fulfillment does not only come from winning or being at the very top of the sport. James Vowles, the Williams team principal, was a key part of Mercedes's serial-winning operation through the second half of the 2010s as it swept to eight consecutive world titles, becoming Toto Wolff's right-hand man. He likened his time there to being part of a "well-oiled machine" where everyone was looking for tiny improvements to improve on an already solid base. At the start of 2023, he left Mercedes to become the team principal of Williams—a step up in role but a big drop down the grid to a once-great team that was suffering from years of underinvestment. Yet the growing pains of trying to bring about overdue change at Williams, and the challenge of taking one of the most historic and successful teams on the grid back to the front, only emboldened Vowles's love for F1.

"I wasn't sure before I came here how much longer I was going to stay in the sport," he said—a rare admission from someone so ingrained as part of the paddock and particularly in such a senior role. "The sport had been great, and I'd enjoyed and spent twenty-five years in, but I'd sacrificed everything else. I didn't really see my family. I only created a family this year. Those were sacrifices I was prepared to make. But it got to a point where I thought, *Do I want to try something else in life?*

"But I joined Williams, and I have zero doubt in my mind I want to bring this team back to where it deserves to be as an organization. I will dedicate what it takes in my life to get there. It's renewed, if anything, my love for the sport."

That love goes back to the basics, back to the initial novelty that we all felt when we first watched F1 on TV. For all of the outside noise and drama, the ancillary matters that can so often detract from the on-track show, the chance to go racing and write their own chapters in F1 history is what spurs every driver and team member on to be the best they can be.

Like Norris, Esteban Ocon also reflected on his earliest memories when it comes to discussing his love for F1, which for him stems from Michael Schumacher and Ferrari, who together ruled F1 through the early 2000s. "I grew up watching red on TV," Ocon said. "To me, it's always been the red helmet with the stars on top, dominating. That's what gave me the love for the sport, the motivation to get to where I am today. If I have to quote someone, or something about Formula 1, it would be Michael Schumacher. That's where it all came from."

It's that kind of magic that, to me, remains at the heart of F1. On the plane home from the final race in Abu Dhabi at the end of an exhausting, seemingly endless season, I type up my interview with Ocon. I listen back to his words and get thinking: Yes, that's where it started for me, too. The early mornings, getting up to watch Schumacher fighting for a world championship in his scarlet red Ferrari—the myth and allure surrounding that team. For newer fans, that same role might have been served by Lewis Hamilton in his Mercedes or Max Verstappen in his Red Bull, or maybe, in the *Drive to Survive* era, someone not quite as successful but with a personality they clicked with, perhaps a Lando Norris or an Alex Albon. Maybe even a character like Guenther Steiner. But everyone who falls in love with this glorious sport will have that pennydrop moment. For some, it'll mark the start of a lifetime of fandom. Others will be spurred on to chase careers in the field, dedicating their lives, personal and professional, with all the associated sacrifices, to F1.

And sometimes, you need a little reminder of what sparked that magic in the first place.

■ ■ ■

Okay, one final trip.

I swore that I was done for the year. That flight forty-six, the one coming home from the final race in Abu Dhabi, would be the last one of the year. I told my friends and family we'd finally get the chance to spend some time together; that they'd have my undivided attention for the next two months until the new season begins; that I'd finally get on top of my Christmas shopping and have the decorations up more than a few days in advance of the twenty-fifth.

But when you get an invitation to go for lunch at Maranello, the home of Ferrari, you cannot say no.

It's only one more night away, only another 1,400 miles of flying in a year when I've covered 118,000 already. And I've promised to make it back home for my friend's birthday dinner the following evening and to bring home some panettone, an Italian Christmas delicacy, to sweeten the deal and make up for my absence throughout the year.

The Ferrari Christmas lunch has become one of the team's end-of-season traditions for the media. It's a chance to debrief after a long year of racing over some fine Italian food and a drop of Italian wine, toasting the team's achievements. This year, that's amounted to only one race win—the other twenty-one races were all won by Red Bull—but for Fred Vasseur, the season will always carry a great deal of significance, given it was his first at the helm of F1's most iconic, famous team. It's an unforgiving role, one that brings with it the weight of a nation's expectation. His predecessor, Mattia Binotto, was axed off the back of a season where Ferrari finished second in the championship and won four races. A tough gig. This year Vasseur has focused on laying the foundations for what he wants Ferrari to be in the future. At lunch, we're set to hear more about what exactly that has looked like.

Maranello is one in a long line of industrial towns running through the heart of Emilia-Romagna. Ferrari put it on the map. From the moment you arrive in the small town (population less than twenty thousand), the brand's hallmark red graces you at each corner, little signals like the red trim on buildings or flags up in support on houses. On the outskirts of the imposing factory that is the heart of both its racing and automotive operations, whole restaurants and cafés are dedicated to Ferrari. For its nearby test track, Fiorano, billboards advertise opportunities to go and drive your Ferrari—because *of course* you own one—around the track for a high-speed thrill.

With the car (a Fiat, not a Ferrari) parked, I walk with my colleagues toward the entrance to the Ferrari campus. All of the neighboring roads are named after Ferrari legends. We turn onto the *Via Gilles Villeneuve*, the street named after the great Canadian driver, and arrive at the welcome gate. Instructions in Italian are agreed to with unknowing nods before our phones are taken and stickers are placed over the cameras. There's a new-spec Ferrari road car being tested out on the track today, and there can be no risk of leaks. It's Ferrari. Of course we oblige.

Under the crisp December sun, we're directed through the

campus toward the main building, where lunch will take place. Running down the middle of the facility is a wall that dates back to the construction of the factory in the 1940s, which has been painted yellow on one side, denoting the "old half" of Ferrari, and red on the other for the "new half" that houses the road car facility. All the buildings in the "old half" retain their original styling and designs, the walls all painted a faded yellow. At the main gate, Enzo Ferrari's office remains untouched, its five brutalist, square windows designed to give *Il Commendatore*, as Enzo was known, a perfect view of every single Ferrari model that would be unveiled and driven out of the factory after coming off the production line.

Closer to the Fiorano test track, Enzo converted a farmhouse, situated on the *Piazza Michael Schumacher*, into another office that ensured he could see the cars being put through their paces. The wooden shutters, painted red, stand out against the whitewashed wall, as does the yellow Ferrari flag over the narrow entrance door. I think of all the F1 greats that must have passed under the brick arch above.

We make it to the main building, where lunch will be held. The red-clothed table, complete with Christmas tree boughs and some subtle decorations, forms an enormous ring around this year's Ferrari F1 car that carries Charles Leclerc's race number. Pictures of great Ferrari cars and drivers hang on the walls, along with a large black-and-white overhead photo of the Fiorano test track back when it opened in 1972, showing nothing but farmland around. After being greeted by Vasseur with a handshake and a wink, we take our seats and, once we've toasted to Ferrari's season, begin our end-of-year Q&A between each course of the meal.

Prior to joining Ferrari, Vasseur always stood out among the other team principals for his humor and ability not to take F1 too seriously. Back when he was Alfa Romeo's team boss, I once spotted him running with glee with a water gun after one of his drivers on a particularly hot day in the paddock. It's rare to get through a chat or interview with him without him laughing at his own jokes. Thankfully, the pressures that come with running Ferrari haven't stripped that from him. He remains in fine form even at the end of a busy season. In a lull during the questioning at the dinner, Vasseur, with a laugh, declares: "Tortellini!" Through two side doors, waiters appear holding bowls of pasta that are carefully placed in front of us. Of course, it's incredibly delicious.

It's this kind of tradition, the pomp and circumstance, that sets Ferrari apart. But when I ask Vasseur how he's found the pressure, he doesn't see it as anything negative, merely "different" to what he's found before. Like the love of the *tifosi*, the pride he feels representing Ferrari is infectious.

He speaks about the future, how he wanted to remove the fear of failure from Ferrari, how this helped ease the inevitable pressure of working and racing for the team. He laughs off questions about sorting new driver contracts anytime soon, despite both Leclerc and Sainz being free agents as of the end of 2024. "We still have thirteen months in front of us," he says after prods from the Spanish journalists present trying to get an update on Sainz, their fellow countryman, in particular.

The tortellini *primo* course is followed by vegetarian mille-feuille *secondo* and capped off by thick slices of panettone for dessert—*dolce*—accompanied by strong Italian espresso. With our questions largely answered and stomachs full, Vasseur circles the table to thank us for our work through the season and to wish a *buon natale*—he is still learning Italian but at least knows the customs—before we head on our way back to the airport.

Departing Maranello feels like going back forward in time. It's been a day of tradition, of history, as much as Vasseur might have been focusing on the future through the lunchtime chat. Ferrari has been there right from the start of F1 in 1950. There is nothing quite like it.

■ ■ ■

Christmas comes and goes. Like everyone else in the F1 paddock, I relish the chance to be at home for more than two weeks without seeing an airport or, in all honesty, a race track. It's a break that allows for a reset before things quickly stir up again, the fire of a new season quickly igniting.

And the new year wastes little time in dropping a major bombshell: Lewis Hamilton announces he is off to join Ferrari from 2025.

Nobody saw it coming. It had always been discussed as the kind of dream move that, surely, could never be realized. Hamilton had always said he'd finish his career with Mercedes, anticipating a relationship that would stretch long after his time on the grid is up, likely as an ambassador while continuing their charitable efforts. Everybody thought that Hamilton racing for Ferrari would always remain one of those what-ifs.

Until it didn't. Over a month before the first race of the new season, before driving a single lap in Mercedes's 2024 car, Hamilton decided to trigger an escape clause in his contract to leave the team at the end of the year and open the door for a move to Ferrari. It was a deal Ferrari's president, John Elkann, and Vasseur were able to get across the line. Vasseur had worked with Hamilton back in his junior career, and they'd always stayed friends. Now, they'd be racing together again.

It was obvious what pulled Hamilton to Ferrari: that heritage, that rare history that nowhere else can boast. In what is likely to be his final flourish in F1, it's a chance to fulfill the dream so many drivers hold but so few actually get to realize: driving one of those famous red cars.

"For every driver I think, growing up, watching the history, watching Michael Schumacher in his prime . . . all of us sit in our garages, and you see the driver in the red cockpit, and you wonder what it might be like to be surrounded by the red," Hamilton said when he spoke about the move for the first time ahead of the new season in Bahrain. "You go to the Italian Grand Prix, you see the sea of red of Ferrari fans, and you can only stand in awe of that. It's a team that's not had huge success really since 2007. I saw it as a huge challenge." Hamilton revealed even as a kid, he would play F1 video games as Schumacher in the red Ferrari. "It definitely is a dream," he said. "I'm really, really excited about it."

Nearing twenty years on the grid, Hamilton has seen it all and won it all. Yet there are still ways to make that passion for F1 burn brighter than ever. The novelty he and so many others felt as a kid watching F1 can still be rekindled. The story of Hamilton and Ferrari is surely going to be one of the most interesting narratives within F1 in the coming years.

That enchantment with the sport is shared by every single person up and down the pit lane, particularly among the drivers. Remember Fernando Alonso questioning whether he might want to stop racing as the demands of being an F1 driver continue to grow? At forty-two years old, he announced a couple of months after Hamilton's Ferrari deal emerged that he too would be continuing (something Hamilton was glad to hear, as it ensures he avoids the status of F1's oldest driver) until at least the end of 2026 with Aston Martin. By then, he will be forty-five years old and on course to become the oldest driver to race in fifty years (Graham Hill was forty-six when he made his final start in 1975). He's making changes to his approach to stop time catching up with him, opting to minimize time away from home and even considering more of a plant-based diet down the line. But what spurred him on to continue was his love for F1. "I love driving so much that I cannot stop at the moment," Alonso said. "The sacrifices that you have to make are smaller than the joy of driving and the passion that I have for driving. I live Formula 1. I breathe Formula 1."

With the start of a new season, that excitement and sentiment, living and breathing the sport, returns to the fore. The drivers have been through another long winter of preparation and sacrifice, hoping to fight for bigger and better things than the previous year. Even as we chat and catch up about winter escapes and pursuits—George Russell never did go skiing, but he started working toward getting a boat license instead—nothing can strip away the fervor they feel to get racing again. That competitive hunger has sustained F1 throughout its history. No matter where or how much we race, nothing is going to change that.

Neither is the fact that this, fundamentally, remains a sport and an industry defined by its people. Returning to the grid again in Bahrain for the start of a new season, I see the familiar faces that have been through a winter filled with some rest but, for the most part, hard work and preparation. There's the nerves and anticipation that fuels and pushes them. All the drivers, team bosses, engineers, mechanics, and everyone else on that starting grid are ready to give their all again for a long year of racing.

It's what makes F1, for all its imperfections, still so compelling. It's a sport that has always been about pushing the boundaries of what is possible, in both its technology and its people. We watch for the thrills, the speed, the breathtaking action on the track. But we also connect with the people making it happen, the commitment and grit of each person standing on that grid before the lights go out, reaching far beyond the paddock.

F1's evolution in the past seventy-five years has been staggering. To think where it may be in another seventy-five is as exciting as it is daunting. But so long as the people at its heart retain the passion that keeps us all so invested and in love with what we do, it will always be so much more than a sport.

Long may that love and humanity endure.

A NOTE ON SOURCES AND INTERVIEWS

All of the quotes and conversations within this book were gathered, unless specified, through my time on the road covering the 2023 F1 season and the early part of the 2024 season, across one-to-one interviews, open media sessions, and press conferences.

ACKNOWLEDGMENTS

When I set out to start writing this book, my hope was always to shine a spotlight on the incredible people who make Formula 1 what it is. Without them, the sport would not exist as it does. The same has proven true for this book, which would not have happened without the support and input of the incredible people I'm fortunate enough to have worked with to make *On the Grid* a reality.

Firstly, my thanks to Gretchen Schmid at HarperVia, and my agent, Allison Devereux at Trellis, for their hard work, support, and vision to see this process through from start to finish. It would be no exaggeration to say without them, this book would never have happened, taking it from an idea first discussed after an out-of-the-blue email from Gretchen—Imola cat, you'll forever be part of this story!—to what you are now reading. I feel so fortunate to have worked with you both on this project.

Across the Atlantic in the UK, my thanks to Frances Jessop from Simon & Schuster for her support and edits throughout the process, particularly helping get it across the finish line (pun totally intended). I must also thank my UK agent, Andrew Gordon of David Higham, for his help and support, as well as the wider teams at HarperCollins and Simon & Schuster for their help at each stage of making the book a reality. It truly has been an honor working with you all.

I must also thank all the F1 drivers past and present who spoke with me for the book, as well as their teams and press officers for helping set up interviews and for their interest in the project. Particular thanks go to Liam Parker, David Leslie, Stephen Duffy, Katie McGuinness, Tom Cooney, Paul Smith, Adam McDaid, Stuart Morrison, Jessica Borrell, Adrian Atkinson, Eve Merrell, Charlie Russell, Sophie Ogg, Sophie Almeida, Michel Berthelemot, Elena Rovelli, Rebecca Banks, Dominique Heyer-Wright, and Connor Bean for their help.

It was also wonderful to shine a light on some of the important yet perhaps lesser-known off-track figures in F1 that became so focal to telling this story of the sport. Thank you to Peter Crolla, Henry Howe, Trevor Carlin, Alice Ashpitel, Ellen Jones, Jonathan Nicholas, Kate Reid, Ben Hodgkinson, Professor Tim Baker, Dr. Maddy Orr, Chris Armstrong, Paul Mills, Anca Raines, Rob Bloom, Bobby Epstein, Matteo Lunelli, Hermann and Carsten Tilke, Martin Whitaker, and the *Paddock Project* crew of Sarah, Tiggy, and Chesa for their time.

Spending the bulk of the past decade on the road in F1 has been (and remains) such a privilege, and an exciting way to see the world. But it would not be nearly half as much fun without the colleagues and friends with whom I share each media center and press session. My particular thanks go to everyone I work with at the Athletic, as well as to the "Groovy Gang" for the countless lifts I've snagged over the years, the shenanigans we've gotten into, and the support when the going has got tough.

To Madeline, thank you for being so selflessly invested in this entire process, acting as the first vibe checker on each chapter and my biggest cheerleader whenever doubt crept in, and for being a dear friend.

To Dan, Phil, Charlie, and Jack—it's amazing how far we've come since starting out, and so cool to share that ride all together. Charlie, you even got good at social media. I'm proud of you, man.

To my friends back at home who have been incredibly understanding for all the birthdays, dinners, and events I've been away for over the years, and who remain so supportive of everything I am doing, thank you all so much. To Lucia, James, Morganne, Damien, Max, Millie, Holly, Esther, and Dan, I'm so grateful for your friendship and love.

To my dad, Martyn, and my stepmum, Sally—thank you both for your unconditional, unwavering love and support, your encouragement, and your excitement for all I do. I love you both so much.

And my final dedication must go to my mother, Angela. It breaks my heart that she never got to see this book happen. She'd have been so tickled by the stories told in it, and I know how excited seeing me go through the process would have made her. Writing this only served as a further reminder of just how great an influence she was, not only in sparking my passion for the sport, but in every aspect of my life. I know how proud she'd have been. This book is for her.

Here ends Luke Smith's
On the Grid.

The first edition of this book was printed
and bound at Lakeside Book Company
in Harrisonburg, Virginia, in February 2025.

A NOTE ON THE TYPE

The text of this collection was set in Minion Pro, an
OpenType update of the original 1990 Minion serif
typeface, released in 2000. The original Minion serif
typeface was designed by Robert Slimbach and released
by Adobe Systems. Inspired by late Renaissance-era
type, Minion's name stems from the traditional naming
system for type sizes, in which minion is between non-
pareil and brevier. Designed for body text, Minion is
classic yet condensed in style, achieving a harmonious
balance between the size of letters. It is a standard font
in many Adobe programs, making it one of the most
popular typefaces used in books.

HARPERVIA

An imprint dedicated to publishing international voices,
offering readers a chance to encounter other lives and other
points of view via the language of the imagination.